Biotraffic

Biotraffic

MEDICINES AND ENVIRONMENTAL
GOVERNANCE IN THE AFTERLIVES
OF APARTHEID

Christopher Morris

UNIVERSITY OF CALIFORNIA PRESS

University of California Press
Oakland, California

© 2024 by Christopher Morris

Library of Congress Cataloging-in-Publication Data

Names: Morris, Christopher Keller, author.
Title: Biotraffic : medicines and environmental governance in the
 afterlives of apartheid / Christopher Morris.
Description: Oakland, California : University of California Press,
 [2024] | Includes bibliographical references and index.
Identifiers: LCCN 2024017899 (print) | LCCN 2024017900 (ebook) |
 ISBN 9780520404014 (cloth) | ISBN 9780520404021 (paperback) |
 ISBN 9780520404038 (epub)
Subjects: LCSH: Botanical drug industry—South Africa—Ciskei. |
 Geraniums—Economic aspects—South Africa—Ciskei.
Classification: LCC HD9675.B683 S66 2024 (print) | LCC HD9675.B683
 (ebook) | DDC 338.4/76153210658754—dc23/eng/20240514
LC record available at https://lccn.loc.gov/2024017899
LC ebook record available at https://lccn.loc.gov/2024017900

33 32 31 30 29 28 27 26 25 24
10 9 8 7 6 5 4 3 2 1

Dear Sir,

The attention of the Medical Secretary has been drawn to a paragraph in the Morning Post of August 15th which suggests that the Imperial Economic Committee is interested in "native medicinal plants" and is compiling an index of such products. I am therefore writing to you to ask if you can kindly give us, in confidence, some information about an African root called Umckaloabo which is said to be imported into this country and used in the manufacture of a secret remedy for tuberculosis.

—Letter from the deputy medical secretary of the British Medical Association to the British Imperial Economic Committee, 1936

The trade in the plant is all underground. It's all skullduggery.

—A South African botanist, 2014

Bantustans are dead—long live the Bantustans.

—Laura Phillips and Ivor Chipkin (2014)

Contents

List of Illustrations	ix
Acknowledgments	xi
Prologue: Two Weddings and a Funeral	xv
Introduction	1
Interlude: "My Boy, You Are in for It" (1897)	29
1. Patent Problems	32
Interlude: A "Secret Remedy" (1901–1909)	58
2. A "Homeland's" Harvest	64
Interlude: "Mountains of Prejudice" (1909–1914)	89
3. On Expansional Belonging and Ethnic Capture	94
Interlude: "The Doom of 150,000 People" (1915–1953)	114
4. Waiting	120
Interlude: The Red List (1920–2024)	144
5. Royal Pharmaceuticals	149
Conclusion: Old Boundaries, New Extractions	172
Notes	183
References	211
Index	233

Illustrations

MAP

1. Map of Eastern Cape Province, South Africa (1986)   xxi

FIGURES

1. *Pelargonium sidoides* tubers   3
2. Sacks of harvested pelargonium stacked in an Eastern Cape warehouse (2007)   71
3. Card instructing harvesters of pelargonium how to sustainably remove plant tubers and sell them to biotraders   82
4. Pelargonium cultivation site in the Eastern Cape (2011)   83
5. Imingcangathelo-area elementary school's bulletin board welcoming representatives of Schwabe (2011)   111
6. Dust jacket of *The Doom of 150,000 People* (1931)   118
7. Anathi revealing a pelargonium plant hidden in a shrub (2011)   124
8. Ntaba kaNdoda on the day of the Heritage Day festival (2011)   159
9. Handwritten access agreement (2018)   168

Acknowledgments

My deepest thanks to everyone in South Africa who made this research possible. Many of these people must remain anonymous here, but they, along with those named in the pages that follow, have my sincerest gratitude for sharing their insights and experiences with me. Without Dabula Maxam, my research assistant, friend, and teacher, this book would not exist. My debt to him is enormous. I had the pleasure of spending the initial months of my research based at the University of KwaZulu-Natal. I thank Gerhard Maré, Shauna Mottiar, Catherine Sutherland, Harald Witt, and Julie Parle for their support and crucial feedback about my project. I'm grateful to the Center for Civil Society and the School of Development Studies at UKZN for hosting me. In the Eastern Cape province, at Rhodes University and elsewhere, I benefited from the amazing and enduring support of Rosalie Kingwill, Michelle Cocks, Tony Dold, and Jeff Peires. Thanks also to those who helped in big ways and small during our interactions in South Africa, including Susan Levine, Tara Weinberg, Katharina Schramm, Jaci van Niekerk, Nolundi Luwaya, Roger Chennells, Sonwabile Mnwana, Luvuyo Wotshela, Aninka Claassens, Mazibuko Jara, Judith Hayem, Steven Robins, and Ben Cousins. Additional gratitude goes to Msindisi Sam for helping me learn isiXhosa. My South

African friends Laura, Lauren, Lazola, Lucy, Marc, Naomi, and Russell brought me so much joy. The scholarship of Rachel Wynberg and Maano Ramutsindela has been a constant source of inspiration. I am indebted to all those mentioned here and below, but all errors in this book are my own.

Biotraffic began as a doctoral dissertation at the University of Colorado at Boulder. I'm incredibly thankful for the mentorship of my dissertation adviser, Donna Goldstein, who was—and remains—an unwavering source of encouragement, inspiration, friendship, and of course, sharp intellectual guidance. I'm indebted to Terry McCabe for the generous and incisive engagement he provided my research from the very outset of my research. I thank Carla Jones for being such a model scholar when it comes to theoretical acumen and intellectual rigor. Others at the University of Colorado inspired me in seminar rooms and conversations, offering insights that have shaped my ideas in ways both subtle and profound. They include Najeeb Jan, Carole McGranahan, Janice Peck, Kaifa Roland, Paul Shankman, and Rachel Silvey. Kathleen Gallagher was a huge help with grant writing, and workshops with Jeff Snodgrass about methods transformed my approach to research. I was lucky to learn from fellow graduate students, including Tracy Bekelman, Jenn Dinaburg, Jamie Dubendorf, Ben Joffe, Kunga Lama, Willi Lempert, Carey Stanley, and Magda Stawkowski. I owe special thanks to Kate Fischer and Marnie Thomson, who were amazing members of a dissertation writing group.

During the extensive research phase for this book, which spanned my PhD studies and post-PhD period, I had the opportunity to embark on two voyages with the Semester at Sea study abroad program, contributing once as a staff member and once as an instructor. This opportunity introduced me to three esteemed anthropologists whose warm encouragement I came to treasure. Thank you to Kathleen Adams, Carrie Douglass, and Joel Savishinsky. Semester at Sea also presented me with the honor of regularly interacting with the late Archbishop Desmond Tutu, an experience I also cherish.

My colleagues at Clarkson University constituted the best kind of intellectual community. I am grateful to them for their kindness, time, and guidance. Laura Ettinger was a special mentor, one who always left me mentally nourished after our many walks and lunches. Christina Xydias gave me invaluable feedback on a chapter of this manuscript and helped me craft an initial version of my book proposal. Stephen Casper and Sheila Weiss helped me quickly settle into life in the Department of Humanities and Social Sciences. Bill Vitek was a thoughtful department chair as well as neighbor in the village of Potsdam. During my time at Clarkson, Michael Garcia, Claudia Hoffmann, and Jen Knack became sources of insight and friendship and this remains so.

Thank you to my current colleagues at George Mason University who have supported me so graciously, especially two charismatic department chairs, Amy Best and Dan Temple. Others in my home department and elsewhere at George Mason have provided fantastic encouragement and collegiality. I thank Benedict Carton, Jamie Clark, John Dale, Shannon Davis, Rutledge Dennis, Nancy Hanrahan, Cortney Hughes Rinker, Niklas Hultin, Yasemin Ipek, Dae Young Kim, Haagen Klaus, Lester Kurtz, Huwy-min Liu, Ben Manski, Patty Masters, Manjusha Nair, Amaka Okechukwu, Rashmi Sadana, Anne Schiller, Joseph Scimecca, Linda Seligmann, Blake Silver, Rick Smith, Eliz Storelli, Susan Trencher, Matt West, and James Witte.

I received helpful feedback at different stages of my writing from Molly Mullin, Colin Bundy, Niko Besnier, and Maxim Bolt. Claudia Hoffman read portions of the manuscript at a crucial time, helping me present my arguments more effectively and providing me with the boost I needed to press on. I am indebted to Pauline Peters, Sara Berry, Peter Geschiere, and William Beinart for their generous commentary and advice. My bonds with friends and fellow academics David Varel, Marco Rossi, and Kyle Kelly have sustained me over the years. Africanists Clovis Bergere and Elene Cloete also became good friends who inspired my thinking.

The fieldwork for this book was generously funded by the Social Science Research Council, the National Science Foundation, and the Department of Anthropology at the University of Colorado at Boulder. Writing was supported by a Dissertation Completion Fellowship from the University of Colorado at Boulder. Portions of this book appeared in *American Ethnologist* (2016) and *Journal of Southern African Studies* (2019). My work also benefited from commentary I received at the Land Divided conference at the University of Cape Town and the Africa in the World: Shifting Boundaries and Knowledge Production conference in Johannesburg in 2018.

I owe so much to my publisher, the University of California Press. I am especially grateful to my editor, Naja Pulliam Collins, for her belief in this project and her expert guidance throughout its development. Her assistance, along with the invaluable input from three anonymous reviewers, has significantly elevated the quality of this book. I also wish to extend my appreciation to Sharon Langworthy, whose meticulous copyediting refined and polished the manuscript, ensuring its clarity and coherence.

Finally, I wish to thank my family. I am fortunate to have my in-laws, Sheila and Larry, whose company is always a delight. They have gone above and beyond in providing support in more ways than I can count. I am equally thankful for the uplift I have long received from the Rettig and Schubert families. My parents, Dan and Nancy, instilled in me the courage to chase my passions and the curiosity to explore through countless family adventures, both near and far. To Mom and Dad: my love and gratitude for you are immeasurable. And to my brother Joel, who has been a steadfast ally throughout my life and in the creation of this book, your backing has been invaluable. From the start of my time in graduate school, my partner Jodi has been my anchor. She encouraged me to pursue a career in research and teaching. What we didn't know was how challenging this path would be. Her support and belief in me have been constants, making every step of the journey possible. This book is as much a testament to her unwavering partnership as it is to anything I've managed to do. As my research unfolded, so did the expansion of our family with the arrival of our two children. Their vibrant personalities and infectious laughter have brought light into what have too often been long hours of study and writing. I love you endlessly, Jodi, Quinn, and Rees.

Prologue

TWO WEDDINGS AND A FUNERAL

This book's primary setting is the contemporary Ciskei region of South Africa, a once-notorious apartheid "homeland." In the chapters ahead, I explore how and to what effect this region became a hub for biological resource access, or a zone where drug companies procured vast quantities of wild plants and converted them into medicines for sale on national and international markets. Between 2009 and 2022, I spent seventeen months in South Africa researching this trade and the diverse cast of people involved in it. I lived with plant harvesters and tracked industry intermediaries. I interviewed corporate actors, government officials, activist nongovernmental organizations (NGOs), and the local elites who became business partners to multinational firms. The story that emerged was one of a problematic industry in which pharmaceutical companies became embroiled in contests over land, regimes of labor, and political power. The story was also one of global environmental governance ambitions and the fraught sociopolitical forces these ambitions have unleashed.

In the pages to come, I show that demand for plant-derived therapeutics can entwine struggles over drug profits with struggles over land, extractive jurisdictions, and political subjects. I ask: What has made this entwinement possible? What is at stake in it and the efforts of different parties to control it?

One event—a wedding—can serve as a tableau to introduce characters and narrative twists that will play prominent roles throughout this book. The wedding, which took place in October 2011, united a prince and a princess in the Ciskei region. When I arrived at the event in the morning, hundreds of guests had started gathering at a rural homestead, standing near a gnarled-wood gate of an impressively large kraal (livestock enclosure). There, the prince's bride would drive a spear into the earth and set the morning ceremony in motion. A cathedral tent towered nearby, erected for the afternoon's tuxedo and gown event. Beyond the tent, hills rolled into the distance, blanketed in thickets of thorny shrubs and succulent trees.

Shortly before the morning ceremony began, I watched as a silver car arrived and two drug company representatives emerged. One of the men worked for Schwabe Pharmaceuticals, a multinational headquartered in Germany that specializes in herbal medicines and health supplements.[1] Both were attending the wedding to bolster their companies' partnerships with the prince. In a few months, the prince would become a chief and claim authority over a jurisdiction from which the companies obtained large quantities of the plant *Pelargonium sidoides*, or what many in the province call *uvendle* in isiXhosa.[2] A popular cold-care medicine made from the plant annually generated tens of millions of dollars for the drug companies.

The prince and his chieftaincy expressed enthusiasm about the partnerships with drug companies. They envisioned themselves receiving drug royalties based on the volume of plant materials local people harvested. At the wedding, a member of the chieftaincy's council ushered the drug company representatives and me into a nearby farmhouse. As we walked into a well-appointed living room, we saw delegates from a kingdom and other Eastern Cape royals dining together in celebration of the wedding. The council member encouraged us to partake of refreshments while we waited for the prince, who eventually entered, clad in his wedding attire. The drug company men said they wished the prince a happy and successful life. They presented him with a wedding gift: a large, carefully wrapped photo album. The council member responded on behalf of the prince, stressing the men's status as special guests: "Mr. X., according to our traditions, the prince is not to be seen by anyone before the wedding. But I have made a small, small opening for you."

The exchange in the house helped me realize that I was witnessing two weddings that day. One married a prince and princess. Another united a chieftaincy and a multinational company. This latter alliance, I came to understand, would have considerable implications for some local residents.

Since the early 2000s, the region had become a focal point where some residents relied on harvesting *Pelargonium sidoides* to earn money. Each morning, those residents had ventured into the forest, pickaxe in one hand and woven plastic sacks in the other, scanning the ground for the plant and its telltale velvety, heart-shaped leaves.

After a day's effort, the harvesters hauled their swollen collection sacks home. They stored the harvested material in various corners of their homesteads, including indoors under their beds, where it amassed for weeks, sometimes months. They then waited for a biotrader, an industry intermediary who purchased the material and coordinated its transport to South African and foreign pharmaceutical companies. And while many locals were well-versed in the art of collecting the plant, most remained unaware of the final destinations of those plants or the companies that commercialized them. This changed with the arrival of the company representatives at the wedding.

The partnership between the chieftaincy and the companies wasn't about collusion; it stemmed from a requirement of new environmental laws in South Africa. To meet the requirement, Schwabe sought out community leaders in areas where the plant was harvested. They established formal "access and benefit-sharing agreements," aiming to direct financial benefits toward people in those areas. The move positioned the chieftaincy, which was seen by government departments and the companies as the de facto authority over the land and people in the area, as community representative and recipient of the benefits.

For its part, Schwabe was doing more than sharing royalties with the chieftaincy. The company had initiated charitable projects in South Africa, including the establishment of a youth scout center and a fruit-tree planting scheme. A Schwabe representative also gave me the impression the company had complied with a government request to identify other actors involved in marketing products derived from the plant. As I understood it, Schwabe provided a comprehensive list and emphasized to the authorities that, unlike others who were operating clandestinely, its own activities were transparent and open to scrutiny.

But matters soon became more complicated for Schwabe and the prince's chiefdom. Recall that delegates from a royal kingdom had also attended the prince's wedding. That kingdom, known as Rharhabe, was looking to enter into its own partnerships with the companies. Its jurisdiction blanketed the Ciskei region, allowing the kingdom to claim authority over forty-two chieftaincies, including the prince's. The kingdom's aim was clear: to position itself above the chiefdoms and centralize control over the trade in *Pelargonium sidoides* and the distribution of benefits from that trade. In reaction, some chiefs complained bitterly to me about their potential loss of drug royalties to the king. "The kingdom knows nothing about the plant and its medicine," one grumbled to me. Muddying the situation further, the Rharhabe king was then mired in controversy after a national commission ruled that his kingship was in fact illegitimate. Out of respect, the commission would allow him to retain his high status until death.

If the list of attendees at the royal wedding told a story of contestation over a medicinal plant, the list of people who were absent was just as revealing in this respect.

Consider that some villagers who lived a few kilometers down the road from the prince and his chiefdom had skipped the wedding in protest. These villagers had harvested *Pelargonium sidoides*, but unlike others, they were better acquainted with Schwabe. From 2007 to 2010, they had collaborated with an activist NGO to challenge patents Schwabe held in Europe that concerned the plant. One such patent granted Schwabe exclusive rights to produce the cold-care medicine. Another gave Schwabe sole rights to use the plant to develop treatments for AIDS and tuberculosis. The NGO, backed by the villagers, accused Schwabe of "biopiracy," or stealing knowledge without compensating people in South Africa and Lesotho, the countries where the plant is endemic.

The villagers' activism had strained an already uneasy relationship with the prince and his chiefdom. Back in the early 2000s, the villagers had established legal associations to manage and maintain the land they occupied. They prided themselves on electing their leaders and crafting their own constitutions—activities that, as they saw it, distinguished them from the nearby chieftaincy, whose callow prince would claim power via birthright. And although they respected the ceremonial significance of chiefs, they did not want them interfering with their livelihoods. Yet the chieftaincy became more assertive, demanding tributes that ranged from supplies for a royal infant to, more recently, livestock for slaughter at the prince's wedding banquet. The villagers held lengthy community meetings to consider a polite response. Tensions escalated when, a year before the wedding, the chieftaincy directed plant collectors to bring their harvests to the chief's compound. There, plants were to be weighed and sold to Schwabe's biotrader. Residents said they learned the chieftaincy intended to deduct a portion of the sales as a levy. Many villagers chose to ignore the directive. However, the presence of drug companies at the prince's wedding signaled the chieftaincy had successfully inserted itself into the trade.

Soon after the prince's wedding, the NGO that had challenged Schwabe's patents organized a meeting in an empty local building belonging to the villagers. Inside, I sat on a wooden bench and listened as an NGO representative described an agreement that appeared to construe the residents as direct subjects of the chieftaincy and kingdom. In exchange for paying royalties to the chieftaincy, the NGO representative feared, drug companies would have access to the plants on the villagers' land. "The companies declared that they had met and consulted with the communities of the region through the kingdom and chiefs," the NGO representative told the gathered group. "And therefore, their understanding is that the people have agreed to this deal." The representative scanned the room for reactions. Quiet discussion erupted. Over the growing chatter, the representative stressed: "The agreement states that the agreement was done with the chieftaincy on the principle that they were doing it on your behalf, as their subjects."

The villagers had relied on the money they earned from harvesting. But with access and benefit-sharing agreements now established between the chieftaincy and pharmaceutical companies, Schwabe's biotrader gave me the impression he would stop purchasing material from the villagers if they kept protesting the chieftaincy. The residents felt that they could meaningfully participate in the industry only by embracing an imposed authority structure that exploited their labor. What is more, they became convinced that the chieftaincy had leveraged the agreements to hoard thousands of dollars in drug royalties.[3] "No one is monitoring their use of the money given to them," one villager told me. "The chiefs are using us as a stepladder to accumulate for themselves (*iqonga lokwenyuka*). All of this at our expense."

Access and benefit sharing had subsumed the villagers into an "Indigenous community" under the political leadership of a chieftaincy and kingdom. As many of them saw it, those leadership structures had captured not merely the drug royalties but also the villagers themselves. Their conscription violated their sense of identity, which among other things, was tied to the powers they maintained over the land they occupied and the citizenship status they claimed in South Africa's democracy. Toward the end of the NGO-led meeting in the village, a resident publicly asked, "I would like to know if our association constitutions state anything about the chiefs and us. Are there any bindings between them and us? I'd like to know." An elected leader of one of the associations replied, "There is nothing whatsoever in them that involves us with the chiefs. Our land and our properties are simply controlled by us. Our association has its own executive committee. We adamantly say we do not want any involvement with the chiefs. We are under the control of our association. We are under the authority of the local municipality."

For the villagers, the situation presented a volatile challenge—one that was distinct from the patent case.

The organization of a former homeland as an extractive zone for the plant appeared to be set.

But then the king died.

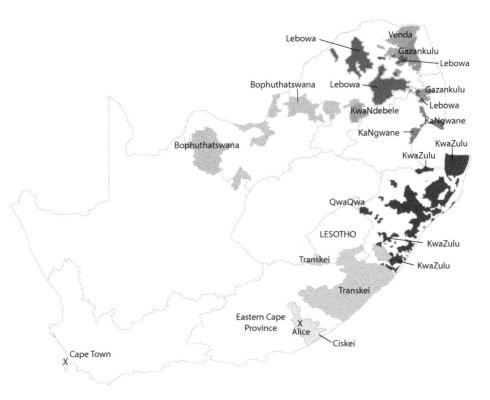

Map 1. Eastern Cape Province, South Africa. A comparative overlay of historical apartheid "homeland" boundaries (adapted with permission from Custom Contested, "Map of Bantustan Authorities, 1986") and contemporary provincial divisions. *Source*: www.customcontested.co.za.

Introduction

When I began my research in South Africa in 2009, I was unfamiliar with many of the elements sketched in the prologue, including plant trade, chiefs, and "homelands." Interested in anti-patent activism, my hope was to learn about the NGO's campaign against Schwabe Pharmaceuticals. I was an anthropology PhD student at the University of Colorado at Boulder, and the potential for a dissertation project about the case intrigued me. In August 2009 I used a preliminary research grant to travel from my home in the United States to South Africa for one month. One of my goals was to engage with the NGO African Center for Biosafety (ACB), which operated from a suburban residence in Johannesburg.[1]

I had previously exchanged emails with the director of the NGO to schedule an interview. But when I arrived on the NGO's doorstep on a low-sky winter day in August 2009, the director appeared to greet me with confusion; our appointment had escaped their memory. Nevertheless, they kindly invited me inside, where I noticed details of a lived-in home: colorful dish towels in the kitchen, family photos on a fridge, and the pleasant aroma of a recently cooked meal. The house radiated warm domesticity—an atmosphere that was at odds with my preconceived ideas about the epicenter of a legal battle against a big corporation. At the same time, the sounds of several employees fervently typing and conversing on phones in adjacent rooms revealed the house's dual purpose.

The director and I began our conversation at a dining table, where they soon conveyed reservations about agreeing to the interview. They understandably underlined their heightened sensitivity surrounding their work and candidly shared their concerns about my presence. In the coming months, they would travel to the European Patent Office (EPO) in Munich, the issuing authority of Schwabe's patents concerning *Pelargonium sidoides* and the site of the challenge. They would not proceed with an interview and would not yet help me contact the Eastern Cape villagers with whom the NGO had allied. I would preferably wait until the case concluded, they indicated. They then cautioned me about the potential complexities my research might encounter, particularly given my identity as a White, male, American researcher in the social and political context of South Africa. I left the house initially jarred, sensing my research had commenced too late. But this feeling quickly gave way to embarrassment at my lack of self-awareness. My privileged naivete had been rightly exposed: after seemingly parachuting onto the NGO's doorstep, I had expected them to welcome a stranger's observation of their activism. I conducted numerous other interviews during that initial trip. Still, I returned home feeling uncertain about researching *Pelargonium sidoides*.

A member of the Geraniaceae family, the plant is indigenous to South Africa and Lesotho and is one of more than two hundred varieties within the *Pelargonium* genus, named from the Greek *Pelargos* for their beak-like seed pods that resemble a stork's bill.[2] *Pelargonium sidoides* (hereafter pelargonium) has velvety, wrinkled cordate leaves and distinctively dark reddish-purple flowers that bloom from late spring to summer. And while appreciated for its beauty, the plant has also found use in Indigenous medicine, whose practitioners have long prescribed it for ailments in people and livestock.[3] Its rugged, rubicund tubers (see figure 1) are central to its medicinal potential.

This potential was thrust into the international limelight in the early 1900s after an Englishman stricken with tuberculosis visited colonial South Africa and Basutoland and credited a local remedy derived from the tubers for curing his disease. That man subsequently commercialized the remedy for tuberculosis in Europe, where he marketed it under the

Figure 1. Pelargonium sidoides tubers. Photo courtesy Tony Dold.

moniker "Umckaloabo." Since the 1980s, Schwabe had intensively marketed Umckaloabo as an over-the-counter treatment for respiratory tract infections like acute bronchitis. Observers have called it a "role model" for African therapeutic products and "one of the most successful phytomedicines in the world."[4] The medicine became available in many grocery stores and pharmacies in North America, Europe, Asia, and Southern Africa.[5]

Unexpectedly, a few weeks after returning home from my research trip in 2009, I received an invitation from the NGO director. After further consideration, they had decided to invite me back to South Africa, suggesting the possibility of meeting the villagers involved in the patent challenge. I was not yet positioned to return, however. And by the time I secured research grants and fulfilled a work obligation that paused my studies for half a year, almost eighteen months had passed. Much had changed during those months. Most notably, ACB's challenge against

Schwabe ended in January 2010. The EPO revoked one of Schwabe's patents, leading media outlets to claim victory for ACB and its community allies. As one South African newspaper proclaimed, "A small Eastern Cape community is elated after challenging a German pharmaceutical giant over a patent to produce extracts from [a] local plant species—and winning."[6] Schwabe, however, contested these triumphant claims, insisting the patent had been revoked due to another European pharmaceutical firm's technical objections, not ethical concerns raised by the NGO. Nevertheless, the NGO's campaign had proved significant. A Schwabe spokesperson told media outlets that the company feared becoming "the scapegoat in a continuing debate on principles that we cannot resolve." Facing a public relations fallout, Schwabe voluntarily relinquished four additional patents concerning pelargonium.

When I returned to South Africa in early 2011 to begin a full year of fieldwork, I wondered if the saga of the plant had concluded. One of ACB's collaborators in the patent challenge described the EPO's decision as "a success in the fight against biopiracy."[7] ACB's director added, "We're happy that the ruling takes away Schwabe's right to monopolize the use of genetic resources and traditional knowledge from South Africa."[8] And yet these same activists implied that the challenge was also merely one chapter in a still-unfolding narrative. "Patents are just another layer of biopiracy," the director said. "There isn't an absence of biopiracy when there's no patents."[9] According to another activist, "the next step will be to fight biopiracy beyond the patent system. Biopiracy is about unlawful use, not only about patents."[10] A documentary film about the case stressed that the campaign against Schwabe was ongoing: "Despite the patents being revoked, [ACB] continues its quest for radical changes in how the plant is traded."[11]

ACB and its collaborators were not alone in their convictions about the trade. My first month back in South Africa, I spent time in urban law offices and shiny government buildings, interviewing people I assumed were preoccupied with questions about drug discovery and immaterial properties like medicinal knowledge and patents. But while discussing those things, my interlocutors frequently turned to the subject of an emphatically material trade in plants. Many spoke of the bulk collection and export of wild pelargonium from seemingly remote parts of the country, about this collection's environmental dangers, and about rural groups who physically labored to make collection possible. The anti-patent activists and government officials appeared to agree: with much of the media coverage focused on alleged misappropriation of knowledge through patents, less public attention was being paid to bulk sourcing of the plant. Schwabe would continue that sourcing, officials told me. And with the patents having been withdrawn and the monopoly ended, it was only a matter of time before other foreign companies followed suit. I began to understand how the issue went beyond patent disputes to include the plant's role in wider debates over resource use and environmental protection—a complexity that would significantly shape the trajectory of my research, directing me away from big-city buildings to rural spaces where large-scale collection was occurring.

Consider that when Schwabe dominated the Umckaloabo industry from the 1980s to the early 2010s, it did so by securing pelargonium as a raw or semiprocessed commodity to produce the medicine. Annual harvest estimates ranged from 26 tons to a staggering 440 tons of material.[12] One South African official told me that between 2000 and 2008, potentially millions of individual plants had been uprooted from the Eastern Cape province for conversion into medicinals. "The resource is appearing all over the world, and we have no way of tracing it," the official told me. His office was engaged in a cat-and-mouse pursuit of the industry's biotraders, whom he perceived as canny operators involved in unauthorized, if not outright illegal, activities. The trade was quick moving and often one step ahead of South Africa's Green Scorpions, the state's environmental management inspectors. According to another official, "We often couldn't effect any arrests because we didn't catch anyone in time. We did see the aftermath of it, and in some areas the land looked like it had been plowed—the plant had been virtually obliterated." As it turned out, the plant was experiencing only limited, localized loss. Still, provincial officials became so concerned that they eventually placed a moratorium on all harvesting of pelargonium.

But the story of Schwabe also showed how these rapid, high-volume movements of plants could indeed converge with more time-intensive processes of drug discovery and patenting that had initially consumed my attention. Schwabe may have used wild-harvested material as a source for testing new treatments, officials suggested. The company had fed the plant into new drug research and development cycles. It organized numerous clinical trials, many of which suggested efficacy for respiratory infections.[13] These efforts led not only to filing of numerous patents in the mid-2000s for new HIV and tuberculosis therapies but also to continued bulk collection.[14] Officials made clear to me their fears that pelargonium was just one example of the country's plants being ferried abroad in mass and becoming source material for medicinal patents.[15]

Such entanglements aren't unique to South Africa. Conventionally understood, commodity trade and drug discovery are distinct processes that operate separately. The former focuses on procuring raw or semiprocessed "biological resources," while the latter involves a more targeted search for "genetic resources"—a subset of biological resources that includes active compounds and useful genes.[16] The volume and type of materials procured vary, presenting ostensibly different environmental risks. For example, while the sampling of plants for drug discovery poses little ecological harm, the story goes, commodity trade requires careful environmental monitoring. Yet the boundaries between these practices can blur. After *Taxus contorta*, a yew tree indigenous to Afghanistan, India, and Nepal, became a source for the chemotherapy drug paclitaxel, exploitation of the tree by Indian and Chinese pharmaceutical companies led to its listing as an endangered species.[17] Such scenarios underscore the argument "that commercial drug development can potentially result in levels of material extraction that are comparable to mining."[18]

As my research progressed, I began to conceptualize the abovementioned movements of biological resources as a form of *traffic*. They weren't unidirectional or one dimensional. They encompassed interacting scalar, temporal, and spatial dimensions, affecting how people engaged with and experienced their dynamics. In terms of scale, I pictured plants like pelargonium and *Taxus concorta* moving along "lanes" of exploitation.[19] These lanes, though separate, occasionally converged, merging a tangibly vast extraction of plant commodities with less tangible processes of discovery and propertization through chemical compounds and patents. Accumulations along these lanes were far from uniform; they varied in intensity: sometimes as dense surges, other times as sparse trickles, or even ceasing entirely.[20] The visual of traffic helped me grasp what scholar Laura

Foster describes as the "different modalities of scale" encompassing such resource movements.[21] I saw how a single plant could take various material forms, assuming different roles and values as it transited scientific and legal realms.

Yet scale was only one dimension of these complex movements. Temporally, the journey of resources like pelargonium spanned swift, if irregular, transits alongside slower, prospective processes of drug discovery, presenting different time frames. This meant that the circulation of resources, as they were enlisted in grand capitalist and commercial schemes by companies and governments, was marked by diverse temporal rhythms, where the urgent economic needs of the present merged with the elongated timelines of future, biopolitical ambitions. Observers experienced these rhythms differently: some saw resource exploitation as a consistent and enduring activity, while others, most notably plant harvesters, perceived it as disjointed, punctuated by intervals of inactivity. One's vantage point within this traffic greatly influenced their temporal experience, with resource movements manifesting as continuous or, in contrast, a sequence of starts and stops. Spatially, the movements unfolded across layered landscapes of geography, law, and politics. Pelargonium's trajectory extended beyond physical environments like biodiverse regions and areas of commercial extraction, moving through legal and political spaces shaped by unresolved land claims, a patchwork of environmental regulations, and the enduring impacts of apartheid segregation.

My heuristic of *biological-resource traffic*—or *biotraffic* as my shorthand—aims to capture these shifting modalities of time, space, and scale that encompass contemporary movements of biological resources. Focusing on pelargonium, this book ethnographically delves into these modalities in two related ways. First, it examines them as they relate to drug companies obtaining biological resources from a region in South Africa that was formerly an apartheid homeland. As I detail, the industry's pursuit of large quantities of pelargonium—a plant that takes years to mature and become commercially desirable—led industry actors to such regions and to their establishment as biodiversity "access" zones. These kinds of interactions between scale, time, and space were also evident in the South African government's efforts to regulate and control access to plants like pelargonium. These efforts are the second focus of the book. State officials became concerned about the potential for foreign entities to use bulk plant material for testing chemicals and patenting knowledge, bypassing benefits to South Africans. The state's concern was also heightened by the lengthy and uncertain process of drug discovery in South Africa, which, in contrast to the ongoing and tangible results of commodity trade, posed a challenge in realizing benefits, especially for those South Africans who lived in regions where companies accessed plants.

The book pays particular attention to how a department of the South African state, responding to these multidimensional complexities, devised a novel governance strategy, one that sought to regulate both commodity trade and drug discovery under a unified legal framework. As I show, the effects of this strategy underscore that, far from constituting unmediated flows, resource movements are sensitive to influence. Indeed, as the pages that follow demonstrate, a seemingly subtle bureaucratic intervention had far-reaching effects in South Africa, altering biotraffic as a social field and in turn reconfiguring subjectivities and experiences within that field.[22] Stated boldly, South Africa's intervention portended a new institutional order, a possible universal gear through which myriad forms of nature and people were made to fit an international legal regime serving capitalist markets and trade. Examining this experiment's effects can tell us much about the kinds of property and people that environmental governance regimes conjure to meet capitalism's changing conditions. It can also reveal the ways such logics of governance are shifting in our current era of commodified nature and turbulent planetary transformation.

THE BLOCKBUSTERS THAT WEREN'T

To delve deeper into the movements of biological resources and their different modalities of time, it helps to have a broader understanding of drug discovery and commodity trade and how their fates have diverged under shifting international governance regimes. The idea of *biodiversity* is now so familiar that one could be forgiven for assuming it is long established. The term is historically recent, however. It materialized in the late 1980s and gained prominence in the 1990s amid scientific and policy concerns about species extinction.[23] The Convention on Biological Diversity (CBD), which entered into force in 1993, became a legal focal point for biodiversity discourse and helped usher in a new era of environmental governance into existence.

Before the CBD, genetic resources and knowledge about their use belonged to the global commons. Northern corporations, research institutions, and other entities advanced their interests through free access to plants and knowledge about them, bearing no obligation to share the profits they generated from the biologically richer Southern Hemisphere. What had been freely available also became patentable after changes in intellectual property law took hold across the world. The landmark US Supreme Court ruling in *Diamond v. Chakrabarty* (1980) was catalytic. Previously, the "product of nature" doctrine had barred patents on most living organisms. The court toppled this doctrine by arguing that human labor can alter biological matter in such a way as to innovate something "markedly different" from its natural state. Based on this Lockean premise, the Supreme Court ruled that a microbiologist named Chakrabarty could lawfully patent a microorganism he had genetically modified to clean up oil spills. The ruling contributed to the spectacular growth of the US biotechnology sector and a proliferation of bioresource-related patents.[24] The World Trade Organization's (WTO's) Agreement on Trade-Related Aspects of Intellectual Property Rights (TRIPS), which came into effect in 1995, globalized protections on such patents by requiring countries aspiring to WTO membership to bring their national policies in line with US standards. According to its advocates, TRIPS would ensure a return on investment and spur innovation. Critics, however, saw it as a cynical reaction to the nascent growth of biotech industries in Southern countries like India, where firms ignored patents and manufactured cheap generic drugs and other compounds, thus threatening US pharmaceutical and agrochemical interests.[25]

During this same period, some analysts feared that synthetic-molecule pipelines for drugs were drying up. Newly efficient bioassay and genetic screening techniques triggered a wave of drug discovery involving biodiversity in what some described as the pharmaceutical industry's "return to nature."[26] Indigenous activist coalitions and representatives of Southern nations who negotiated the CBD between 1989 and 1992 feared this development and fiercely opposed the broader shift toward exclusive property rights over genetic resources. Seeking ways to address long-standing imbalances in South-North exchange and anticipating the privatization of their biological heritage under TRIPS, these coalitions managed to imprint some of their interests in the CBD. Genetic resources and knowledge were "removed" from the commons and placed under the control of nation-states. To promote equity in exchange, the convention also endorsed the use of intellectual property rights, albeit a favorably refashioned version in the form of access and benefit sharing—a "grand bargain" between companies and Indigenous knowledge holders.[27] The CBD obliged signatory states to ensure that companies obtain consent and share benefits with the people who provide access to genetic resources or knowledge about them. The Nagoya Protocol to the CBD, enacted in 2014, outlined more specific mechanisms for executing benefit sharing. While recognizing the potential for multilateral approaches, both agreements predominantly adopted a bilateral approach, with the Nagoya Protocol promoting contracts as the favored tool for benefit sharing.

The decade that followed the launch of the CBD was one of anticipation. Some envisioned benefit sharing transforming biodiversity sectors into engines of economic growth, engendering rural and Indigenous development, new medicines, nature conservation, and scientific infrastructure building across the South. And Southern countries had arguably positioned themselves to negotiate the terms of genetic resource exploitation. Some states were also placed to overturn corporate patents on resources.[28] Yet fundamental asymmetries bedeviled the implementation of the CBD. With terrestrial species diversity concentrated in the South, the heaviest conservation burdens fell on countries in that hemisphere. Many of these countries had only recently experienced decolonization, and they later reeled from externally imposed fiscal austerity measures. Northern signatory countries, for their part, mostly failed to incorporate CBD provisions into their legal systems. Concerns about species extinction and the loss of species abundance have only intensified.

The circulation of genetic resources slowed in the 2000s.[29] Cases of alleged "biopiracy" continued to appear.[30] Nevertheless, a prevailing sense emerged that the development potential of genetic resources would only be realized over the long term, if at all. Interest in such resources among higher-technology companies and research institutions also diminished due to legal uncertainty about compliance, as well as growing public fears about misappropriation. "Access" increasingly entails the "digital mining" of databases that contain genetic sequence information—a "dematerialization" of genetic material that can enable parties to bypass benefit-sharing obligations altogether.[31] Meanwhile, marketing and consumer demand for botanical medicines continued to spur commercial interest in biological resource commodities.

The book *Therapeutic Revolutions* describes "narratives of therapeutic revolution" as stories that correlate medical modernity with, among other things, sudden and dramatic revolutions in advanced science and laboratory-based research.[32] I suggest that in the 1980s and 1990s, across governmental, activist, and academic worlds, drug discovery involving biodiversity emerged as one such revolutionary narrative. For a large body of postcolonial science and technology studies literature, the transformational potential of drug discovery became a prominent matter of inquiry.[33] This work elucidated the politically charged nature of knowledge claims and production in the realm of therapeutics. It also highlighted the competing directives of neoliberal governments as they endeavored to monetize nature to conserve it. Yet this literature also tended to minimize the fact that most pharmaceutical development worldwide does not occur via biodiversity. The use of plant genetic resources has always been limited and has only become more marginal.[34] As a therapeutic revolution, the pharmaceutical industry's return to nature never really came to pass. Furthermore, it became apparent that commercial demand for genetic resources alone was unlikely to motivate biodiversity conservation. The transactions facilitated by the CBD have not yielded significant conservation benefits to date.[35]

The narrative of drug discovery from biodiversity, once heralded as a transformative force, has not dissipated, but rather, as Lauren Berlant might suggest, has entered a state of "animated suspension."[36] This condition reflects a peculiar limbo—one in which the anticipated revolutions in pharmaceuticals via biodiversity remain on the horizon, yet their realization is frequently deferred. In this state, a seeming momentum is paradoxically stilled, framed by an ongoing anticipation of the next discovery, legal development, or shift in the global landscape.

GOVERNING BIOTRAFFIC

This backdrop can help us understand recent developments in South Africa. The country is regarded as "mega-biodiverse," ranking among the seventeen countries that collectively account for 70 percent of the world's biodiversity. South Africa's Department of Science and Technology (DST) has framed this status as key to South Africa's "tremendous yet untapped potential" to become "a world leader in biotechnology." In 2007 the DST unveiled plans to work alongside university and corporate partners to nurture "one of the top three emerging economies in the global pharmaceutical industry, based on an expansive innovation system using the nation's indigenous knowledge and rich biodiversity."[37] A subsequent government strategy aimed to ignite a national "bioeconomy," citing South Africa's biodiversity as a "comparative advantage" and biopolitical boon, with species richness "providing an important basis for economic growth and development that underpins the well-being of our society."[38]

Seemingly frustrated with the slow progress in the country on these and other fronts, South African president Cyril Ramaphosa launched Operation Phakisa for the National Biodiversity Economy in 2018. Meaning "operation hurry up" in Sesotho, this effort aimed to economically supercharge the biodiversity sector to the tune of $2.5 billion in revenue by 2030. Drug discovery remained an active and potent site for imagining a future in which economic growth, public health, and therapeutic innovation interlink. But the government's own inquiries into markets and biotech research revealed something consequential about the potential of biodiversity exploitation: in the shorter term, it was the more ecologically perilous commodity trade in plants that could fuel the bioeconomy. The country would likely have to wait for longer-term efforts at drug discovery to contribute.

During my research, I found that South African policymakers perceived these movements of plants as boon and bane. They consequently endeavored to control *and* exploit them. To this end, officials expanded the scope of the country's benefit-sharing laws beyond conventional drug discovery and thus beyond what is articulated in the CBD and Nagoya Protocol.[39] Rather than attempt to loosen the knot of im/material resource movements, South Africa's laws embraced it. They packaged plant-commodity trade and drug discovery together, obligating commodity-trading companies to engage in benefit sharing the same way drug discovery companies would. The circle of responsibility was widened to include new corporate players who obtained biological resources. While seemingly banal and technocratic, this regulatory move was unusual and ambitious, especially when it came to making an instrument like access and benefit sharing responsive to the postcolonial realities of biodiversity exploitation.

Pelargonium epitomized these realities. In a region of Africa with notably contentious struggles over biological resources, many high-ranking South African officials told me they considered pelargonium the most contentious.[40] After decades of unconstrained extraction, officials wished to curb an industry that flourished in the regions they most associated with apartheid segregation. Officials considered the two former "homeland" regions—the Ciskei and Transkei—of the Eastern Cape province the "hubs" of commercial access to the country's wild plants. One reason, they told me, is that the Eastern Cape is a biodiverse province where drug companies found the wild biological resources they sought. A second reason had to do with the difficulties of securing those resources. Plants traverse spatial and political boundaries, growing across South Africa's provinces, including the Eastern Cape.[41] But some grow slowly, requiring years to mature and become commercially desirable. The industry's biotraders were consequently on the move to new areas in search of mature plants for their drug company employers. And in contrast with private land, which was practically and legally inconvenient to access, the communal lands established in the province's two former homelands during apartheid provided more contiguous and accessible harvesting zones. The land was contiguous because its ownership remained unresolved; at the time of writing, it continued to be state held and considered the political jurisdiction of chiefs.

The durability of homeland spaces mattered in other respects. South Africa's Green Scorpions occasionally managed to apprehend biotraders who engaged in unauthorized trade. According to the inspectors, however, biotraders were difficult to prosecute, complicating efforts to learn the identity of their employers and the overseas destinations of the materials they transported. "The industry is largely underhand and mostly illegal—blatantly illegal," one official told me. "And the problem is that we don't know where the products are going." Assisting the biotraders were homeland-era nature conservation laws that remained active in the Eastern Cape. The laws left resources differentially protected across three different zones within the province. Biotraders exploited such spatiolegal disjunctures for decades. If they could evade the Green Scorpions long enough to transport illicit materials to spaces of the province where plants lacked legal protections, they could avoid arrest.

The CBD and Nagoya Protocol remain unique in the context of environmental governance; whereas equity is a guiding principle in other frameworks, it is the primary aim of access and benefit sharing.[42] South African resources and knowledge may on occasion become sources of information for drug innovation and patenting. But where was the equity, officials understandably asked, if access and benefit sharing failed to concern the more immediate and high-volume trade in plants like pelargonium? Their aim became to monetarily improve the lives of people living in resource-access areas, but it also went beyond this; access and benefit sharing was intended to promote resource conservation and research, among other things.[43]

The problem relates to another apparent limitation of the CBD and Nagoya Protocol. Activists negotiating the CBD in the late 1980s and early 1990s considered intellectual property rights to be a problematic mode of empowerment. Yet despite this wariness, "property" was not ultimately excised from the CBD's end product. Anthropologist Cori Hayden reminds us that access and benefit sharing finds a footing in decidedly Lockean ideas.[44] Benefits belong to those groups that can be rewarded for the identifiable input of mental labor and innovation they put into a genetic resource and its stewardship. To reward such labor and innovation is to incentivize stewardship. And to incentivize stewardship entails rewarding it where it occurs. Thus, built into access and benefit sharing is an intellectual property–modeled logic that assumes a great deal about relations among plants, people, and knowledge. It imagines that these things will be "found together—localized and localizable—in one discrete package."[45]

But such tidy packaging is not a given. As numerous scholars have stressed, even in instances where the origin of knowledge appears discernible, spatial *distance* often characterizes the relationship between Indigenous knowledge holders and the material resources their knowledge concerns.[46] Groups like the San and Khoi are commonly considered the original holders of Indigenous knowledge concerning plants in Southern

Africa. Yet due to a prolonged and violent history of displacement and relocation, these groups frequently do not reside in areas like the former homelands of the Eastern Cape, where the extraction of biological resources booms. Those who do occupy such spaces and wish to involve themselves in the industry cannot as readily identify themselves as Indigenous knowledge holders. According to environmental scholar Rachel Wynberg, these dynamics reveal a larger "disconnect between, on the one hand, the realism of contemporary biodiversity custodians and knowledge holders, and on the other, a worldview, supported to a large extent by international agreements and global movements, that essentializes indigenous peoples."[47] By broadening access and benefit sharing, officials wish to ensure that rural groups—who may hold some knowledge or simply engage in plant collection to make ends meet—gain more from commodity trade than the small amount biotraders pay harvesters per kilogram of plant material collected. Officials saw the potential monetary rewards for the country as significant—they hoped to direct hundreds of millions of dollars in annual funds toward goals like poverty alleviation.

"LISTEN TO THIS ONE" (ABOUT "HOMELANDS")

If the spatial and temporal dislocations described here are problems, South Africa's approach to access and benefit sharing is nevertheless a fraught solution. The CBD's version of the instrument reflects a supranational interest in shaping national policies on exceedingly complex cultural matters.[48] It has unleashed—and obliges signatory states to try to manage—wildly generative forces in the realms of nature, property, and collective identity. By modifying access and benefit sharing and regulating commodity trade and drug discovery under the same national regulatory framework, South Africa's laws have released these forces into new sociopolitical domains, scrambling their stakes. This book shows how and to what effect a former homeland, the Ciskei, came to be a locus of those swirling forces. In the chapters that follow, I specifically argue that these forces entrenched, and in some instances expanded, boundaries and configurations of power that some South Africans associated with illiberalism and apartheid. The state and corporate task of producing communities amenable to biodiversity commercialization and conservation became entangled with processes of homeland reconsolidation. Resource rights in this context foregrounded forced enrollment and the expansion of Indigenous group membership as modes of capitalist accumulation in an extractive economy.

In the old South Africa, the ten homelands stood as pillars of segregationist ideology and policy. When White nationalists seized control of the South African government in 1948, they initiated a formal campaign to make racial separateness—*apartheid*—the most total possible reality. To engineer a White-majority nation, the nationalist regime sorted millions of Africans into different ethnic groups, concentrated them in separate territories, and stripped them of their citizenship. In a move antiapartheid activist Steve Biko would call "the greatest single fraud ever invented by White politicians," the territories later became nominally autonomous "countries" known as Bantustans or "Bantu homelands."[49] "The whole idea," Biko wrote, "is made to appear as if for us, while working against our very existence."[50]

Each of the homelands was different, but on the whole, their creation had devastating consequences. Millions of people were forced to live in haphazardly planned rural slums where poverty, disease, and ecological ruin characterized everyday life. Many also became the subjects of customary chiefs, who were the only point of access to government.[51] After the end of official apartheid in 1994, Nelson Mandela's government dissolved the homelands and absorbed them into the new Republic of South Africa. In the view of many observers, however, the regions' histories have cast them indefinitely to the country's margins, where they remain the forgotten waste products of empire.[52] Indeed, although seventeen million South Africans remain attached to the former homelands, these regions have been largely erased from the social imagination of the country.[53] What, scholars have started asking, has actually become of the homelands? What is their place in the wider political economy of the country and beyond? "It is time to think about [the homeland] phase in a longer perspective," historian William Beinart insists.[54]

To think in this longer perspective, I take inspiration from South African geographer Maano Ramutsindela's description of former homelands as "resilient geographies."[55] Homeland configurations of power and space haunt South Africa; they are undergoing reconsolidation and expansion. But if boundaries are sociological facts that form space, what kind of spaces did homeland boundaries produce?[56] And how does the character of these spaces shape experiences and understandings of reconsolidation in the present?

Drawing my attention to these questions was a conversation I had with Dabula, a Xhosa man in his sixties who acted as my research assistant for the duration of my fieldwork in the Eastern Cape. On a cold winter day in 2018, Dabula and I meandered around the city of Bhisho, viewing the results of a recent program to revitalize this Eastern Cape capital's government offices. Dabula had not visited Bhisho in many years, and when I asked him for his thoughts about the creation of the city after the Ciskei was declared an independent homeland during apartheid, his reply seemed like the delivery of a punch line. "Listen to this one. Kaiser Matanzima, the president of Transkei homeland, was the first to take independence. That was 1976," Dabula told me. "In 1981, the president of Ciskei, Lennox Sebe, followed by also taking independence. And in an instant, from then on, we found ourselves living in a foreign country called Ciskei."

Dabula had grown up in the region that became the Ciskei homeland and had been in his twenties during the Ciskei's consolidation. He likened the experience to being swept up in a surreal tragicomedy. He recalled listening to radio reports about the Ciskei national independence celebrations, shaking his head with repulsed incredulity upon hearing that the Ciskei national flag, when raised for the first time at the celebrations, had prophetically toppled over because the flagpole snapped. Dabula remembered other absurdities. Lennox Sebe and his government conjured Bhisho as a "historic" capital of Ciskei by transforming rural fields into a stadium and state buildings. To create a site for national worship, they ordered the construction of a massive temple on a forested mountain. The regime appropriated as its national anthem "Nkosi Sikelel' iAfrika," a widely recognized hymn and emblem of the anti-apartheid movement. It also sought to transform Dimbaza, the notorious settlement camp and symbol of forced removals, into a showcase industrial center. "We heard that they were manufacturing tracksuits for the Taiwanese there," Dabula said, beginning to laugh. "The entire situation was like a fucking joke."[57]

The establishment of indirect rule represented another farce, Dabula said. The White nationalists' push for the "separate development" of the "races" was legislatively initiated in the Bantu Authorities Act of 1951, which, for the sake of governing the areas that would become the homelands, sought to co-opt and strengthen the power of chiefs. In the Transkei, which was considered a model homeland, this process proved relatively straightforward. The Transkei had, after all, been a largely coherent and contiguous entity since the early 1900s. There, chiefs had held longer-standing and more meaningful powers.

But circumstances were more complicated in the neighboring region that would become the Ciskei homeland. Neither a "geographical nor a tribal entity," this region constituted a patchwork of White-owned farms and areas set aside for Black South Africans.[58] An ambitious program of land acquisition and reallocation ensued, and a territorial block over eight thousand square kilometers in size began to take shape. Into this block, the apartheid state relocated hundreds of thousands of people, resulting in the creation of what anti-apartheid activists called a human "dumping ground."[59] On the eve of its independence as a homeland in 1981, the Ciskei had the second-highest population density of the homelands. Although there were attempts to foster industrial development and job growth, most residents did not benefit. Unemployment rates exceeded 30 percent, with most people barely getting by.[60]

The Ciskei was not a "tribal entity" for an additional reason. As one high-level apartheid commissioner stated in the 1950s, "the power of the chiefs had gone" in the region.[61] This absence can be traced back to the late eighteenth century, when British colonial forces instigated a series of violent conflicts known as the Wars of Dispossession, or the Cape Frontier Wars. Through these conflicts, the British expanded their rule into the area, crushing Xhosa chiefs and others who resisted. In the aftermath, colonial officials opposed hereditary leaders. They cast aside the trappings of chiefly power, incorporating the Ciskei zone into the Cape Colony under liberal common law.

It was this backdrop that prompted the commissioner I quoted previously to object when Hendrik Verwoerd, the National Party politician and so-called architect of apartheid, later ordered that a process of "retribalization" begin in the Ciskei. Verwoerd's aim had been to resurrect chiefly power in the region and anchor in it a centralized, patriarchal power that European officials had long (and mistakenly) understood to be the norm of rule in precolonial Africa. But the commissioner objected because the material context for chieftainship no longer existed.[62] His protests meant little. He was removed from his position, and a more agreeable commissioner was installed. To create "tribal authorities," administrators granted new powers to local leaders, who were renamed "chiefs." In other instances, chieftaincies were resuscitated or wholly fabricated. They were jurisdictionally positioned to foster ethnic belonging and consent for homeland rule. Lennox Sebe, the former schoolteacher who claimed power as president of Ciskei for life, was a case in point. He secured a chieftaincy, land, and subjects of his own, all by crafting a story about his descent from an anticolonial warrior chief.[63]

"We knew there was no such thing as independence as a homeland," Dabula insisted to me during our stroll around Bhisho. "Sure, independence was what we wanted. But not as a homeland. We wanted independence from the White nationalists." Within a few years, civil resistance to Sebe's regime boiled over. As a hegemonic project, indirect rule proved tenuous, failing to generate any durable nationalist sentiment.[64] Having more to do with patronage than primordial loyalty to traditional leaders, resuscitation also established a clear link between chiefs and colonial rule.[65] In 1990 the brigadier general of the Ciskei's military ousted Sebe in a coup. The brigadier's new regime lashed out at civil opposition, climaxing in the government massacre of twenty-eight protestors in Bhisho in 1992. Two years later, after several coup attempts against the new president, a popular uprising led to the resignation of the brigadier and plans for democratic elections.

During our visit to Bhisho, Dabula and I peeked inside the shiny, $5 million House of Traditional Leaders, completed in 2009. The national government has called the building "the first of its kind": a state-funded headquarters for provincial chiefs. Our visit prompted Dabula to note how much chiefs had resurged in the post-apartheid period. The resurgence was surprising, he told me, because after Mandela's government had absorbed the homelands into a unitary South Africa in 1994, chiefs had been relegated to the sidelines of governance plans. But they eventually secured recognition in the country's constitution, which proved foundational to a series of laws introduced by parliament in the new millennium. The laws legislate state salaries for chiefs as Indigenous leaders and strive to invest them with statutory powers concerning land administration, welfare allocation, the adjudication of justice in traditional courts, and economic development. Over the course of our research together, Dabula and I witnessed multiple groups of villagers—numbering in the thousands—subsumed under the authority of chiefs via benefit-sharing agreements involving pelargonium. Having grown up in the region, Dabula expressed bewilderment. Some scholars of South Africa I spoke with put it in more extreme terms. When I mentioned chiefs involving themselves in bio-traffic in the region, one scholar reacted sharply: "But there are no chiefs there." Another explained it to me in more nuanced language: "The power of chiefs was always relatively diluted in Ciskei, and it's supposed to be a less chief-obsessed region today."

In the former homelands of South Africa, the re/centralization of chiefly authority evokes what some have termed "reBantustanization."[66] Put differently, critics argue that new laws that empower chiefs to control land and resources reinscribe the homeland boundaries, constraining people's ability to organize themselves on any other basis than as "tribal" subjects.[67] One scholar has invoked Giorgio Agamben's concept of "bare life" to describe the resultant status of such people; they "are not included in the normal juridical terrain but are excluded from it, living as they do in a state of exception."[68] For these scholars, chieftaincy is not merely some remnant of the institutions White settlers erected. It is, as historian Sara Berry argues, "but one element in ongoing, multifaceted struggles among local, national, and international actors over practices and meanings of ownership, authority, and belonging in postcolonial Africa."[69]

When I use the names "Ciskei" and "Transkei" to refer to contemporary regions, I aim to underscore the continued sociospatial salience of apartheid's boundaries, not to reproduce those boundaries uncritically.[70] Benefit sharing is not alone in driving the reconsolidation of homelands. It is merely one facet of larger processes involving contests over land and political power.[71] Nevertheless, interventions like benefit sharing can serve as a window into such processes, helping us mark the often-unmarked hyphen in terms like "re-consolidation" and "re-Bantustanization." Put another way, they invite us to pay attention to what—if any—historical and institutional scaffolding "re-consolidation" requires.

Explosions in rights consciousness, extractive capitalism, and the durability of chiefly leadership are profoundly linked phenomena in South Africa. An examination of biotraffic and its governance reinforces this finding, while highlighting less explored features of it. For one thing, it contrasts with existing scholarship—which focuses almost exclusively on mining industries—by revealing medicines to be an increasingly prominent frontier of chiefly recognition and legitimacy in the former homelands.[72] Second, it contrasts existing scholarship—which largely describes contexts characterized by historical continuity in the leadership of chiefs—with a situation in which rights expand customary subjectivity into areas of the country where chiefs were virtually nonexistent for well over one hundred years. Third, it offers a window into ethnic boundary construction in Indigenous claims to resources. It does so, however, by shifting attention from the exclusionary nature of this construction to the dangers of exclusion's concomitant: forced inclusion or membership.

This book highlights these developments to engage a larger conversation about colonial histories and their recursions. According to Ann Stoler, this conversation has too frequently been characterized by divergent analytic postures, one of which emphasizes marked ruptures between the colonial past and postcolonial present, while the other emphasizes continuities.[73] Echoing Stoler's interpretation, an examination of former homelands renders such oppositions difficult to maintain. Apartheid's afterlives endure, yet their frequent occlusion and submersion demand that we ask precisely how they work and how their effects may be differential. They also demand that we ask how and to what effect they intersect with or diverge from contemporary logics of governance.

CONFRONTING MY POSITION AS A RESEARCHER

Most of the research informing this book unfolded in 2011, but I continued to make numerous return trips to the Eastern Cape until 2022, with most of these trips lasting about a month each. During this research, I spent spells living on my own in the city of Makhanda and other periods with rural families in the Amatole District. I lived with these families to understand everyday life in the Ciskei region (though I visited the neighboring former Transkei as well). I also wanted to conduct in-depth interviews with the residents involved in the pelargonium patent challenges. The translocal nature of the plant trade and the actors involved kept me on the move, however. I drove throughout the Eastern Cape to interview biotraders, plant harvesters, government officials, land-policy researchers, farmers, and traditional leaders, including chiefs.

In Makhanda I frequented the Cory Library, where I consulted books and learned much from the library's director, the historian Jeff Peires. It was during these visits that I came to understand better the hurdles the apartheid state had faced in its efforts to formalize "separate development" by transforming the country's existing "native reserves" into "self-governing" homelands. I also spent time in the cities of Bhisho and Qonce. In the latter, I visited the provincial archives repository and deeds office. In addition, I interviewed officials at the Eastern Cape Department of Economic Development and Environmental Affairs. I visited the bustling taxi rank area to speak with medicinal plant hawkers, "African chemists," and Indigenous healers to learn about the availability and uses of medicinal plants like pelargonium. To get a better sense of the national landscape upon which biological and genetic resource politics played out, I spent several weeks in Pretoria, Johannesburg, Cape Town, and Durban interviewing "policy intellectuals" in government departments, NGOs, companies, and law firms.[74] Finally, I spent numerous weeks digging through archives in Cape Town and London, learning about the Englishman who commercialized pelargonium as a medicine in Europe. This Englishman's story is the topic of the book's five interludes.

I began my research in 2009 as a PhD student in anthropology at the University of Colorado at Boulder. From the outset of this research, I tried to "study up" by gaining access to elites making decisions about resource trade. I did not expect to be successful. But in the case of state officials, corporate actors, and most chiefs, access opened up relatively quickly and sometimes to uncomfortable effect. For example, after I learned that drug companies had initiated access and benefit sharing with chiefs in the Ciskei, I endeavored to observe the partnerships firsthand. In 2011 I learned of plans for a "stakeholder meeting" about an agreement. I sought an invitation from Schwabe's biotrader, whom I presumed was the meeting's organizer. The intermediary could not grant me permission, however. He insisted I contact the "community representative," who turned out to be the chiefly secretary and self-described "CEO" of the Rharhabe kingdom's corporate arm. It took me weeks to get the attention of the busy chief, who eventually agreed to my request. But what I had anticipated would be a large gathering of harvesters and other stakeholders turned out to be an exclusive meeting between the biotrader and the chief in a house belonging to a relative of the chief. During the meeting I sat beside the biotrader as he urged the kingdom to rapidly establish an independent access agreement—separate from Schwabe—with him to get plant harvesters working at capacity. "The people are suffering," he said. Far from viewing me as a passive observer, the two men watched me for reactions, even appealing to me as a third party when persuading one another on specific points.

I have contemplated various explanations for my unquestioned access to such meetings, but the reasons remain unclear. One possibility is that representatives of companies like Schwabe were tired of receiving bad press about their activities and hoped I would depict them in a more positive light. Over the previous decades, Schwabe's activities had epitomized what South African officials wished to curtail. In more recent years, however, the company had reversed course and started helping officials confront "illicit" trade.

Other early fieldwork encounters were more sensitive, revealing the problematic nature of my research and positionality.[75] When I began exploring professional affiliations with departments at South African universities, more than one South African scholar I met spoke frankly of their exhaustion with assisting funded American PhD students. They were open to helping me, but they lamented how their South African students often languished, securing the scarcest resources to conduct research at home.[76] South Africa is certainly a popular research location for American scholars. Adding insult to injury, some Americans have positioned themselves as antagonists to South African scholars, brashly criticizing them for willfully disengaging from matters of moral and political urgency in the country (see Ramphele 1996; Robins 1996).

I soon learned how easy it was to see hypocrisy and simplism in American critiques of South African scholarship. During my research in 2011, I attended a public talk at Rhodes University, an Eastern Cape institution that would later become a site of the "Rhodes Must Fall" protests calling for free, decolonized education at South African universities.[77] The talk had drawn public interest due to its headline speaker, a White South African scholar named Samantha Vice, who had that year published a series of controversial writings, including an op-ed in the country's largest newspaper. Vice's writings called on White South Africans to refrain from publicly commenting on the country's political problems. Indeed, Whites should "feel shame at their White identity" and "cultivate humility and silence, given their morally compromised position in the continuing racial and economic injustices of this country."[78]

The talk at Rhodes included a panel of scholars who deliberated on Vice's arguments and, upon finishing, invited questions and reactions from the audience. Many in the audience raised their hands, and their comments reflected an embrace of Vice's perspective. I raised my hand, too, and waited to be called upon to pose a question. In the meantime, the audience reactions had proved so receptive to Vice that one White panelist appeared to think a small proviso was in order. The panelist implied that the audience members were being too critical of themselves as White South Africans. To paraphrase, the panelist said: "Look, at least we aren't Americans, whose imperial footprint and carnage around the world far exceed that of South Africans." The implication was that if anyone should be silent about the world's political problems, it was Americans. At that time, the US military's ongoing operations in Iraq and Afghanistan reflected a troubling pattern of interventionism, marked by a significant and often contentious global military imprint that raised serious concerns about the implications of American foreign policy and its disproportionate impact on world affairs.

My eyes grew large upon hearing the comment. I sheepishly withdrew my hand, knowing that my accent would expose me as an American if I spoke. But even if everyone had discovered my nationality, they still would not have known the entire truth. It was one thing to be a White South African publicly weighing in on South African political issues. It was quite another to be a White *American anthropologist* who intended to weigh in on them. What is more, my research examined the South African government's application of provisions of the CBD, a treaty that the US government has never bothered to sign but whose elaboration the United States has sought to dominate (in an example of what some have called "bio-imperialism").[79] Continuing this trend, the United States stood alone among UN member states in not adopting the Kunming-Montreal Global Biodiversity framework that emerged in late 2022.

What is this book if not me figuratively raising my hand and speaking when I should arguably be heeding Samantha Vice's advice to cultivate humility and silence? The words on these pages are a kind of hauntologist production; their disciplinary and broader structural scaffolding predates me, but this scaffolding nevertheless conditioned the very possibility of my arrival in South Africa and the construction of the story I get to tell.[80] Many of the South Africans I encountered understood this intuitively, and some tactfully pointed it out to me. They knew that I would use representational tactics to represent—and thereby fit—local dynamics into a narrative that produced and secured value. This would entail the haunted production of academic value (and the employment that comes with it). As my relationships with South Africans developed over time, we worked toward common goals. The relationships made me deeply aware of my own presence, instilling a greater degree of humility and a deeper sense of gratitude to the people who granted me their time. My understanding was continually refined by the insights of individuals who shared their experiences and perspectives. Each interaction became an instructive exchange—one that frequently called on me to mobilize my research to new and unexpected ends. This interplay of observation and response guided my research approach, involving me as both listener and participant attuned to the interests of my interlocutors.

The trajectory of my research was particularly influenced by my emerging awareness of connections between medicinal resources and land rights. Through dialogue with villagers who contested both pharmaceutical companies and local chieftaincies, I learned of their dual concerns over intellectual property and landownership. As my fieldwork unfolded, it became increasingly clear that villagers' struggles for sovereignty over medicinal resources was deeply entangled with broader struggles for recognition and identity within the postapartheid landscape of South Africa. Such insights, gleaned from interactions in the former Ciskei region, compelled me to expand my initial focus. I came to realize that land politics was as pivotal to their narratives as patent disputes. This shift was not just a change in research direction; altering the scope and implications of my anthropological work also created new and uncertain positional entanglements, notably my involvement in land rights advocacy. Throughout this book, I demonstrate that for many, land represented a more stable and lasting asset than the ephemeral nature of the plant trade could provide. This advocacy, as much as I may have subconsciously hoped it would, did not absolve me of the complicities and power imbalances I embodied. It merely produced new positional entanglements. Like a ghost, my troubled production of this book seemed "neither present, nor absent."[81] It permeated my research and was never resolved.

OUTLINE OF THE BOOK

Before sketching the ground the book's chapters cover, it's worth stating what they don't.[82] This book is not an ethnography of Indigenous knowledge. It will not describe detailed interactions between healers and plants, nor will it provide prescriptions for combating "biopiracy." And although I touch upon "multispecies" dynamics between plants and people, readers steeped in such epistemologies will find my account inadequate.[83] This ethnography arguably aligns more with a long-standing anthropological engagement with governance interventions and their effects. It particularly examines how governance initiatives, informed by political rationalities, identify and intervene in issues impacting populations, thereby producing distinct subjects and spatialities of authority.[84] As articulated by Tania Murray Li, the "identification of a problem is intimately linked to the availability of a solution. They coemerge within a governmental assemblage in which certain sorts of diagnoses, prescriptions, and techniques are available."[85] This perspective sheds light on the dynamics at play in my research, where the exercise of power was often rationalized and rendered technical. In such contexts, interventions became depoliticized, transforming complex and inherently political issues into mere bureaucratic challenges. The transformation risked obscuring the nuanced facets of environmental governance, often sidelining their vital sociopolitical implications.

To explore these themes and others, the book presents a twofold narrative structure using five chapters and five interludes. The five interludes chronicle pelargonium's tumultuous absorption into international medicinal markets, beginning in the early 1900s. For the most part, the interludes move chronologically through time, focusing on an Englishman named Charles Henry Stevens and his role in establishing pelargonium as a prominent yet contentious tuberculosis remedy in Europe and eventually a popular common cold treatment globally. An important proviso is in order, however. The interludes draw from sources whose narration of events is potentially unreliable, inviting readers to engage with a discerning lens. And that engagement may take the form of reading the interludes as they appear (enriching the understanding of the more contemporary narrative the chapters unravel) or exploring them in succession from the outset.

In contrast with the interludes, the chapters recount and further unravel a more contemporary story. They collectively analyze the dynamic interplay of time, space, scale, and the diverse experiences of individuals ensnared within the social field of biotraffic. Much like the Rashomon effect, they present multifaceted perspectives, offering a deeper exploration of how these dimensions shape an unfolding narrative. The chapters take a step back, rewinding that narrative to the initial skirmishes led by the NGO ACB against Schwabe Pharmaceuticals, which I introduced at the outset in this book's prologue. This rewind, along with a narrative that unfolds in a manner that reflects my gradual understanding of this book's story, aims to provide structure to numerous interweaving threads. This approach also embraces reflexivity, as omitting my voice could be misleading, perhaps even deceitful.

Chapter 1 provides an account of the transnational legal battle waged at the EPO from 2007 to 2010, challenging Schwabe's pelargonium patents. It documents the concerted efforts of the NGO ACB and its allies within a group of Eastern Cape villagers, examining the complex interplay between drug discovery and the trade in plant commodities. The chapter explores how these intertwined dynamics proved resistant to anti-patent strategies, demonstrating that the implications of their resistance reached beyond the confines of anti-intellectual-property activism and into the broader sphere of global trade and regulatory practice. Chapter 2 examines biotraffic involving pelargonium in the Ciskei region at ground level, showing how both apartheid afterlives and new policies contribute to an economy characterized by insecurity and unpredictability. In chapter 3 I return to the topic of the NGO and the villagers described in chapter 1. Presenting the situation of villagers as a case study, I investigate the influence of recent environmental legislation in fostering partnerships between chiefs and pharmaceutical companies in the former homelands—partnerships that fortified and in some cases extended apartheid-associated boundaries and manifestations of authority. In chapter 4 I argue that the unresolved status of land rights shapes biotraffic's inequities in contemporary South Africa. Continuing to spotlight the villagers involved in the patent challenges, I detail the complex interplay between land reform policies, zones of legal exclusion, and the governance of biological resource movements. Chapter 5, finally, expands the analysis of South Africa's governance of biotraffic beyond the villagers involved in the patent challenge. The chapter frames the book as a cautionary tale about prevailing legal regimes to address pressing social and ecological concerns. It critiques tick-box regulatory compliance, which, in service to an extractive imperative, hazardously reproduces illiberal modes of government.

INTERLUDE

"My Boy, You Are in for It" (1897)

In 1897 Charles Henry Stevens, a seventeen-year-old mechanic from Birmingham, England, felt unwell. He visited his family physician, Dr. Taplin. Upon examining Stevens, Dr. Taplin told the teen, "My boy, you are in for it." Taplin had discovered a lesion on Stevens' left lung, indicating that Stevens had contracted tuberculosis, the largest single source of mortality and chronic illness in Britain during the nineteenth century.[1] Concerned, Taplin encouraged Stevens to travel from England to southern Africa's Central Plateau. There, he could convalesce at a high elevation—perhaps somewhere in the Transvaal or the Orange Free State. Soon after his appointment with Taplin, Stevens began arranging his travel south.

We cannot know for certain why Stevens took the advice of his doctor, but the weak provision of care available to "consumptives" likely played a role. Germ theory was in the ascendancy, with Robert Koch's postulates on bacteriology and his related case study explicating the life cycle of anthrax firmly placing germs at the forefront of disease etiology during the last decades of the 1800s.[2] Yet while Koch had himself convincingly explained the pathogenic nature of tuberculosis and had won the Nobel Prize in medicine for this work in 1905, there were no antibiotic therapies at hand. Therapeutic trial and error ensued until the early 1940s, when streptomycin was discovered. In 1890 Koch insisted that he had isolated an element of the infectious bacilli—what he called tuberculin—which would, upon injection, "render harmless the pathogenic bacteria that are found in a living body and so this without disadvantage to the body."[3] Koch's tuberculin was used in some hospitals, but it quickly proved ineffective as a cure. However, the substance would later become key to detecting latent tuberculosis via skin tests.

Nevertheless, given Koch's evidence that tuberculosis was pathogenic, one might assume that by 1897, Charles Henry Stevens would have greeted a medical landscape buzzing with activity aimed at combating the disease. Consider also the scale of suffering and death wrought by the disease: by 1900, an estimated quarter of a million sufferers and fifty thousand annual deaths had been recorded in Britain. Demand for care and treatment was considerable. And yet, as historian Michael Worboys notes, none of the abovementioned factors mattered; tuberculosis was not yet a "public health disease" and "was ignored at almost every level of medicine."[4]

Perhaps Stevens could have applied as a voluntary patient in a specialist consumption hospital. Fourteen such institutions were open in Britain by 1900. But between them, these institutions provided only one thousand beds.[5] State-run sanatoria would not proliferate for another fourteen years in Britain, and the more rapid growth of private sanatoria there began in 1900.[6] This timeline was too late for Stevens.

Given this backdrop, Dr. Taplin's recommendation that Stevens become a medical tourist to Southern Africa was far from unusual. Alongside tonics, many general practitioners viewed the open-air recovery method as a good course of action. Their hope was that clean, cool air inhaled at high altitudes, coupled with rest, exercise, and nutrition, would stimulate an immune response to infection.

In pursuit of this recovery, Stevens arrived in the Cape Colony of South Africa in 1897, some fourteen years before the country's union. He made his way to the Central Plateau, stopping in the city of Bloemfontein, the so-called fountain of flowers and capital of Orange Free State, a Boer republic granted independence with the British Empire acting as suzerain. In Bloemfontein, Stevens encountered an Afrikaner who suggested he do more than breathe the air, however. The Afrikaner told Stevens to consider Indigenous medicine.

This was no chance recommendation. Stevens arrived at a period when African therapeutics were rapidly becoming popular among White settlers. According to historian Karen Flint, this was especially the case among Afrikaners, who prided themselves on self-reliance and were sometimes wary of a biomedical health sector dominated by English speakers (a wariness that grew during and after the First Anglo-Boer War, which unfolded between 1880 and 1881).[7] The trend was also fueled by the increasing urbanization and professionalization of African healers, who were becoming proficient at advertising their medicines and their efficacy.

The Afrikaner encouraged Stevens to consult a particular African healer whose ethnicity remains uncertain.[8] The healer was an older man who lived in a village in the nearby Maseru District of the mountainous Territory of Basutoland, which, like the Cape, was a British colony at the time. The man's name was Mike Kijitse, the Afrikaner said, and he had a cure for lung diseases. Upon Stevens's departure for Basutoland, the Afrikaner gave Stevens a tarp he could pitch—something to sleep under for the months Stevens would be under Kijitse's care.

According to Adrien Sechehaye, a Swiss physician and the source of this account of Stevens's trip to South Africa, when Stevens met Kijitse and told him of his disease, Kijitse "fetched a bag, from which he took some roots which he crushed between two stones and boiled" in a kettle pot.[9] After drinking the decoction, Stevens felt sick. He vomited profusely. However, as he continued to drink the medicine over the following weeks, his condition improved. His appetite returned. "Very thin at the outset," Sechehaye says, Stevens "put on weight and got stronger; after two months there was a complete change; after three months he no longer coughed or expectorated at all, and felt as well as he had ever been."[10]

Stevens soon returned to Birmingham and met again with Dr. Taplin. Taplin percussed Stevens's chest wall and heard the kind of resonance air-filled lungs would make. He detected only a slight dullness in one area of lung tissue. Stevens was cured, Taplin said.

1 Patent Problems

Nomthunzi Api sat quietly, her back ramrod straight. She waited. It was January 2010, and the middle-aged South African woman was seated at a large conference table inside the EPO in Munich. Beside her were representatives from the NGO ACB and their lawyer. Occupying one end of the table were delegates from several European pharmaceutical companies. Stationed at the head were members of the EPO's Opposition Division, the unit responsible for challenges to patents. They stood, methodically sorting legal documents into neat little stacks, preparing to speak.

Finally, the announcement came: the EPO was to revoke a patent held by one of the pharmaceutical companies—the German multinational Schwabe.

Nomthunzi exhaled, then smiled.[1] The revocation was what she and the NGOs had sought. They had argued to the EPO that Schwabe's patent replicated existing knowledge about pelargonium from Southern Africa and therefore lacked the novelty required for patentability. The patent had amounted to "biopiracy," they said—Schwabe had stolen knowledge from South Africa and Lesotho.

Soon after the EPO's announcement of the patent revocation, the South African newspaper *Mail & Guardian* published an article titled "Locals

Win Patent Dispute." The newspaper declared that "a rural South African community has won its case against German homeopathic giant Schwabe Pharmaceuticals over a traditional medicine the company had sought to patent."[2] Nomthunzi, a representative of the community, voiced her satisfaction at a media event. "This is the first time that a patent is challenged successfully by Africans," she announced.[3] An ACB representative added, "This is quite a big victory for us. It sends a very clear sign to international companies that we will not tolerate this kind of exploitation."[4]

Schwabe quickly disputed such portrayals. "The headline 'Locals win patent dispute' (January 29) is misleading," a spokesperson for the company complained in a rebuttal in the *Mail & Guardian*.[5] The patent had been revoked on technical, not substantive, grounds, they insisted. "The accusation of 'biopiracy' was rejected" by the EPO.[6]

It was too late. The narrative of victory against corporate misappropriation seemed to stick. Sensing its reputation was at stake, Schwabe soon voluntarily withdrew four other patents it held at the EPO that concerned the plant.

What, precisely, was the patent challenge about? Who was the "small Eastern Cape community," and why had it become involved with an NGO? What is more, what had this group's ostensible victory against a "German homeopathic giant" meant? This chapter frames the patent challenge as an act of activism aimed at addressing biotraffic, particularly the intricate interplay between drug discovery and plant-commodity trade across multiple scales. It explores how these practices, when intertwined, proved resistant to anti-patent strategies, demonstrating that their implications reached beyond the confines of anti-intellectual-property activism and into the broader sphere of global trade and regulatory practices.

"UNPRONOUNCEABLE, BUT PRONOUNCEDLY GOOD"

When people ask me about the research reflected in this book, they frequently ask if I identify as a "plant person" and if my status as such explains how I became aware of pelargonium. In truth, I first learned of the plant when I was an anthropology PhD student on a month-long research trip in Germany. It was 2008, and I was in Bonn to conduct interviews with representatives of German ministries and agencies, trying to understand why and how they were promoting "good governance" on the African continent, advising states there to become more "efficient" and "transparent." I had become particularly interested in good-governance initiatives aimed at reorganizing the health and environment sectors of selected African governments.

I had arrived in Bonn a week after the city hosted the Ninth Conference of the Parties of the UN CBD, and I had been reading news about the event with interest. One article in the magazine *Der Spiegel*, published in anticipation of the conference, sketched its stakes to me. The article expressed doubt that the roughly six thousand attendees at the conference would do anything consequential to slow global loss of ecosystems and species—a goal the parties to the CBD sought to achieve by 2010. The conference would ideally "bring meaning to what might otherwise be empty words and phrases," the article stated. At worst, it "will end in little more than bland declarations of intent."[7] The article foregrounded one challenge in particular: balancing the interests of Southern countries with rich biological diversity and Northern countries wishing to commercialize that diversity. Parties from Southern countries would enter the discussion with mistrust, "because bio-pirates have already hijacked parts of their biological treasures."[8] After all, firms already earned $43 billion in yearly revenues via remedies made from Southern resources, the article noted. It even named one alleged "biopirate" from Germany: Schwabe, whose patents concerning pelargonium were attracting international scrutiny.

On prominent display at a Bonn bookshop was a German-language book titled *The Biopirates: The Pharmaceutical Industry's Billion-Dollar-Business with Nature's Blueprint*.[9] I purchased it and became engrossed in its case studies of alleged "biopiracy." One such case involved Schwabe patenting a method for manufacturing Umckaloabo, the pelargonium-derived medicine that earned Schwabe €80 million in annual sales. The book posited a glaring regulatory gap: no laws had hindered Schwabe's attempt to privatize what was commonly held knowledge in South Africa and Lesotho. Only an international regime of access and benefit sharing could bridge this chasm.

Talk of such a regime struck me as familiar. German development parastatals and other agencies actively promoted benefit sharing in some

African countries as part of their reform agendas. NGOs were also involved. The closer I looked, the more the effort resembled what I had come to understand about "good governance" more broadly. It was hybrid and constellatory, with a multiplicity of government and government-like players orbiting a belief in the transformative power of administrative "capacity."

Indeed, benefit sharing appeared to be just one example of a shift in international development policy and discourse—a deviation from the overtly economic ideology of a modernization paradigm (establishing conditions for the "take off" of national economies for full-throttle industrialization and agricultural production, for example) that had characterized so much of the twentieth century. To be sure, the new approach, which became prominent in the early 1990s, was also about fostering economic growth. Yet its means to this end was different. It zeroed in on the state bureaucracy and its functioning. According to Gerhard Anders, the specific aim was to increase "transparency" and "efficiency" by establishing systems of management and autonomy, features that purveyors of "good governance" suggest are missing from states in Africa due to their "dysfunction."[10] But anyone who understands benefit sharing knows that its administration would bedevil any government in the world. Its dynamics of rights and property are notoriously unwieldy. So how and to what effect, I wondered, would bureaucratic procedures attempt to order what were recognizably complex matters of culture and structural inequality?

I had previously lived in Germany and maintained friends and other contacts there. When I asked them about Umckaloabo, they told me it was popular in the country; parents give it to their cough-stricken children, and doctors prescribe it to adult patients with respiratory infections. *The Biopirates* quoted a Schwabe ad informing consumers that relief from mild or acute bronchitis "doesn't come from the research laboratories of giant chemical corporations" but rather "from the savannahs of South Africa."[11] This relief, the ad claimed, also comes from "the knowledge of the South African herbal healers," which is "a thousand years old," "is passed on from generation to generation," and thus provides "detailed information about the application and efficacy of native plants."[12] Another Schwabe ad I saw showed a cliché image, a kind of visual shorthand for "Africa" in which spear-clasping figures stood under an acacia tree while silhouetted against a setting sun. The ad drolly described Umckaloabo as "unpronounceable, but pronouncedly good."[13] Taken together, the two ads reminded me of mediation that William Mazzarella calls "close distance."[14] The ads were their own form of commodities, whose "elements are sourced from an existing repertoire of resonances and meanings."[15] Playing on desires to consume a known (essentialized) "Africa" and its healing knowledge, they produced value by appealing to what is at once invitingly quotidian and grippingly distant.[16] Their commodity image radiated reified cultural difference, but one that evoked familiarity and safety. After all, the knowledge behind the medicines is "a thousand years old," and the medicines themselves come from nature (savannahs) rather than the more alien laboratories of "giant chemical corporations" (*Chemie-riesen*).[17]

I discussed the ads with my German contacts, some of whom suggested that fantasies about African medicines have particular resonance in their country, especially those that frame the African continent as a source of age-old remedies that have avoided biomedical tampering. The phytomedicine sector booms in Germany, a country with a robust history of such commercialization, and one in which Schwabe played a role.[18] My interlocutors linked demand for phytomedicines to the country's reputation as a nation that is deeply suspicious of medical biotechnology. The idea confronted me in bold print while I was perusing a South African newsstand in 2009. The front page of the international edition of *Newsweek* stated that "technophobia," including fear of medical biotech and its capacity for ethical overreach, "holds Germany back."[19] According to the magazine, many Germans view such biotech as "a dangerous meddling with nature" and "an attack on human dignity reminiscent of Nazi eugenics."[20]

Whatever the drivers, the country has ranked fourth in the world as a medicinal-plant importer, with most of this material arriving unprocessed and thus primed for profitable value adding.[21] In 2015 those imports were valued at US$250 million, which is likely an underestimate and signals that Germany is by far the largest trader of such plants in the European Union.[22] The country also acts as a "turntable" for phytomedicinal materials, ranking third as an exporter of medicinal plants to the rest of the world.[23] Within this national setting, Schwabe's engagement in the plant-commodity trade would seem unremarkable. But the company's patents had apparently crossed a line, publications like *Der Spiegel* and *The Biopirates* concluded.

The prevalence of Umckaloabo extended beyond Germany, as I discovered during my own encounters with the product. Upon my return to the United States from Bonn, I found versions of Umckaloabo on the medicine shelves of most grocery stores I visited. I was living in Boulder, Colorado, and I saw the product in major chain-retail companies like King Sooper's (a Kroger company) as well as in smaller natural food stores, including an independent retailer called Alfalfa's. In the latter, I reached for a bottle of Umckaloabo and studied its label, looking in vain for information about its source location. A store employee approached me and, after asking me if I was fighting a cold, began extolling the medicine and its efficacy for "stubborn" coughs, something that I admittedly struggled with due to a congenital condition that causes gastroesophageal reflux disease. I later mentioned the medicine to my mother, a teacher who lives in a small rural town in Colorado. She told me that some of her colleagues at school used a version of Umckaloabo called Umcka, which is sold by Schwabe's US subsidiary Nature's Way. These anecdotes spurred me to look deeper into the case against Schwabe and to read social science scholarship about drug discovery involving plants. By 2009 I began to think about studying the patent challenge, observing it as best I could as it unfolded. That year, I received a small grant to travel to South Africa. It was on that trip that I visited ACB at its headquarters in Johannesburg for the first time.

A LONELY CAMPAIGN

During that same trip in 2009, in an office building on a bustling city street, I interviewed officials in South Africa's Department of Environmental Affairs (DEA).[24] When I asked them about Schwabe's patents, they said they were aware of Schwabe's portfolio at the Munich EPO, which included seven patents concerning pelargonium. They knew that one of the patents protected a method Schwabe used to manufacture Umckaloabo from pelargonium. They also recognized that other patents granted the company exclusive use of extracts from the plant to develop medicines for a range of afflictions, including HIV/AIDS, tuberculosis, and disease-related changes in behavior. The idea that the company had privatized knowledge originating from South Africa troubled the officials. Speaking frankly, however, they said that Schwabe had likely taken a chance with its patent applications at the EPO and had been fortunate to succeed. Now the company risked losing both its patents and its public image. Still, the results of the challenge were pending, the officials said, and it remained to be seen if Schwabe had in fact patented existing knowledge.

One thing was certain, the officials insisted: the DEA was not interested in challenging the patents. As I understood it, to do so and shame drug companies in the media would have undermined the department's grander ambitions. Consider that, at the time of this conversation, critics from within the government were reproaching the DEA for being unnecessarily hostile toward drug discovery. South Africa's National Environmental Management: Biodiversity Act (NEMBA) came into force in 2004, but its sections regulating discovery and plant-commodity trade became active only in 2008. The first iteration of the sections required parties interested in discovery to apply for government permits at the very earliest stages of research on plant samples, long before the commercialization of a plant-derived product would be conceivable. Frustrated with this demand, employees of the South African National Biodiversity Institute (SANBI) disparaged the policy in a publication in a scientific journal. So "onerous" were the permit application regulations, the authors argued, they would drive industries away from drug discovery and into "closure."[25] The article seemed to have offended DEA officials. They saw the DEA as the parent institution of SANBI, and the authors had not bothered to consult the DEA before publishing their criticism. But disapproval of the policy appeared to be widespread. "NEMBA is stillborn" due to its strict requirements, one South African intellectual property lawyer told me around the time I had spoken with the officials.

In 2009 the DEA amended its legislation. The early "discovery phase" would no longer require a permit (only later, if research progressed to the "commercialization phase"). Parties needed only to notify the minister of the environment of their *activity*. Even if this notification were written on the back of a napkin it would be legal, DEA officials joked to me, punctuating their department's newfound flexibility. The move foreshadowed what was to come: a two-front effort to first, invite new companies and research organizations into drug discovery, and second, steer existing discovery companies out of the shadows and toward transparent benefit sharing with South African communities. Reflecting just how far the DEA was willing to go to bring existing companies to the table, the DEA carved language into NEMBA allowing companies to continue their discovery activities without national permits, provided they applied for permits during a transitional period, before the discovery regulations became active in 2008. This move proved to be unlawful. But the department soon responded by proposing an amendment to NEMBA that would grant amnesty to companies awaiting permit decisions.[26] The whole endeavor proved challenging; most companies were either unaware of the laws or reluctant to engage with the complex directives they spelled out.[27]

But if DEA officials did not see patents as part of this larger problem, ACB appeared to understand the matter differently. The conviction that drug companies were obliged to be, but often were not, engaged in benefit sharing in South Africa was a mainstay of the NGO's campaign against four of Schwabe's patents at the EPO. The NGO collaborated in this campaign with the Berne Declaration, a Swiss NGO that had previously contested a European patent on a plant endemic to Africa, *Swartzia madagascariensis*. ACB also received funding from Church Development Service (Evangelischen Entwicklungsdienst), a German association led by Michael Frein, one of the authors of *The Biopirates*.

The NGOs' case stood on two pillars. The first was the claim that the four patents were entwined with improper commercial practices. The European Patent Convention recognizes provisions of the CBD, a treaty to which both Germany and South Africa are signatories. Under CBD provisions, a company like Schwabe would seek prior informed consent and establish benefit-sharing agreements with any community that grants the company access to resources and knowledge. According to the NGOs, Schwabe had failed to follow such steps. Its patents thus violated Article 53 of the European Patent Convention, which states that an invention is not patentable in Europe if the commercial activities underpinning that invention are unethical.[28] The NGOs cited this same article to draw a connection between Schwabe's patents and the company's role in plant-commodity trade. Stated differently, Schwabe had violated the article because the inventions its patents protected were tied to unsustainable plant collection. This collection was decimating pelargonium in the wild, the NGOs feared. They submitted to the EPO an affidavit from a conservation official in the Eastern Cape warning of such a risk. What is more, the patents exploited the local harvesters upon whose labor the trade hinged. According to the NGOs, harvesters earned a pay rate ten times below an already meager minimum wage for farmworkers under South African labor laws. They were often otherwise unemployed, and if working without plant-collection permits, they also risked arrest while harvesting.

The trouble with the patents went further. In the language of intellectual property law, Schwabe's patented method of producing Umckaloabo allegedly lacked "novelty." It was missing an "inventive step" when compared to "prior art" in existing production methods. Three European drug companies joined the NGOs at the EPO in challenging this patent, insisting that it was a standard textbook procedure in herbal chemistry. However, the NGOs differed from the three competitor companies in two crucial respects. First, the NGOs said that prior art in the method was visible in South African Indigenous knowledge systems.[29] Second, the NGOs argued that by monopolizing the primary production method of pelargonium-derived medicines in Europe, Schwabe had privatized the plant itself as a life-form.

These two claims constituted a second pillar of the NGOs' challenge, and they resonated with broader critiques of intellectual property laws and their international expansion. To understand, consider a concluding section of *The Biopirates* titled "No Patents on Life." The section bemoans the US Supreme Court's decision in *Diamond* v. *Chakrabarty* (1980) because it "expanded the concept of technology" without "appreciating the social and ecological ramifications of such a move."[30] One ramification of the decision was the capitalization of life itself, or the ability of companies and research institutions to patent living organisms by "modifying" their DNA to "innovate" something that ostensibly did not previously exist in nature. Article 53 of the European Patent Convention prevents the EPO from granting patents on plant or animal varieties as life-forms. However, this same article stipulates that "microbiological processes or the products thereof" are a different matter. Reflecting our post–*Diamond* v.

Chakrabarty world, patents on "modified" organisms remain possible within the European Union (as in the United States and elsewhere).[31]

If one imagines these developments in intellectual property law as a swelling and deep-carving river, then critics view drug discovery involving biodiversity as one of this river's largest tributaries. It is what Vandana Shiva addresses in her landmark book *Biopiracy: The Plunder of Nature and Knowledge*, explicitly situating the practice and its capacity for ruinous exploitation in global histories of European conquest. "The freedom that transnational corporations are claiming through intellectual property rights protection ... is the same freedom that European colonizers have claimed since 1492," Shiva argues.[32] Western powers "are still driven by the colonizing impulse to discover, conquer, own, and possess everything, every society, every culture. The colonies have now been extended to the interior spaces, the 'genetic codes' of life-forms from microbes and plants to animals, including humans."[33]

Political economists draw similar historical through lines, describing the capitalization of life as a present-day version of what Karl Marx called primitive accumulation. As Marx described it, primitive accumulation entailed eighteenth-century elites enclosing land and resources, reconstituting the people who subsisted on such things as "free workers" who, with few alternatives to make ends meet, became willing sellers of their labor power to capitalists. And by divorcing people from their "social means of subsistence and production," elites also remade these means; like money and commodities, after all, "they need to be transformed into capital.[34] In Marx's view, primitive accumulation was part of capitalism's "prehistory"—an early but foundational mechanism for producing the "capitalist-relation." Yet some scholars argue that dispossession via enclosure remains foundational to capitalist accumulation today.[35] Working from this premise and describing unethical drug discovery as a case in point, Carol Thompson suggests that "the most comprehensive enclosure, one that invokes future calamities, is the increasing enclosure of the planet's gene pool, both animal and plant. This enclosure involves privatization not just of the means of production, but of life itself."[36]

Schwabe's NGO challengers told the EPO that one of the company's patents similarly enclosed a life-form, allowing it to unfairly capitalize life. However, the argument supporting this accusation presented a twist.

Whether Schwabe had or had not modified pelargonium as an organism was not in question; the company had not. The NGOs instead suggested that Schwabe's procedure for making Umckaloabo was so exceedingly simple and common—a "standard textbook procedure in herbal chemistry," they said—that its enclosure effectively monopolized pelargonium itself. The patent was "a clever way by Schwabe of circumventing Article 53 of the European Patent Convention, which expressly disallows patents on life (patents on plant varieties)."[37] The reason: exclusive rights of use to such a common procedure meant exclusive rights of use to a species.

If true, the patent embodied what legal scholar Ikechi Mgbeoji says is often ignored about the appropriation of plant genetic resources: such resources are patentable even when no modification has occurred.[38] Keep in mind that when Northern patent offices like the EPO assess whether an invention (including a procedure for producing a medicine) is novel, the concept of novelty that informs their decision can operate to ignore Indigenous knowledge.[39] Why? Without any standard or meaningful guidance concerning global or absolute novelty, the EPO is prone to identify what may be common knowledge in one setting (e.g., South Africa) as novel knowledge in another (Europe).

For ACB, this reality reflected a fundamental mismatch between intellectual property regimes and Indigenous knowledge systems. The TRIPS industrial model recognizes intellectual property rights as private rights, a move that collapses shared knowledge into an atomized, exclusive conception of knowledge.[40] Such atomization is "designed to encourage industrial innovation and creativity through market incentives," the NGO said.[41] Indigenous knowledge is different. It "is based on cultural heritage and developed through several generations for noncommercial use," and it is also "mostly an outcome of a collective, which is not only intergenerational, but also sometimes also trans-cultural and trans-national."[42]

Given the arguments, critics of patents could reasonably disagree with the DEA officials I interviewed in 2009, who expressed their department's lack of interest in challenging patents. When discussing Schwabe's patents, the officials had implied to me that Schwabe had likely taken a chance and been fortunate with its patent applications. However, ACB seemed to see structural conditions at play in the applications' success more than fortune. State inaction—the "government-is-not-interested-in-challenging-patents" part of the conversation with the officials—was no static variable in the equation of "biopiracy." It was part of the problem, according to the NGO. As ACB put it, "Patent systems are seriously flawed. It is inherently unfair that public interest NGOs should have to challenge patents, at enormous effort and expense, to bring about equity and justice in protecting resources and traditional knowledge from the South."[43] The NGO repeatedly insisted in its publications that governments play a central role in the protection of Indigenous knowledge concerning biological resources.

A South African legal scholar agrees and has pushed the claim further. The South African government's absence was *the* problem the case against Schwabe underlined, Andre Myburgh says, because "the patent system can deal with those cases where an outsider attempts to patent plant-based traditional knowledge. The true problem is one of access to justice."[44] Access to justice entails "state-supported activism" to protect biological and knowledge diversity, including "keeping watch" to ensure that no one registers patents and other intellectual property concerning this diversity internationally.[45]

MEETING NOMTHUNZI

A self-described "activist organization" established in the early 2000s, ACB developed a reputation in South Africa for research-driven, advocacy-focused campaigns concerning biosafety, biodiversity, and food sovereignty. Among these campaigns, the NGO opposed the introduction and spread of genetically modified organisms in African agriculture, voicing concern about ecological and socioeconomic harms of such organisms. It produced reports examining the influence of multinational seed companies on the continent and the incursion of genetically modified maize, decrying their impacts on local seed diversity and farmer independence. The NGO particularly strove to influence regulatory and commercial practices, and South African officials repeatedly told me they took ACB's policy opinions seriously. Those same officials and others suggested this focus on national and international policies distinguished the NGO's approach from others focused more directly on "local community" support and interventions. They implied that, during the mid-2000s at least, the

NGO's activism had tended to emanate from its headquarters in the city of Johannesburg, rather than being deeply rooted in the more rural spaces its activism concerned.

But even if such impressions were accurate, ACB's campaign against Schwabe's pelargonium patents seemed a departure from the patterns discussed previously. While the campaign was tied to the NGO's longer-running efforts "to contribute to debate, public awareness and improved policy, legal and administrative reform," the organization was, in its own words, "a newcomer to the discourse on bioprospecting and biopiracy" in 2008.[46] Moreover, the campaign entailed the NGOs collaborating closely with a group of rural South Africans. To make their case against Schwabe, the NGOs presented the EPO with affidavits from villagers in the Eastern Cape province.

In its legal filings and initial publications, ACB referred to these villagers as "the Alice community," revealing only their proximity to the Eastern Cape town of Alice.[47] Offering the affidavits and providing direct testimony from Nomthunzi, the NGO argued to the EPO that the members of the Alice group had used the same method as Schwabe to produce a medicine from pelargonium that treated respiratory infections. "This procedure is not only commonly used in the phytomedicine sector," ACB asserted, "but also has for eons been used by traditional healers from the Alice and other communities in South Africa."[48] The Alice collaborators also exemplified Schwabe's noncompliance with the CBD; the NGO said that no benefit-sharing agreements concerning pelargonium had ever been made between the company and the villagers. This was so even though Schwabe had obtained pelargonium from them via a third-party biotrader.

After I first visited ACB's headquarters in 2009, the NGO's director left the door open to future interactions with me, provided we continue to correspond via email. Upon my return to South Africa in 2011, the director gave me Nomthunzi's contact information, and early that year, Nomthunzi invited me to visit her where she worked during the week, a museum in a city located a couple of hours from Alice by car. When I arrived, the museum's info desk gave me Nomthunzi's office number. As I neared the office, a sign above its door came into focus. It read, "Anthropology Department." Taped to the door was a flyer advertising a "Traditional Xhosa Dance Performance" in the city the following week. I entered the room, which was filled with tables, mannequins, and brown boxes. Across one table lay carefully labeled dolls, pottery, wooden objects, and beaded jewelry. Behind the tables and piled high against walls were coded containers packed with additional museum objects. "We have a very large collection of Xhosa cultural items here," Nomthunzi told me. In addition to cataloging and maintaining the items, Nomthunzi used them to create themed displays in the museum's exhibits. She took me on a tour, describing the contents of glass-enclosed displays she had arranged. She said she was particularly proud of one fertility-themed display, which included fecundity dolls, twine necklaces for teenage male initiates made from veld fig trees, and charm necklets for nursing mothers made from Cape honeysuckle trees.

When we sat down to talk, Nomthunzi recounted how she and other residents became involved in the patent challenge. Representatives of ACB had contacted a botanist in the Eastern Cape to learn more about pelargonium in 2006, and the botanist introduced the NGO to Nomthunzi. The botanist knew that people living in and around Nomthunzi's village used pelargonium to treat illnesses. Moreover, the botanist was aware that some residents in the area actively collected the plant and sold it to a biotrader. Soon after the botanist's introduction, the NGO began organizing meetings in Nomthunzi's village. Nomthunzi stressed that the NGO had approached the residents carefully to gauge their interest in assisting with the campaign. After numerous meetings and discussions, the residents agreed to help.

"When the dispute actually went to the EPO," Nomthunzi told me, "the NGO and the community agreed that a person from the community should go to Germany—someone to represent it and confirm our knowledge of the plant and its use by the Indigenous people of the area." They specifically "wanted someone to dispute the German company's claim of ownership and their claim of first knowledge [of pelargonium's medicinal uses]." The villagers nominated Nomthunzi and another woman.

Nomthunzi made two trips to Germany. During the first, the NGOs announced their challenge to media outlets. Nomthunzi was asked to speak with reporters. She told me she had arrived in Munich on a Saturday and was introduced to the Swiss lawyer helping the NGOs. "It was my first time to be involved in a case of such magnitude. So when I arrived, I was fearful and tense, unsure if I could cope well with all of it." Adding to her anxiety, the other woman from her village could not join the trip because her passport was delayed. But Nomthunzi recalled that the NGOs and their lawyer had prepared her. "They sat down with me and briefed me as to how I was to handle the media questions. I was told I should simply tell all that I know in an honest manner. This calmed my fears (*sayipholisa*)."

During the second trip, Nomthunzi once again spoke with reporters and was also present in the EPO when representatives of the office announced their ruling in front of Schwabe delegates and others. By this time, Nomthunzi had steeled herself. She described a publication from ACB called "Knowledge Not for Sale." "I had a slogan. There's that red pamphlet the NGO made. When you first open it, it has a quote from me that says, 'They [Schwabe] are like thieves because they have stolen our traditional knowledge and also our traditional plant'. I found strength in that position (*ndafumana amandla*)," she said. "Of course, I was required to explain what I meant, which I did. I told the story from beginning to end."

A VERSATILE MEDICINE

One of the healers the NGO had interviewed about pelargonium used the term *izifozonke* to describe the plant, likening it to a jack-of-all-trades medicine whose therapeutic versatility was its strength. She had learned about the plant from her father, who, himself a healer, regularly prepared decoctions from it for his patients. "When he used it to heal stomach problems," she told me, "he would crush the tubers and boil them in water. Once the water had cooled, he'd have the sick person drink it." His treatment for coughs was slightly different. "He boiled the crushed tubers and told the person to drink the water while it was still hot or warm." Over the many decades that the woman had practiced as a healer, men and women came to her requesting the medicine, citing complaints like a persistent cough, stomachache, and weakness in their appendages. I interviewed one woman who had been treated for tuberculosis in a nearby hospital but upon returning to the villages had struggled with an aching foot that hindered her walking and prevented her from sleeping at night. She drank a brew derived from pelargonium and attributed to it her foot's improvement. The healer's location in a farming community also meant that farmers (whom she described as "too lazy to prepare their own medicines") occasionally came to her requesting a brew from pelargonium for cattle infected with red water disease, a tick-borne disease that causes fatigue and possible death. She initially sold one-liter medicine bottles for $1.20, but later for $2.40 after demand increased in the mid-2000s.

Indigenous medicines are a booming business in South Africa. An estimated twenty-seven million South Africans are consumers, and they annually purchase about 700,000 tons of plant material to the tune of $150 million.[49] Pelargonium is consumed in rural locales, but as a traded commodity, it is more likely to go abroad than to be found in the medicinal plant markets of South African cities.[50]

In 2013 I visited the Eastern Cape city of Qonce's taxi-rank area. It was a Friday near the end of the month—when people receive paychecks and thus have money to spend. The rank was buzzing with activity. Queues of people stretched from ATMs. Minibus taxis unloaded and reloaded travelers. Many were arriving from villages surrounding Qonce to spend their day browsing street vendor goods and dipping in and out of grocery stores, often lugging hefty bags of cornmeal and rice upon their exit. Some were ducking into the nearby shop of a Xhosa chemist (*Iikhemesti*). The sign on the front of the shop translates to "swallower of witchcraft makers" (*Ginyabathakathi Kwa Ntongambini*). Inside, the chemist conversed with a customer while five others sat waiting. The customers were fixated on a TV showing that appeared to be a British version of *WrestleMania*. Glistening, muscle-bound men in leotards were tussling about, threatening one another with charming English accents. Hanging by wires from the walls in the shop was an assortment of animal skins and furs, which the proprietor sold to healers to help them channel specific healing powers.[51] Against another wall were shelves of cardboard boxes, still imprinted with their original, biomedical-sounding labels—Betadine Oral Antiseptic, Bioplus Syrups, etc.—but brimming with plant material.

The Qonce chemist embodied the hybridity of Indigenous medicine and its capacity for treating illness and disease.[52] He wore a white laboratory coat while wrapping various plants in newspaper for his customers. "If you want to bewitch a woman (*ukuba ufuna ukumthakatha umntu obhinqileyo*), this is a good medicine," he told me, nodding at the materials he was currently wrapping. "She'll fall in love with you (*uyakuba seluthandweni kunye nawe*), and she won't take an interest in other men." When I asked him about pelargonium, he spoke of using it to treat illnesses, including stomach ailments, rashes, and weakened immune systems. The plant grew around his house outside of Qonce, he said. However, he was too preoccupied with the running of his shop to collect it himself. He relied on harvesters when his clients requested it, though he did not receive many such orders.

Some travelers in the taxi-rank area were also stopping by the medicinal plant [*amayeza*] market area, where vendors sat on plastic crates in the shade of a building, pointing at and describing to their customers their impressively large and varied selection of plants, which were laid out in front of them on top of plastic sheets. I noticed one man who had stepped off a minibus walking immediately to the medicine market, and I approached him to talk. He was in his mid-thirties and wore a black peacoat with a Bafana Bafana scarf draped over his shoulders. He told me he had traveled by bus overnight from Cape Town, where he currently lived and worked. He was on his way home to a village near Qonce to support a younger brother who was being initiated into manhood. The man could only stay for a couple of nights, meaning his return trip to Cape Town would bring him through Qonce again on a Sunday, the only day of the week the medicine market would be closed. He did not want to miss the opportunity to stock up. Plants were fresher and cheaper than in Cape Town (because their prices were less affected by transport costs), he insisted. He made his selections and began filling a woven-plastic luggage bag with an assortment of barks, tubers, and thicket leaves, most of which he said he and his friends in Cape Town would use to treat colds and asthma. They would also consume some to guarantee personal and professional good luck.

The man did not purchase any pelargonium, and only one of the six vendors present that day offered the plant. When I asked the venders about this, five of the six said they knew of pelargonium. However, they typically only received special orders for it, especially from local Xhosa chemists. The one vendor selling pelargonium that day suggested that the plant's popularity in South Africa had grown over the last five years. The plant grew abundantly in a forest near her house, and she supplied it to chemists in Gqeberha, Port Elizabeth, Johannesburg, and Cape Town. However, rangers from the provincial environmental offices often harassed her and others for collecting without permits. She and her children consequently harvested at night using flashlights. She never held permits for any plants, but rangers only pursued traders like her in the forests, she said. In other words, they showed little interest in policing once resources arrived at the market.

IN THE FIELD, AND IT'S AN ANTHROPOLOGY DEPARTMENT

The involvement of Nomthunzi and other villagers at the EPO arguably embodied what some scholars say is a trend: marginalized groups and their allies using the law to contest or clinch rights. The hope is to use such rights to redress past and present-day injustices. Jean Comaroff and John Comaroff call this strategy "lawfare" by the historically dispossessed—a tactic that, together with the proliferation of law-oriented NGOs that help carry it out, reflects a "planetary culture of legality" in which "people almost everywhere, even in the most remote of places, are finding reason to behave as *homo juralis*."[53] This culture of legality, anthropologists of law tell us, is simultaneously about the expansion of a standardizing *legality of culture*. Global policy principles invite groups of people to make collective assertions in the name of culture and prescribe normative pathways for them to articulate such assertions.[54] Frameworks like the CBD and the UN Human Rights Declaration shape how groups understand and express themselves to be Indigenous; as constituting, in the language of the CBD, "local communities embodying traditional lifestyles"; or as territorially bounded holders of traditional medical or environmental knowledge.[55]

The relationship between law and subjectivity concerns questions of individual autonomy and agency. In contrast, the relationship between law and collectivity introduces other thorny questions, including those of cultural legitimacy.[56] This legitimacy can demand difference. Collective subjects that are legible in the eyes of the law tend to be those who can manifest as culturally—and coherently—distinctive.[57] The trend underlines that law's generative capacity goes beyond material entitlement and enforcement; law is also "a form of social mediation, a locus of social contest and construction."[58] To paint a caricatured picture of a very serious process, one might say that the machinery of law seems not unlike the "very peculiar" machine used by Sylvester McMonkey McBean in Dr. Seuss's story *The Sneetches*.[59] Social contest compels some groups to enter the machine. Upon their exit, they have been rendered identifiably distinctive as a collectivity.[60]

And in an era of renascent, identity-based politics and surging cultural consciousness across the world, such social contest and construction can be especially bound up in assertions about property.[61] According to Shane Greene, "Indigenous representatives across the world now commonly speak about themselves not merely as representatives of distinct cultures but also as part-owners of collectively propertied cultures."[62] The claim echoes a broader anthropological literature describing the historically recent nature of "Indigenous movements" and indigeneity as a new frontier of "culture possession."[63]

The case of *Hoodia gordonii*, the southern African succulent, demonstrates this pattern in the context of benefit sharing.[64] In 1996 a South African governmental organization called the Council for Scientific and Industrial Research (CSIR) patented the use of *Hoodia* for appetite suppression. CSIR eventually partnered with a UK-based company to develop and market what many hoped would become a blockbuster weight-loss supplement. Activists and reporters disparaged the patent as "biopiracy," insisting the knowledge of *Hoodia*'s medicinal effects had been stolen from Indigenous San groups. In response, San representatives established a political body called the South African San Council and secured the assistance of a human rights lawyer. By 2003 the San Council had negotiated a benefit-sharing agreement requiring the research organization to pay 6 percent of all royalty income earned from *Hoodia* products into a San community trust. To date, the deal has generated limited revenue for San people. But it did foster concern among some San about group membership and belonging. According to Comaroff and Comaroff, "the effort to assert their intellectual property rights ... required that 'the' San assert a collective social and legal identity."[65] "San-ness" as an identity thickened and sedimented, resulting in "an increase in conflicts arising out of people accusing each other of 'not being San.'"[66] The boundaries of "community" began to contract.

Developments like these were admittedly on my mind when I arrived at Nomthunzi's workplace. That this workplace was an anthropology department certainly did not fit any conventional ethnographic arrival trope (that fetishization of finally *being in the field*—that Other place where the anthropologist, as author, tells you the research actually began). After all, I had merely traded one anthropology department for another. Still, I was guilty of fetishizing something else: my own discipline. In Nomthunzi, I encountered another anthropologist and thus another author of sorts. I wondered what this might signify about the EPO case and its effects on the villagers involved. Consider that the arrival trope long served to enhance the ethnographic monograph as the literary property of the anthropologist. By marking "the presence of the ethnographer in the field," it also "ratified his or her observations and lent authority to a monograph that suppressed all ambiguities in his or her authoring of the society's culture."[67] As I understood it, lawfare as an analytic foregrounded the possibility of similar authorial moves, such as writing culture in legal narratives and documents and deploying "strategic essentialism" to assert possession of culture.[68]

When I started spending time in Nomthunzi's village and others nearby, some residents I interviewed suggested they did view their community as a kind of "collective figuration of the possessive individual property holder."[69] According to one resident, Nomthunzi had returned from Germany "with great news: we had won the case. It was declared that we own the traditional plant" (*kwagqitywa ukuba singabanini bechiza*). Another similarly insisted to me that the community "had won the patent right" (*siphumelele ilungelo elilodwa lomenzi weyeza*). I began asking myself: Had Nomthunzi, the anthropologist, alongside the lawfare-oriented NGOs, sought to render "the Alice community" distinctive and in possession of culture? If so, to what effect?

A RED HERRING?

Those statements by villagers soon proved to be outliers that did not reflect any shared convictions. I had been myopic in my fascination with cultural production and the possibility that the group was engaged in strategic essentialism. As a result, my questions had misapprehended the

EPO case and the larger sociopolitical forces in which Nomthunzi and her neighbors were being enveloped.

Ironically, one person who helped me begin to grasp the limitations of my thinking was Roger Chennells, the South African human rights lawyer and scholar who helped the San Council navigate its benefit-sharing agreement with CSIR. I met with Chennells on a fall day in a café in Stellenbosch in 2011. While we sipped rooibos tea, I ask him for his opinion about the pelargonium patents and the activism against them. "I'm worried they are a red herring," he replied. He feared that myopia about patents would prevent South Africans, including the Alice group, from "milking rightful benefits" from drug companies like Schwabe. As he saw it, if activism to overturn patents did not entail meaningful advocacy for a community, then it was a missed opportunity.

To contextualize Chennell's view, I should emphasize that when CSIR eventually recognized that knowledge about *Hoodia* originated with San people, it did so without pressure from the San Council and Chennells to withdraw its patent. This move was vital, Chennells told me. The San trust's coffers may not have filled as anticipated, but the benefit-sharing agreement nevertheless proved catalytic. It showed doubters that such arrangements were feasible. It also helped place the San at the forefront of future negotiations to commercialize biological resources in the region.[70] And the San Council has indeed gone on to establish other agreements that may prove more lucrative. In *Reinventing Hoodia*, Laura Foster describes the San negotiations with CSIR and mentions a conversation she had with Chennells about them. Chennells recounted how international NGOs initially sought to persuade the San Council to dispute the CSIR patent.[71] According the Chennells, "We said no, we are actually going to make a lot of money out of this patent if it works. So why on earth should we oppose our own patent? Because we now had a 6% share of the patent actually. It became the San patent."[72] Given the perspective, Chennells's befuddlement about pelargonium activism at the EPO is understandable.

In my conversation with Chennells, he further contrasted the stories of pelargonium and *Hoodia*. When the NGOs and the Alice collaborators fought Schwabe's patents, they did not claim exclusive rights as knowledge holders. They instead fought them on the grounds that the Alice group was one among *many groups that shared* knowledge about pelargonium. They did so, moreover, without requiring that Schwabe give the Alice group anything. To be sure, the NGOs relied on language and concepts from the CBD demanding that companies from signatory countries access resources like pelargonium through "prior informed consent," "material transfer agreements," and "benefit-sharing agreements." However, this reliance proved helpful to the NGOs only insofar as it helped show that Schwabe had violated the European Patent Convention's "public order" mandate. The aim was to cancel the patents, not to activate instruments of the CBD.

The title of ACB's first publication about the patent challenge—"Knowledge Not for Sale"—said it all. Knowledge of pelargonium was "not for sale"; it was not to be reduced to a commodity form and not to be traded through a market-based approach like benefit sharing. A South African group had the right to reject the patenting of medicinal knowledge they and other South Africans held. Should any reparatory gestures be possible on the part of Schwabe, the NGO said, they could take the form of "compensation" (not "benefits"), the "localization of production," and the satisfaction of "local demands and priorities."[73] In a different publication, the NGO made its opposition to benefit sharing even more explicit: "We are concerned that benefit sharing through bilateral agreements with select communities will divert attention away from interventions that should be addressing the need for support for locally adapted food and health systems."[74] "For me," the director of the NGO once told a journalist, "there is an inherent inequity in the system that is unacceptable even if a benefit-sharing agreement is agreed with a community and you give them clinics and schools and bursaries." Why? Because "you do not interrogate this inequity and say 'Okay, Schwabe, we would like shares in your company. But it's not about money. How about we also have a stake in the production . . . the manufacturing of the product?' You see, then it becomes a very different thing."[75]

Chennells understood this stance, but questions remained for him. The first question emerged from his view that NGOs often cleave into two distinct categories: those that are "cause or project-oriented" and those that are "community-based." Did ACB fall into one of the two? If it landed in the former, did its position on benefit sharing reflect what all members of the Alice group wanted? Chennells formalized a second set of questions in a publication and foregrounded the complicated matter of shared versus exclusive knowledge. The EPO case may not have been about exclusive rights. But rights were nevertheless part of the equation, Chennells insists, and they were "deemed sufficient to provide [the Alice group's] *locus standi*, or legal standing, as indigenous knowledge holders."[76] If Xhosa groups claim knowledge rights, as Chennells says one did in the pelargonium case, "What is the nature and extent of this indigenous community? The Xhosa people comprise a powerful South African tribe strongly represented in government, having produced both recent presidents Nelson Mandela and Thabo Mbeki. Therefore, how does one define the extent of a knowledge holding community when it might represent a significant proportion of a country's citizenry, such as the Xhosa people?"[77] Of course, raising such questions was likely part of the point for ACB. The questions demand that we evaluate benefit sharing as an answer. Bilateral agreements reflect an effort to take groups of knowledge holders who are dynamic and congeal them into fixed "communities." The aim is to be able to define and single out collectives as select realizations of the CBD's "grand bargain." Could such piecemeal arrangements truly serve the larger "public interest," as South Africa's National Biodiversity Act required? No, ACB appears to have responded.

CONCLUSION: LOSING BUT WINNING

In the weeks after its oral decision revoking Schwabe's production method patent, the EPO released a written decision revealing that, despite the many media reports suggesting otherwise, the NGOs had not technically won. Consider that at the end of Nomthunzi's second trip in January 2010, and after the EPO had made its oral ruling, the NGOs released the following statement to the media:

> The Opposition Division of the European Patent Office (EPO) has today revoked a patent granted to Dr. Willmar Schwabe (Schwabe) in its entirety. The patent was opposed by the African Centre for Biosafety (ACB) from South Africa acting on behalf of a rural community in Alice, in the Eastern Cape, in collaboration with the Swiss anti-biopiracy watchdog, the Berne Declaration. The patent was in respect of a method for producing extracts of

[pelargonium] to make Schwabe's blockbuster cough and colds syrup, Umckaloabo. It was revoked because the Opposition Division found that the patent did not satisfy the requirements of the European Patent Convention dealing with inventiveness.[78]

The statement accurately reflected the rationale behind the revocation. However, as noted by lawyer André Myburgh, "ACB's proclamation of victory after the oral hearing neglected to mention that its attack based on illegal misappropriation was unsuccessful."[79] In reality, the EPO had withdrawn the patent on the grounds that one of Schwabe's corporate competitors had identified and submitted evidence of prior art in a production technique used in Germany. This evidence provided the EPO with a conventional means of invalidating a patent; the Opposition Division could base its judgment on the nearest written prior art, rather than on an affidavit from a South African knowledge holder submitted by the NGOs. As a result, the EPO avoided a ruling in which Indigenous therapeutic use, if shown to be prior art, was assessed against an invention for therapeutic use as claimed in an EPO patent.[80] The actual decision said nothing about the method having replicated knowledge held by the Alice group or anyone else from South Africa, and it remained an open question if the NGOs' evidence would have been strong enough to invalidate the patent had the corporate competitor not produced its evidence.

Moreover, the EPO refused the NGOs' less conventional objection that Schwabe's patents had violated the European Patent Convention's public order mandate. "The granting of a patent would not necessarily and exclusively lead to uncontrolled exploitation and damage to the environment," the EPO appeared to reason.[81] More generally, Schwabe's ostensibly illegal activities could not in themselves serve as grounds for a patent's invalidity; the EPO said such matters went beyond the purview of intellectual property law.[82] Nevertheless, in a seemingly extraordinary move, the EPO had asked an inventor (Schwabe) to prove that it had the legal access to a genetic resource (via prior informed consent and material transfer agreements). In doing so, the EPO implied that legal access could be an issue under Article 53 of the European Patent Convention.

Whatever the nuances, the NGOs' declaration of victory appears to have been effective, for it added to the hefty public pressure the NGOs had already directed against Schwabe—pressure that Schwabe's corporate competitors, for their part, had not meaningfully applied. In a media statement, Schwabe indirectly cited the NGOs' accusations as a reason for the withdrawals, stating that the company wished to avoid falling "victim to a policy debate about the differing goals of these various international rules and regulations that we as manufacturers cannot resolve."[83] The NGOs justifiably took credit. "We regret that such action comes only after such patents have been challenged by us," ACB's director stated in a media release.[84] With Schwabe's other four patents withdrawn, ACB's opposition to them never proceeded to a hearing at the Munich EPO.

Despite this success, the questions raised by Chennells about the "nature and extent" of the Alice community and the effectiveness of the NGOs' approach would prove prescient as new struggles emerged. Following the patent challenge, the NGO pressed on with policy activism. It invited representatives of the Alice group to join it before Parliament's Portfolio Committee of the Department of Trade and Industry. Together, they warned the committee about South Africa's new Intellectual Property Laws Amendment Bill and its capacity to subsume Indigenous knowledge into the country's intellectual property system, facilitating commodification and privatization. The NGO emphasized in its publication about its visit to Parliament that such knowledge "does not belong within the intellectual property regime that is designed to provide ownership for technological inventions within the context of industrial applications."[85]

As I would learn, however, the more pressing issue for the Alice group was not the Intellectual Property Laws Bill, but rather the trade in bulk plant matter and the country's Biodiversity Act, which aimed to regulate the plant trade through access and benefit sharing. As the pages that follow show, if the NGO thought it had merely raised questions about the complicated "nature and extent" of stakeholder communities, it soon learned otherwise. Like a drug company navigating benefit sharing, the NGO found itself mired in the complex dynamics of group membership and belonging that had also surfaced in the case of the San and Hoodia. However, unlike the San case, where the boundaries of the community were contracting, the Alice group faced a different challenge. Their community boundaries were being dissolved as the group was being absorbed into larger polities—a chieftaincy and a kingdom. The forces behind this absorption had been unleashed by access and benefit sharing, the very instrument intended to resolve problems of biological resource exploitation. The Alice group and their land had become sites of struggle over biotraffic and its governance in the country.

INTERLUDE

A "Secret Remedy" (1901–1909)

In 1901 Charles Henry Stevens returned to Southern Africa and volunteered to fight in the Second Anglo-Boer War. Mike Kijitse's medicine for tuberculosis remained on Stevens's mind, however. Stevens began contemplating how he could distribute it in the Cape Colony to treat consumption. After the war abated in 1902, he returned to Kijitse in the Maseru District of Basutoland. There, the healer revealed his ingredients. Stevens sought to establish a supply chain. To Stevens's happiness, on his return journey from Maseru to Cape Town he located a farm where the plants appeared to flourish naturally. The farm was near the city of East London in the Cape Colony's eastern frontier, which would later become the Eastern Cape province. It was situated nearly one thousand kilometers from Cape Town, but delivery could be arranged.

In Cape Town, Stevens tried to persuade physicians and medical societies to take an interest in Kijitse's medicine. Tuberculosis mortality rates among Black and White South Africans were peaking in Cape Town. However, such rates were far worse among Black residents, who tended to develop rapidly fatal disease in settlements that were both medically underserved and increasingly crowded.[1] Whites, in contrast, usually experienced more chronic courses of illness, with infections limited to the lungs.

Stevens tried his hand at other ventures, none of which proved successful. He established a bicycle and motorcycle repair shop in 1903. It burned down. He sold alcohol but was arrested for selling to Africans. By 1904 he was nearing financial ruin. In what may have been a final attempt at remaining in Cape Town, he set up a joint stock company on St. George Street in Somerset West. Under the name Stevens and Co., he began producing and promoting Kijitse's medicine, which he marketed as "Sacco."

Stevens advertised Sacco in local newspapers. He also mailed promotional correspondence and free product samples to South African physicians. On Stevens's instruction, a friend named Wightman traveled to London to contact English physicians, imploring them to use the free samples he had ferried with him from the Cape. Most of the physicians who received the letters "sent no answer; but some others were interested and wrote to tell him of the good results obtained; only they asked not to be named."[2] They likely feared ignominy.

Stevens may not have attracted the attention he desired, but he turned heads at the British medical journal the *Lancet*, which published a scathing criticism of Stevens in an issue in the summer of 1905. The denunciation, titled "The Latest Quackery," quotes Stevens and Co. advertisements for Sacco, providing a glimpse into Stevens's promotional claims and the medical establishment's skepticism about them. "South Africa, if we may judge from the advertisements which appear in the local newspapers, is an even happier hunting ground for quacks than are these islands. The latest dodge is a nostrum called 'Sacco.'"[3] The *Lancet* article quoted one of the ads and lambasted its assertions:

> We learn that "about seven years ago an Englishman travelling in a remote part of South Africa became cognizant of some remarkable cures effected by a native in cases of consumption and kindred diseases which affect more particularly the pulmonary organs. The successful treatment by what appeared primitive means so impressed the Englishman (who is now one of the proprietors of Sacco) that he was constrained to test its curative powers." Then follow the usual statements about the wonderful efficacy of "Sacco" and remarks about the conscientious beliefs of the proprietors. We have heard all of this before. Sometimes the drug has been discovered in North America among the Red Indians, sometimes, as in the case of "Corazza" in Mexico and we fully expect one day to see some enterprising quack bring out a remedy, the receipt for which has been discovered on the top of Ararat, having been left

behind by Noah. The usual testimonials are attached and also, as usual, we cannot find any of the London addresses given in the Post Office Directory. According to the conscientious proprietors "*This* preparation has never been known to fail to *Perfectly cure any case of Consumption, Hæmorrhage, or Asthma*. . . . We claim that if a person has half of his or her lungs left we can effect a permanent cure, providing, of course, the patient does his or her share by keeping to our directions." We have no hesitation in saying that the statements in this circular are wicked perversions of the truth.[4]

A month later, the *Lancet* published a supplemental comment, gently amending its criticism of Stevens. "We have had an interview with a representative of Messrs. Stevens and Co., the proprietors of 'Sacco', who convinced us of his good faith but not of the value of his secret remedy."[5] According to the comment, Stevens also provided the journal with letters from two "medical men" who had prescribed Sacco to patients with tuberculosis and witnessed improvement in their condition.

Despite such testaments, Sacco did not prosper. Stevens's company on St. George Street folded. Stevens relocated to Johannesburg, where he began personally administering the medicine to receptive consumptives. He was twice fined for practicing medicine illegally. Bankrupt but flush with Sacco supplies, he eventually returned to England in 1907. He established CH Stevens Co. and rebranded Sacco as "Stevens' Consumption Cure." The product consisted of a bottle containing two ounces of liquid. Each bottle cost five shillings and came with a direction sheet suggesting the following regimen: "One teaspoon in a wineglass of water (as hot as can be conveniently taken for preference) one hour before breakfast and two hours after the last meal of the evening, unless the patient be in the habit of waking between 12 midnight and 3 a.m., in which case an extra dose may be taken then. After the first week's treatment half-an-hour before breakfast is quite sufficient."[6]

Business records show CH Stevens Co. netting over £4400 in 1908, suggesting that the company's marketing tactics, including press advertisements proclaiming its medicine to be "an absolute cure for the White plague," were having some success.[7] Interest grew to such an extent that Stevens hired five women, who were stationed in the attic of his company headquarters, a Wimbledon house, to respond to the nearly one hundred letters of inquiry the company received each day.

The British Medical Association (BMA) took notice of the success and included Stevens's cure in its national campaign against "fraudulent medicines." As part of this campaign, the BMA thought it "useful if not instructive to make analysis of some of the secret remedies, the virtues of which are so boldly advertised, especially in popular monthly magazines and weekly newspapers, and in diaries and almanacks pushed under the front door or dropped over the area railings."[8] The BMA especially targeted purported cures for life-threatening diseases, such as tuberculosis and cancer, and it hired a London chemist to assess the medicines' contents.

In 1909 the BMA published *Secret Remedies: What They Cost and What They Contain*, a book that directly accused Stevens of fraud and "quackery." Like other swindlers, Stevens had sent "one letter after another to any sufferer whose name he may have obtained"—a system that appeared "to have been invented in America" and was "certainly cheaper than bold advertisements in newspapers."[9] The BMA sarcastically noted how Stevens, in an additionally similar vein to other swindlers, had "considerately" cautioned afflicted consumers "against American quacks and imposters and against the preposterous and wicked swindles of Polish or German Jews."[10]

The BMA's hostility centered on Stevens's secrecy. Stevens said the medicine came from Africa but often lied when offering additional details. He said it originated in Liberia, among other places. Secrecy, Joseph Masco argues, is "wildly productive," creating "unpredictable social effects, including new kinds of desire, fantasy, paranoia, and—above all—gossip."[11] For Georg Simmel, secrecy "is one of the greatest accomplishments of humanity," procuring "enormous extension of life" and "the possibility of a second world alongside of the obvious world."[12] *Secret Remedies* implied something similar about secrecy, suggesting that its productive capacity is what made "quack" medicines appealing:

> One of the reasons for the popularity of secret remedies is their secrecy. It is a case in which the old saying *Omne ignotum pro magnifico* applies. To begin with, there is for the average man or woman a certain fascination in secrecy. The quack takes advantage of this common foible of human nature to impress his customers. But secrecy has other uses in his trade; it enables him to make use of cheap new or old fashioned drugs, and to proclaim that his product possesses virtues beyond the ken of the mere doctor; his herbs have been culled in some remote prairie in America or among the mountains of Central

Africa, the secret of their virtues having been confided to him by some venerable chief; or again he would have us believe that his drug has been discovered in chemical research of alchemical profundity, and is produced by process so costly and elaborate that it can only be sold at a very high price.[13]

Nevertheless, not unlike the *Lancet*, the BMA saw Stevens's behavior as curious. His advertisements and letters had "a character of their own." Stevens offered free samples to any doctor interested in experimenting with the medicine. He offered "guarantee bonds" that allowed customers to receive a refund under specific conditions. One such condition: consumers must adhere to the strict treatment regimen over a period of three months. Another condition: consumers were to invite an attending physician to observe and record the medicine's effects continuously. The product came with a counterfoil form upon which a physician could provide answers to an extensive list of questions. "How long have you attended to this patient? Do you consider this a mild, severe, or hopeless case? Do you consider this patient has a fair chance of recovery?"

Whatever Stevens's intentions may have been, *Secret Remedies* suggested that his product contained substances "devoid of any medical activity."[14] In one of his circulars, Stevens confessed he had never revealed the formula. He conceded his failure to do so had made him a target of the medical profession. But the secrecy "is now done away with," he announced in the same circular. The formula was as follows: "80 grains of umckaloabo root and 13 and 1/3 grains of chijitse to every ounce, prepared according to *British Pharmopœia* methods."[15]

In *Secret Remedies*, the BMA mocked Stevens's big reveal, calling it "one of the oldest dodges of the quack medicine man."[16] Indeed, the BMA had done its research and found no person, government department, or publication in South Africa aware of the names "umckaloabo" and "chijitse." *Secret Remedies* even mentions that the Native Affairs Department of the Cape Colony had initiated inquiries about the ingredients and their possible use by Indigenous groups in the Transkeian territories. "Nothing was known of any such plants, nor was it even possible to identify their names," the BMA insisted.[17]

The BMA provided its own answers about the medicine's constitution. Its analytical chemist suggested that the medicine "agreed in all respects with the solids of decoction of krameria."[18] The finding was critical: *Krameria*, a plant from the Americas whose dried roots evinced astringent powers, was considered ineffectual against tuberculosis.[19] The BMA chemist said that, in addition to krameria, the medicine possibly contained kino, a botanical gum that also constricted tissues but would do little to help consumptives.

2 A "Homeland's" Harvest

When I began my formal research in 2011, I knew little about the trade in plants in the Eastern Cape. One person I encountered that year provided me with an initial and memorable sketch. I was touring a South African company that specialized in the manufacture of plant-derived medicines. In a candid moment during the visit, the middle-management employee guiding me explained how he had recently been involved with and thus observed trade in wild plants from the Eastern Cape. "Many plants grow there naturally, and people collaborate to get them out. It's where I saw the system from within the system."

"What is this system?" I asked.

"It's for any plant, but they use the same 'mules' if you want to call them that. Although now it's not even mules. It's large, mechanized transport—trucking companies."

After the tour, the employee and I walked outside, where he began telling me about the trade's intensification in recent years. "After the economic downturn started in 2007, people got more and more desperate. Before, you wouldn't even bother getting involved in something like that because you knew the risks were too high. But now you've few other options." The employee leaned against a building wall, lit a cigarette, and continued.

"You have access to land, but you have no money. Or maybe you have access to trucks, equipment, or you've got connections—you know people who have these things. Maybe there are thousands of cycads [*Encephalartos*] in an area, for example.[1] But it's illegal to trade them. If you own the land, there are ways to donate a cycad, as long as it's not a mother plant."

"But what about trade on a larger scale?" I asked.

He paused, nodded his head, and then answered: "On a larger scale, there's a facilitator, a middleman, and that's where the logistics come from. It used to be done with Black [minibus] taxis. But they got stopped and searched, mainly for *dagga*, or marijuana. So the officials asked them, 'What's that?' and the mules replied, 'It's just traditional African herbs.' 'Okay, fine. Go ahead.' There was never any question until Nature Conservation started getting involved and started searching for other things."

In the months and years since this conversation, I have interviewed many environmental affairs officials who have affirmed what the company employee implied to me. First, until the mid-2000s, much of the commodity trade in plants from the Eastern Cape occurred beyond government scrutiny or even interest. Second, as officials came to understand the trade better, they recognized that it was a highly coordinated but also secretive effort involving numerous parties and large volumes of plants. Third, because most of the trade was organized without state permits, officials understood it to be "illicit." Summarizing the state of the pelargonium trade in 2011, one official insisted to me that "all of the plant material not collected with permission from private land—so all of the stuff from the former homelands like the Ciskei and Transkei—is going to role players who have not applied in terms of our country's laws. In terms of South African regulations, it's all illegal."[2] A South African botanist who served as an expert witness in court cases against industry intermediaries put it even more bluntly to me: "The trade is all underground. It's all skullduggery."

Internationally, plant trade has grown exponentially over the past two decades, powered by an explosion of consumer demand for natural therapeutics and changes in biodiversity use. Trade in medicinal plants in particular has tripled in value since the late 1990s and is likely to see further expansion in years to come. The United Nation's valuation of this trade, which now surpasses $3 billion annually, is undoubtedly an underestimate. Much of the trade is considered invisible to governments.[3] It also tends to be ignored by conservation policy communities and a public more interested in endangered charismatic animals—an example of "plant blindness," or the anthropocentric tendency to rank plants as inferior to animals.[4] The blindness is consequential. Only a small percentage of the world's traded wild plants has been assessed in terms of international extinction-threat criteria. Some ecologists suggest that one in five wild plants is threatened.[5]

This chapter examines the dynamics of time, space, and scale that characterized movements of pelargonium from the former Ciskei homeland. It also explores how departments of the South African government sought to tame those dynamics of biotraffic, making them more visible and governable.

HOW ONE PROMINENT VALUE CHAIN WORKED

I met a man named Khwezi at a weekend social event in a rural village in early 2011.[6] At that event, the sixty-something Khwezi approached me and asked if I liked the song "Islands in the Stream" by Dolly Parton and Kenny Rogers. We soon began spending time together and he told me about his participation in the pelargonium trade. Frequently, women are the primary actors in the trade of plant commodities.[7] In the case of pelargonium, however, I found that roughly equal numbers of women and men were involved as harvesters.[8] Khwezi, like some of the other men I encountered, told me that he preferred harvesting pelargonium to "tapping" juice from *Aloe ferox*, another plant commodity traded in the region. Indeed, tapping was seen as too time intensive. In addition to waiting for a biotrader to buy, one had to wait many days for the juice to drain and collect in a container. Khwezi saw such work as more suited to women, whom he viewed as more patient than men.

Pelargonium was a quicker means of making money, he insisted. To sell pelargonium to a biotrader, Khwezi would drag his sacks of the plant to a meeting point, an old vacant building that was also the source of the area's local name, which translates to "Dress." In the 1800s, as one of the Wars of Dispossession raged, the building's site served as a British military post. The Wars of Dispossession stretched between 1779 and 1879 and have been described by one historian as both "the main formative experience of South Africa" and "a powerful formative influence" on the British Empire as it approached its zenith.[9] The wars brought about the decimation of Indigenous Khoisan communities, the expulsion of Xhosa people, and the seizure of African lands for British settlers. Upon the arrival of the settlers, the building Khwezi and others now used as a trade rendezvous had been constructed as a store to supply the settlers with implements and other wares, including dresses. In the early 1980s, at the height of apartheid and during the consolidation of the Ciskei, the White settlers left. The old store building subsequently sat empty, save for a hive of bees in recent years.

Biotraders were often on time. But they also sometimes failed to appear and purchase Khwezi's yield. When they did show up, a transaction might go smoothly. At other times they haggled pettily over the value of plant material, flexing their power to control price. If they arrived long after scheduled pickups, they might insist that material was too old to warrant full payment. Officials told me that delaying purchase was an intentional practice. Dry plants weigh less and consequently fetch a lower amount of money. "You see, they're paying the collectors on the fresh-harvested weight," one official told me. "So if the buyers aren't coming and the weight drops drastically, collectors get a lot less per pound. It's on a per-kg payment system, and this benefits the biotraders because they want the dry stuff anyway." Biotraders also visibly tampered with the scales they used for weighing, harvesters said. Given these disadvantages, harvesters sometimes added old shoes or stones to their collection bags to make trade fair. But fairness was always unlikely when collectors lacked information about the market value of the plant, severely limiting their bargaining power.[10] Indeed, they were disadvantaged by "information asymmetry," or conditions under which one group involved in a transaction has less knowledge than another, opening the door to their exploitation.[11]

Khwezi and other harvesters in the region constituted the first link in what officials described as the country's most prominent value chain involving pelargonium. The principal biotrader (hereafter "the biotrader") in this chain had started procuring wild-harvested pelargonium for Schwabe in the early 2000s. A White South African man, he employed at least two Xhosa men as coordinators to schedule and carry out pickups from local plant harvesters on his behalf. The biotrader and his coordinators purchased the plant material from harvesters and hauled it out of rural areas, initially storing it in a warehouse in the Eastern Cape. From there, the material was transported to a facility in the Western Cape that dried and cut the material, and then on to a South African drug company called Parceval, which produced its own pelargonium-derived medicines but also supplied pelargonium to Schwabe.

I learned much of this from officials in the Eastern Cape Department of Economic Development, Environmental Affairs, and Tourism. This provincial office has numerous locations, and these locations can be a study in contrasts. The central office is in Qonce and looks architecturally state of the art. Its multistoried, glass edifice glistens. Inside, the scene is corporate in feel. Sharply clad employees in crisp button-down shirts, blazers, dresses, and polished shoes bustle about, ferrying documents here and there or conversing with colleagues while consulting graphs, tables, or paragraphs on laptop screens. Much of the daily work appeared to be happening within the building, I recall thinking. In contrast, the satellite district offices I visited were often older and more architecturally conventional in appearance. They were by no means rundown, however. And despite their mortar—rather than glass—walls, they were more "permeable" than the central office in the sense that employees frequently came and went from the field. Though they sat behind desks and computers, many employees were clad in army-green ranger jackets and government-issued caps, ready to spring into a government bakkie, or truck, at a moment's notice. Where groups gathered in corners of the office to chat, they might appear as a copse of legs typically adorned in hiking boots, brown socks, and khaki shorts cut at the mid-thigh.

In 2011 I visited a district office to interview two White officials I call Tom and Kenneth.[12] When I arrived, Kenneth stood with a doorknob in his hand. He was trying to reinsert it into the bore hole from which it had fallen. Tom was speaking with a colleague who, apparently visiting from another office, had stopped by for a quick chat. The conversation alternated between the topics of trout as an invasive species in the province and doorknobs, which Tom implied were loosening all over the building.

The colleague asked Tom how things were going with work. Tom exhaled, his mouth shaping into a sardonic smile. "A lot of work and no pay," he replied.

I had first heard Tom's name from one of the biotrader's coordinators (hereafter "the coordinator"). The coordinator implied that he was in regular contact with Tom, and he encouraged me to telephone Tom if I wished to attend an upcoming "stakeholder meeting" that would bring biotraders, chiefs, harvesters, and state officials together to discuss the trade. When I sat down with Tom and Kenneth, I quickly mentioned the meeting. Tom reacted with confusion. He knew nothing of it. "Listen, I've only spoken with [the coordinator] when I'm arresting him," he said. Tom sensed that industry players depicted themselves as having professional relationships with state representatives. In reality, he saw them as duplicitously "running with the foxes and hunting with the jackals." He paused and looked at me soberly. He said he was concerned about my interacting with the coordinator. "You must be very careful with him. He's been involved in some dangerous activities."

Tom told me the coordinator asked for and received money from harvesting communities by deceitfully promising "to process their harvesting applications and ensure they got their permits." I had spoken to residents in those communities, and they told me that they had recognized the deception too late. Some of them had been familiar with the coordinator, and though he had a track record of unethical behavior, they hoped that his business partnership with the biotrader, which they knew to be close, would secure them permits. But as Tom put it, the coordinator "had instead quietly disappeared into the sunset." Knowing the coordinator would be greeted with hostility, Tom added, "I'd like to see him go back to some of those communities."

Officials saw the biotrader and his coordinators as exploiters of spatial uncertainty—uncertainty about where the plant could or could not be harvested and by whom. Scholars have described the legislative circumstances in the Eastern Cape as "detrimental to both conservation and livelihoods" because "confusion prevails regarding if harvesting is permissible, and if so, under what conditions."[13] During the time of my research, regulations concerning harvesting in the province were under revision, leaving resources differentially protected under various still-active homeland conservation acts. With a new provincial Environmental Conservation Act still in the works, pelargonium was uniformly protected by law only in the Ciskei region. Outside of the Ciskei, a collection permit was required only if the plant was removed from protected zones or nature reserves. Written permission from a landowner was required if it was collected from private land.

Tom and Kenneth specifically described how the biotrader and his team took advantage of the homeland borders by collecting from the former Ciskei and then rapidly transporting the material out of that region for processing, hoping to reduce the risk that they would be prosecuted if apprehended by the environmental management officers tasked with making arrests. This strategy was also the subtext of a 2002 newspaper report in which an Eastern Cape conservation official expressed concern about the environmental consequences of the pelargonium trade. "We are very perturbed at the amount [of the plant] being removed—several tons per week—as this is doing particular damage to that species," the official told the newspaper.[14] "[The official] said the [biotrader]—whose identity was known—had no permit and was therefore collecting the plants illegally. The department and police are investigating but needed 'to catch him at the right time,' he said."[15]

Harvesting permits issued from the early 2000s onward were intended to control biotraders by allowing them to collect from limited zones within the communal areas of traditional leaders in the Ciskei and Transkei. Yet some took more than their permits allowed, and they also took from areas where permits did not apply, allowing them to acquire large quantities of the resource. As Kenneth explained it, "The permits that we issued in the past are used as a conduit to launder stuff illegally collected on private property. And that is the essence of the problem of enforcement. If you had a legal permit to collect, unless we physically caught you collecting on someone's land, no one could touch you. If you got your tubers out and got them to your place, your point of collection that's written on your permit, we could do nothing."

The coordinator, who was based near the town of Alice, had such intentions in 2007 when he assembled a team of harvesters to collect pelargonium from a private farm near the town of Cathcart. He told the farm's owner he represented a local university science department and that the department required pelargonium to investigate it as a treatment for HIV and AIDS. His documentation made the farmer suspicious, however. The farmer later told me that she contacted the police after scores of harvesters appeared on her land and started digging. Upon investigating,

Figure 2. Sacks of harvested pelargonium stacked in an Eastern Cape warehouse (2007). Photo courtesy DEDEAT.

the provincial office learned that the research project was, to quote Tom, "a load of bullocks; a smokescreen." Officials confiscated a minibus and trailer loaded with pelargonium, headed for the biotrader's Eastern Cape warehouse, where officials found additional bags of "illicit" pelargonium (figure 2). Provincial officials arrested and charged the coordinator and biotrader with contravening various provincial laws, including permit forgery.[16] The two men were never convicted of the charges, however. The confiscated material—two weeks' worth of harvesting—amounted to over three hundred satchels, each weighing roughly thirty kilograms.

Provincial officials rarely uncovered such unambiguous crimes in progress, however. The department's poor success at prosecuting the coordinator and the biotrader frustrated officials. As early as 2002, the *Financial Mail* reported that officials had "arrested two teams of *Pelargonium* pickers and two [biotraders]" over the past year, but the officials found "it difficult to enforce the law."[17] The provincial office was "hamstrung by a 70% staff shortage and the courts' reluctance to pursue environmental crimes," that same news report stated. This was partly due to the plant's lack of legal protection outside of the Ciskei.[18] "These transporters, the middlemen, they make quite a bit of money out of the trade, with very little risk to themselves," Tom told me. "I mean, our enforcement officers go out and arrest harvesters who are collecting without a permit, and these are the people who suffer in the long term." Tom said that "in the former Ciskei and Transkei, we will arrest the drivers of the trucks that are in transit. But inevitably what happens is that the trucks have a finance agreement on them, meaning we can't seize them. This is where we have come short twice. If there's a finance, then the asset-forfeiture unit becomes less interested in the trucks and nothing happens with them."

Between 2003 and 2008, sales of Umckaloabo in Europe doubled.[19] This period was a free-for-all of pelargonium collection, Kenneth said. Concern about the sustainability of demand drove the provincial office to impose what restrictions it could on harvesting permit holders, requiring for example that they replant a percentage of collected pelargonium.[20] Eventually, in 2007, the provincial office stopped issuing harvesting permits entirely and placed a province-wide moratorium on all pelargonium collection.

The moratorium did not curtail the disorder, however. Further complicating matters was the National Department of Environmental Affairs and its efforts to shape the relationship between conservation and commercialization from the top down. The National Biodiversity Act (hereafter NEMBA) was signed into law in 2004, but its sections regulating drug discovery only became active in 2008. Notably, the national department's vision of the bill reflected a discovery-friendly approach, which contrasted with the provincial office's stricter stance. For example, NEMBA allowed companies already engaged in drug discovery to continue their activities without national permits, provided companies applied for permits during a transitional period, before the discovery regulations became active. Parceval and Schwabe were both active companies, and because both submitted applications during the transitional window, the national department subsequently sanctioned their continued access to pelargonium without actually granting them national discovery permits.

On paper, at least, and to Parceval and Schwabe's annoyance, the provincial moratorium initially prohibited the companies from accessing pelargonium in the Eastern Cape. In 2009, however, the provincial office fell in line with the national one by partially lifting the moratorium and authorizing the biotrader to sell to Parceval (and thus Schwabe) only. The NGO ACB expressed consternation about the continued confusion characterizing the industry, pointing out that "the harvesting and collection of *Pelargonium* can be authorized by a provincial department in accordance with provincial legislation (in this case old-order apartheid legislation) at a time when a bioprospecting permit application under NEMBA and the [Bioprospecting and Benefit Sharing] regulations has not yet been decided."[21] ACB also criticized the NEMBA section permitting companies to collect without minister-granted permits, correctly identifying it as *ultra vires*. Indeed, the active homeland conservation acts did not give "the issuing authority [the national department] the statutory power to make such conditions." In reaction, national officials sought a legal opinion. They later acknowledged to me that the condition was "null and void," adding that "we were not adhering to our own legislation." The department then crafted an amendment to NEMBA allowing the minister to declare a period of amnesty for companies like Parceval and Schwabe. As an official clarified, companies "can apply and they can await a decision on the permit application while they continue their activities." In late 2017 the national office invited public comment on a proposal to make amnesty a consistent national policy.[22]

Beyond creating further confusion, the provincial and national strategies had appeared to create a legal monopoly for Parceval and Schwabe. And while some biotraders and harvesters continued with unauthorized collection, when Parceval and Schwabe unexpectedly elected to stop buying pelargonium in 2011, many otherwise unemployed harvesters complained bitterly to me about their loss of earnings.[23] Neither of the departments' approaches had seemed to work in their favor. An additional irony was not lost on them: Schwabe and Parceval had never actually held a national drug discovery permit, yet somehow they were the only companies authorized to buy the plant. Some locals continued to harvest, but others felt they were left with nothing.

WAITING FOR A PREDICTABLE FUTURE

Khwezi told me that pelargonium remained abundant near his village. I asked if I could accompany him to harvest a plant, as a neighbor had requested a fresh one for medicinal use. We walked for ten minutes from his homestead, eventually arriving at a handful of plants located in a field. Under a clear blue expanse of sky, Khwezi heaved at the ground with a pickaxe. He wore a wide-brimmed hat and a well-worn, blue work jacket. The ground around him was sparsely vegetated, the plants low and scrubby. In a short period, he carved out the soil surrounding a plant, forming a shallow pit. The plant's network of roots was exposed. Its leaves, with their delicate serrated edges, stood out in fresh green contrast against the muted tones of the dug-up earth. Loose soil clung to the roots and edges of the pit, where the earth's texture varied from fine particles to small aggregates. Khwezi removed much of the plant but was careful to leave a portion of its tuber in the ground, allowing the plant to begin its regeneration.

We soon returned to Khwezi's house, where a small but motley set of old collection bags with pelargonium in them rested against a wall. This was material that Khwezi had harvested but never sold. The bags, mostly made from muted green and red plastic fibers that were fraying at the edges, lay open, unfastened. The roots in the bags were gnarled and earth-stained, their hues a spectrum of sienna, umber, and the dark tannins of spent tea leaves. Some were thick and knobby, others slender and twisted, and all were coated with the fine patina of dirt. Amid the tangled heaps were roots with small green sprouts, suggesting a continued burst of vitality.

When provincial officials issued their collection moratorium, they had not aimed to harm harvesters like Khwezi. On the contrary, they told me that some residents in the Ciskei and Transkei had become financially dependent on harvesting, and the NEMBA provision was at least in part intended to keep trade active. And despite misconduct by biotraders and their associates, locals were readily available to supply them. As the provincial official Tom had put it to me, "There was a large migrant labor force in these former homelands, but employment in the urban areas can't absorb the numbers, so many of them come back." Many of those returning, he added, "were never involved in the industry before. But they get to hearing and say, 'Hey, we can make 40 or 50 bucks' or whatever the case may be for a bag. 'Here's an opportunity for me,' they say, 'because there is basically nothing else for me.'"

Securing work during apartheid was an easier prospect than it was now, Khwezi insisted. The problem was that at that time the available work was likelier to get one killed. "During apartheid, you could only leave the Ciskei through your reference book, or identification papers." If one were found in a White area without such documentation, arrest or deportation would follow. Government-imposed "pass laws" regulated the outflow of migrant workers from the Ciskei and other homelands to major cities. "You would be permitted to seek work that you could hold onto for only a period of months," Khwezi said. "After those months, you had to go back home to renew the permit to work again."

Mining near Johannesburg was an especially common means of employment for people in the homelands. In urban areas of the Ciskei, mining companies set up employment bureaus to recruit laborers. This is how Khwezi ended up in Johannesburg. A book, or invoice, was issued to the recruitment agency, and transport was arranged. "We didn't have to pay. This book would come from the employer who needed workers, and it would state how many the employer needed."

I asked Khwezi why he went to the mines.

"You have to remember that back then we were simply part of the family unit (*ubumbano losapho*)" Khwezi said. "When we were growing up, we did not have our own cattle or homestead, and as such, for growing up, one would almost have to work in the mines. Up there in the mines, you would work and always send some money home. That's how it used to go (*yayiyindlela ekwakuqhubeka ngayo*)."

"And what was it like working in the mines?" I asked.

"When you go underground in the mines you are all loaded into a cage lift. Thousands go underground. And you all go down, each to a relevant station until the deepest or last level." Khwezi said that he had worked in Carletonville at TuaTona Mine, also called Western Deep Levels. "I think it was in 1986 that Western Deep was confirmed . . . [as] the deepest gold mine in South Africa. The depth probably measured from here to Stutterheim [a town nearby in the Eastern Cape] two times! That's how deep and also hot these mines were."

Khwezi began speaking about the dangers in the mines. "The gold was found very deep and heavy dynamite was used. There were many fatalities." His eyes grew large. He swung his arms upward and outward. "Limbs would be scattered (*amalungu omzimba ayeya kuthi saa*)," he said. Unsettled by this and other events he witnessed at the mine, he decided to break his contract and leave. "We could see we were getting killed and that the best plan was to go home and rather die at your own home than die horribly in the mine."[24]

As we spoke, it was getting late and dim. Khwezi often waited to feed his prepaid electricity meter until long after it was dark. He lived in his family's house, which had been constructed through the country's Reconstruction and Development Program and was therefore what he called a tiny house. Khwezi, like others, called the houses *oovezingyawo*, or "those that show your feet outside (while you sleep)." In the growing darkness, he reflected on the violence of the mines. "That's why, you see brother, things in our country don't get right. It's because many people's limbs from the mines were never buried correctly near their homes. The bodies couldn't be identified from the blasts underground. They were like pulp; they were like dough. It's been a bad omen for us in South Africa. It haunts us as a nation (*ifikelela qho ezingqondweni kuthi njengesizwe*)."

In recent years, Khwezi had found work repairing potholes on a local dirt road, earning $35.00 every two weeks. He was annoyed to have paid nearly $4.00 for a uniform. "Also, my employer is very cunning, as our salary is channeled through the post office rather than a bank. So if you can't get to the post office on the exact payday, the money can be returned to the employer." Traveling to the post office in town was inconvenient; a round trip with a mini-bus taxi cost Khwezi money and consumed most of a day.

Young people in the area recognized the dearth of work opportunities and sought to avoid ending up like Khwezi. This is what compelled a man in his mid-twenties named Luthando to leave school after Standard Nine, one year before matriculating.[25] "I left to make money," Luthando told me. "There was not enough for me to continue in school anymore, so I stayed at home to look after the few cattle we have. After that I went to the city of Gqeberha to work at its deep-water port." But after his contract ended, he returned home to the Ciskei, and he was drawn into the plant-commodity trade. One of his sisters had died in early 2011. His was now a household of three—himself, his twenty-something sister, and his father. His father had remained unemployed for some time but was not yet sixty, meaning he was still too young to receive an old-age pension. His mother was employed as a domestic worker in a nearby city but earned little, preventing her from remitting much to her husband, son, and daughter. Consequently, the family relied heavily on his living sister's disability grant. Through a work injury, she had lost her sight in one eye, and after a period of waiting, the state eventually approved her enrollment in a welfare program. "This means she is currently the main breadwinner in our home," Luthando added.

To help his family, Luthando had worked for several months on a citrus farm near the town of Kirkwood. The job went well at first. "You see, the way I pushed myself, I could fill nearly two hundred bags of oranges a day, filling up my truck fairly quickly while other harvesters fell behind with theirs. The *umlungu* [White] boss even came to witness this, as he had a hard time believing I could fill that many sacks. I proved it to him, but then things went sour with the other workers, and I decided to leave." Since leaving the citrus farm, Luthando had picked up odd jobs around his village, including clearing dandelions from the yard of a better-off neighbor who wished to help him financially. He had not been selected for any five-month contract positions in the area that paid $6.50 per day, like clearing rocks from dirt roads. His inability to secure a job had left him feeling bored, with each day passing seemingly more slowly than the last. Luthando's long-term plans entailed moving to a different location to address these problems.[26] He told me he wished to one day relocate to Cape Town, where he felt he could find a steady job if only he could demonstrate his efficient and tireless work ethic to employers.

Frustrated with a life deprived of consistent work, Luthando also told me he and other harvesters planned to resume plant collection as soon as biotraders reappeared. Luthando's continued interest in harvesting was not shared by everyone in his area. Some harvesters I interviewed there had stopped harvesting years before Parceval and Schwabe stopped buying. Working conditions had become too challenging.

"But what about the low payment?" I asked Luthando, curious about his desire to resume harvesting.

"We were not happy after hearing that the biotrader was paying us far less than what he earned from selling overseas," he insisted.

"And how about contract jobs, like trench digging for water pipe projects?" I asked. "If harvesting were to resume, which job do you think people would prefer?"

Luthando did not hesitate: "No, the people would prefer to harvest pelargonium than be engaged in those short contract jobs. The plant makes money (*esisityalo senza imali*)." With local contract jobs, a worker could toil until they are exhausted but only earn $9 a day for their efforts. Moreover, some employers had recently failed to pay contract workers in the area. "Myself, I could harvest as much as ten satchels per day," he said, echoing what Khwezi had implied to me (and in contrast with *Aloe ferox*). "This means it is quick money, at the end of the day. And money is like food ready to eat."[27] A young and able-bodied man, Luthando considered industries organized through state infrastructure to be less desirable, given their unreliability and their inability to fully utilize his physical capabilities. To be sure, harvesting was also unreliable, but the risk was more worthwhile, provided one leveraged one's body effectively.[28]

Luthando's calculus was sensible in the context of the Eastern Cape. When the province inherited the Transkei and Ciskei, it absorbed some of the country's poorest people and highest levels of structural and socioeconomic disadvantage.[29] The decentralization of government also severely curtailed the state's capacity for development and had severe implications for industrial and public sector employment. Opportunities to secure income were often characterized by precarity, a lack of benefits, and low wages.[30] In this light, South Africa's transition to democracy presented a deep irony to the country's poor: "As democratization largely benefitted business, the deep crisis of waged employment amplified social marginality."[31] The Eastern Cape typifies the situation, with scholars describing the province using negative superlatives. One scholar has labeled it South Africa's "most stressed" and "most deprived" province.[32] Unemployment rates were among the highest in the country, with only 31 percent of the working-age population in work in 2015.[33] In the Amathole District, where a significant part of the former Ciskei homeland is located, the monthly weighted household income averages $240, significantly below the national monthly average of $383 for provinces.[34] Roughly 17.3 percent of households in the district earn between 5 cents and $52 a month, and an estimated 14.0 percent earn no income at all, with a total of 74,500 households (or 31.3 percent) living below the poverty line.[35]

An urban bias dominated state development efforts in the province.[36] In contrast to strategic "industrial development zones" like cities, which received investments in public resources, rural spaces within the former homeland boundaries were "still, after 1994, governed distinctly and differently."[37] For example, the Integrated Development Plan in one rural area of the Eastern Cape states that in localities with low development potential, government spending "should focus on providing social transfers, human resource development and labor market intelligence to enable people to become more mobile and migrate, if they choose to, to localities that are more likely to provide sustainable employment or other economic opportunities."[38]

I learned that Luthando did eventually make his way to Cape Town, in 2020. He had even managed to find consistent work there as a security guard. He traveled home for holidays and funerals. Yet not everyone can achieve such mobility. "If there was some validity in referring to the Bantustan population as a 'displaced proletariat' in the 1970s, today this is nonsensical because only 5% of the population of the Ciskei and Transkei are currently active migrants," Ashley Westaway argues.[39] "Of the diminished number of migrants, 60% do not remit money to their homes at all. There is a widening and deepening chasm between the urban and the rural in South Africa. Fewer people migrate from the country to the city than did ten years ago, and less money is remitted from the city to the country."[40]

Given the economic realities, the connection between the economic struggles of many in the former homelands and the environmental consequences of the plant trade was clear enough to provincial officials. "What has resulted," Tom told me, "is totally unsustainable harvesting of pelargonium [in some areas]. Especially in the Kolomani area of the Chris Hani District, pelargonium has been virtually obliterated. It was relatively common at one stage but is virtually non-existent in that area now."

WAITING FOR THE PLANT

The problem of inconsistent plant protection under still-active homeland laws had been remedied for law enforcement, a provincial official insisted to me in a 2018 interview. The official mistakenly claimed pelargonium had been officially listed as a threatened species, a move that would have blanketed the province with new laws concerning the plant. In reality, the plant's listing had been proposed in 2015, but Parliament had yet to rule on the matter.[41]

The conservation status of pelargonium was uncertain in other ways. Due especially to wild harvesting in former homelands—where concentrated overharvesting occurred in areas densely populated with people and livestock—state actors used a categorization of threat for pelargonium that was contentious.

To begin to understand, consider that Tom told me residents had paid the Alice coordinator for harvesting permits they never received. They paid him because they "are under such duress." "We've got to be realistic about it," Tom pressed, "pelargonium drives the economy in some of the very isolated areas. Apart from social grants, child maintenance grants, etc., there's no other money coming in." Shackleton and colleagues similarly suggest that "the use and commercialization of non-timber forest products is especially significant to rural livelihoods in the [Ciskei] region."[42] The degree of this significance is debated in the broader literature on such products, however. Scholars generally disagree about whether earnings from harvesting primarily fill shorter-term gaps in income or more meaningfully alleviate poverty.[43] According to former pelargonium harvesters, both sides in this debate proved accurate at different times. Living in a region with a high unemployment rate, families I interviewed stated that cash from harvesting had made a real contribution to their income in the past. "We earned good money," one woman told me. "We used that money to buy food at the market in town. We filled our electricity meters." But collection was not a long-term livelihood strategy. Harvesters tended to lack transportation, and collection was consequently concentrated near villages. The work became increasingly difficult: "We had to go deeper and deeper into the farm camp because the plant would be finished in the areas closest to home."

Reports of harvester overexploitation of pelargonium led SANBI to organize a resource assessment. The assessment, which Schwabe helped finance to demonstrate its commitment to conservation, concluded in 2010. Citing the review, SANBI reported that while pelargonium was experiencing "limited localized loss from overharvesting," the plant was "widespread and not threatened" in South Africa.[44] SANBI; the wildlife trade monitoring group TRAFFIC; and a working group consisting of industry, state, and NGO-sector representatives later used the findings of the assessment to craft a Biodiversity Management Plan for the plant.[45] The plan recommended legally binding conditions for harvesting and trade, with limited details on monitoring. It argued that pelargonium "does not qualify under one of the IUCN [International Union for Conservation of

Nature] categories of threat (Critically Endangered, Endangered or Vulnerable)."[46] Under South Africa–specific conservation criteria, the plant was categorized as "declining."

Some stakeholders were puzzled by the *declining* status, as it was not an official International Union for Conservation of Nature (IUCN) category. A Parceval representative suggested to me this classification implied a presumed decrease in numbers due to usage. But they insisted the plant was being inaccurately labeled. SANBI eventually agreed, revising the plant's status on the Red Data List of South African plants from "declining" to "least concern" in 2013. Parceval further investigated the plant's status by commissioning an independent environmental assessment in 2018, the results of which were presented to SANBI. Considering this study and the management plan, Parceval and other parties came to view pelargonium as one of the most thoroughly researched species in the country.[47]

Still, the Parceval representative I interviewed acknowledged localized overharvesting and agreed with the management plan that "incorrect harvesting practices," such as not leaving part of the lignotuber for regeneration, had been harmful.[48] The use of a pick or hoe, rather than a shovel, was seen as one way of addressing this problem (see figure 3). A related challenge was the collection of the still-regenerating young plants. Since this could lead to permanent destruction of a population, Parceval had for many years instructed its biotraders to avoid purchasing young tubers, which are characteristically lighter colored.

But if wild harvesting was controversial and caused localized decline, I wanted to understand why the industry continued to focus on this approach rather than large-scale cultivation. The Parceval representative suggested a multifaceted rationale, emphasizing the company's commitment to supporting the local communities involved in collection. The company valued ensuring that these communities benefited financially from the resources, rather than money being directed solely to commercial farmers. Additionally, economic considerations played a role in this decision. There were apparent financial benefits of wild harvesting, such as the absence of expenses related to planting, soil preparation, land acquisition, and equipment maintenance—costs typically incurred in cultivated farming. The primary expense for the company in the wild harvesting process appeared to be the actual collection of the resources.

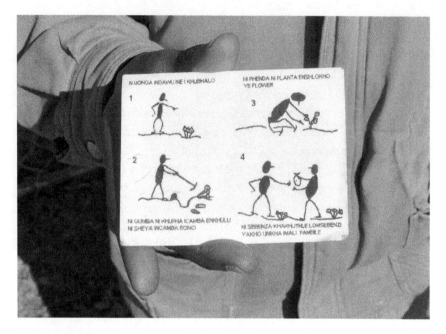

Figure 3. Card instructing harvesters of pelargonium how to sustainably remove plant tubers from the soil and sell them to biotraders. Photo by the author.

Studies have explored cultivation as an alternative to wild harvesting, focusing on whether cultivated pelargonium plants can match the bioactivity of wild ones. Some argue that greenhouse-grown plants can achieve this, while others propose micropropagation and plant part substitution as promising methods.[49] However, some observers suggested the plant "resists" cultivation, with a scientific paper published in 2023 concluding that "populations of *P. sidoides* are not easy to cultivate."[50] Parceval abandoned its forty-five-hectare pelargonium plantation in 2009 due to "unsuitable" growing conditions.[51] By 2011, none of the four cultivation sites established in the Eastern Cape by the Amathole District Municipality and other actors had yielded harvests, despite Parceval's financial and horticultural support. (See figure 4.) Schwabe and Parceval's test plantations in Mexico and Kenya also produced disappointing results, a person with knowledge of those sites told me. Above all, however, Motjotji has rightly pointed out that "it is unclear what the *Pelargonium* industry considers as commercially acceptable for . . . tuber characteristics."[52]

Figure 4. Pelargonium cultivation site in the Eastern Cape (2011). Photo by the author.

In 2011, I interviewed a professional plant grower, a former Parceval employee, who had conducted the trials to identify suitable conditions for Schwabe and Parceval to cultivate pelargonium abroad. He told me, "I did the trials in Kenya to find which climatic condition would be the right one for them to farm it." He said he had also been asked to take pelargonium seed to Mexico and advise a Mexican grower about cultivating the plant. He refused to take the seed, however, feeling it would have been illegal. His concerns were shared by scholars who questioned whether the plant material had been exported in compliance with South African regulations and whether such actions would deprive South Africans of benefits.[53] Some observers note that "it is precisely this sort of activity that led to the negotiation of the CBD and the promulgation of national laws in the first instance."[54]

A White South African, born and raised in the country, the grower also saw the act of taking the seed to Mexico as an affront to his heritage and identity. "You don't take my blood from Africa and plop it on another continent. Doing that in Kenya? Fine, no problem. That's still Africa. It's the same place and the birds can carry the plant there. Mexico? No way. Adios. Goodbye."

The grower believed the trials aimed to protect against a potential ban on wild harvesting in South Africa, ensuring a future supply of raw material for the growing medicinal market (a view corroborated by Parceval's CEO to van Niekerk and Wynberg).[55]

"Schwabe and Parceval have got a market happening," the grower told me. "And what if suddenly the South African government says, 'No, we don't want you accessing this plant anymore [from the wild].' What do those companies do then?" According to the grower, "What if you can't convince the government to change its mind? That's all it is—you know you can maintain a supply. And you need to maintain that. After all, the Americans have been buying the medicine off the shelf like hotcakes."

"So this isn't about the plant being difficult to cultivate in South Africa?" I asked.

The grower replied: "It's really an easy plant to grow. It can grow in difficult circumstances. If you grow one hectare of plants this year, then next year you can grow five hectares of the same, from the same plants, without touching the roots. You simply strip the tops off and plant them. At the right moment and the right way. In our climate, you must do it in a wet winter. The climate can make a difference to propagation and production. But to select a climate for where pelargonium could grow—you can probably pick nine out of ten."

"So the notion that the plant 'resists' cultivation, which is something I keep hearing—that's incorrect?" I asked.

"It's bogus," the grower said. "It just takes a long time for the production of the plant's root." He suggested that Parceval's farms had experienced some difficulties, but he attributed those to human error.

"So how much of the material on the international market comes from cultivation?" I asked.

The grower suggested that, to the best of his knowledge at the time, none of the material came from cultivation.

"But why not? Why wouldn't they cultivate instead of wild harvesting if there's more controversy in harvesting?"

The grower rubbed his fingers together, indicating that money was the reason.

"Okay, the money. Because it costs a lot more money to maintain a farm that's growing it rather than paying somebody a little bit to harvest it?"

According to the grower:

> Parceval makes a whole lot of money on the wild harvesting. The guy between Parceval and Schwabe is a botanist who also makes money—he does some of the processing of the harvested material, like drying and cutting it up for transport. This was also the guy Schwabe paid at the beginning of things to travel this country backwards and forwards like a network and assessing what plants were available where. The guy between that botanist and the people is the biotrader. He makes a medium-sized amount by operating it all. Getting all the harvesting, the depot, the work in, speaking all the isiXhosa to the Ciskeians, getting harvesting permits from Bhisho. It's the first guys [on the supply chain] that are doing the hard, horrible work—that's the Black people digging the roots. They're hitting their pickaxes into what's just a little bit short of cement. That's what the soils feels like after two years with no rain.

Further answering my question, the grower added that at the time, South Africa's wild roots were generally older and more mature than farmed ones, yielding more extract, or medicines. Therefore, he understood why wild harvesting was more productive for a company engaged in large-scale production of those medicines.

Whatever the characteristics of commercially desirable tubers, the management plan for pelargonium underlined that regrowth of such tubers is "very slow," severely limiting opportunities for return harvest.[56] Indeed, the regrowth period was estimated to last between four and fifteen years. Industrial actors like Parceval subsequently recommended to national and provincial officials that harvesting periods be rotated among participating villages. A Parceval representative emphasized to me the importance of not overharvesting in a single area to avoid the risk of collecting newly sprouted plants, which could endanger the resource. The company's approach was to harvest an area thoroughly for a season or two and then allow it to remain untouched for an extended period to enable plant regeneration. Parceval believed that a five- to six-year interval between harvests might be sufficient, while acknowledging that the conservation organization TRAFFIC advocated for a longer, ten-year gap. The representative mentioned that since the company started wild harvesting, it has not revisited the same locations, describing the operation as mobile in nature.

A mobile business was precisely what harvesters did not want, however. The literature on plant-commodity trade argues that increased global demand for resources can result in large-scale cultivation efforts, which in turn foster the capture of benefits by those controlling the means of production. While this is undoubtedly accurate, residents I interviewed also viewed wild harvesting as a system of elite accumulation—a system that would be further imbalanced by limiting community participation for the sake of plant regeneration.

The management plan for pelargonium also emphasized that apartheid-associated population crowding was a malign legacy for plant trade. The plan asserted that "the greatest threat to *Pelargonium* is currently not harvesting of its rootstocks, but habitat transformation and degradation mainly due to livestock overgrazing."[57] The pelargonium resource assessment report stressed that in the Eastern Cape, "many of the known localities [with localized extirpations] are situated on communal grazing land, much of which has been degraded by historical and ongoing overgrazing and erosion."[58]

CONCLUSION: ENDURING BORDERS

Even when benefit sharing is taken out of the equation, governance strategies aimed at balancing commercialization and conservation can be fraught with ambiguities and unintended consequences. As I have shown in this chapter, structural poverty in rural spaces, where initial transactions in plant commodities often occur, drew local people into plant trade, creating conservation dilemmas.[59] The livelihoods of such people were exceedingly vulnerable; they were affected by a host of unpredictable variables, including fluctuations in commodity supply and demand, disparities in information about the market value and price of resources, and shifting ecological and climatic factors affecting resource availability.[60] Moreover, plant species themselves arguably played a role in the conservation-commercialization nexus; their slow growth and distribution patterns complicated harvesters' desires, shaping the organization and inequities of the commodity chain.

In the Eastern Cape of South Africa, each of these issues was entwined with—and often exacerbated by—homeland-associated spaces and temporalities. As officials sought to balance commercialization and conservation of pelargonium, spatial dynamics associated with homelands and provinces also exposed consequential fault lines within the South African state. Provincial and national departments implemented different legal strategies to address the inconsistent protection of the plant across the Eastern Cape. They especially sought to control the activities of the industry's biotraders, who exploited legislative disjuncture to unlawfully purchase the plant from harvesters in the Ciskei and then transport it to companies in the Western Cape for further processing and export. The departments' approaches proved conflicting, however, and were ultimately muddled by still-active homeland conservation laws. The result was not only further confusion but also a monopoly for the trade's most prominent companies.

As provincial and national officials grappled with legal continuities and confusion associated with the apartheid era, they simultaneously attempted to fulfill the South African constitutional mandate of aligning and integrating spheres of government.[61] In this context, "the state" revealed itself not as some "monolithic entity whose interests can be presumed."[62] "The state" was instead instantiated via the political construction of scale, through which "decisions about political-institutional design, networks between strategic actors across and within various scales, as well as in decisions about which functions to decentralize to them" were made.[63]

This chapter has also drawn a link between contemporary spatial development strategies, labor insecurity, and concentrated overharvesting of plants. While unusually high levels of migration continue to characterize the Eastern Cape, urban areas of South Africa had arguably not improved in their capacity to absorb the rural unemployed who spilled into their centers. With some residents of the Ciskei consequently returning home and finding few opportunities for work, medicinal plant harvesting offered an exceedingly low yet vital wage. Of course, due to the arduous nature of collection and the exploitative behavior of industry biotraders, many residents stopped harvesting. That the plant became increasingly scarce in village areas due to overharvesting mattered little for biotraders and the drug companies employing them, as long as the migrating business could find new harvesters, new villages, and new, unexploited spaces within former homeland jurisdictions. The former Ciskei was more than a marginal space from which migrant workers continue to seek access to South Africa's "formal business sectors." The region became a crucial link in a system of transnational accumulation initiated within its enduring borders.

INTERLUDE

"Mountains of Prejudice" (1909–1914)

By 1909 Charles Henry Stevens had renamed the medicine he sold Umckaloabo.[1] This name, while perhaps etymologically derived from isiXhosa or isiZulu influences, was likely created by Stevens. Stevens sought to boost sales of Umckaloabo by linking its efficacy to expanding scientific and public discourses about germ theory in the early 1900s. He argued that African medicines could target disease agents in the same manner as biomedical drugs. But the claim made Stevens himself a target. After all, the *Journal of the American Medical Association* stated in 1910, "One of the worst and most heartless features of quackery is the exploitation of such disease as tuberculosis and cancer, which are unamenable to drugs."[2] Nevertheless, Stevens claimed his medicine was "a vegetable germicide, fatal to all disease germ growths." Likewise, he promoted Umckaloabo's capacity to "safely be advantageously given wherever a germ disease exists or is suspected."[3] The only obstacle to the medicine's potential was widespread doubt, Stevens said: "In spite of the mountains of prejudice to be overcome, I intend to prove that at last something has been discovered that will destroy the *Tubercle Bacillus* without being detrimental in any way to the human system; in fact, besides destroying this germ, it is a strong tonic, and will invigorate a healthy body as well as bring back to its normal condition a consumptive one."[4]

Stevens actually embodied prevailing views about African and biomedical healing systems and their differences. Writing on this era of medicine, Karen Flint remarks that recognition connecting African medicinal plants to Africans was typically derogatory. "Indeed, it was in the process of scientific inquiry in which chemists and pharmacologists extracted African plants that made African *muthi* (medicine), formerly cloaked as superstitious and unscientific, both knowable and valued to the scientific world."[5] Stevens's use of the word "discovery" in his discourse about Umckaloabo was operative in his attempts to shift the medicine out of an unscientific and unknown framing and into something doctors and patients could value. The following excerpt from one of Stevens's letters is illustrative:

> Now you must know that throughout the world our clever Scientists and most Prominent Specialists on Consumption have for ages past spent their lives trying to find something which will destroy the Tubercle Bacillus without injuring the human system. They have everything at their command; the most up-to-date Sanatoria, the cleverest Nurses, and the pick of climates, yet they have failed, through every drug and remedy known, including every ingredient contained in any proprietary medicine or cough mixture ever heard of has been exhaustively tested in every shape and form. My treatment differs in this one great respect, that none of the ingredients have ever been used before by any Chemist or Doctor, and are an entirely original discovery.[6]

To Stevens's detriment, the BMA's *Secret Remedies*, which excoriated Stevens for quackery, was widely distributed to British physicians, who in turn gave copies to patients. Word spread quickly, and the publication's impact on CH Stevens Co. was severe. Sales dipped at home in England and in Europe more broadly, where Stevens had recently expanded his marketing. In response, Stevens sued the BMA for libel in 1912.

The legal firm Tindal Atkinson and Rowsell represented Stevens as plaintiff. A publication titled *Medical Evidence Given in the Consumption Cure Libel Case* describes the case this way: "The book 'Secret Remedies' had had a large circulation, and the attack was one on the personal reputation of the plaintiff, and one calculated to ruin the business in which he was engaged. The jury would be asked to reward Mr. Stevens substantial damages."[7]

In court, Stevens produced plant materials for analysis. He also provided numerous witnesses—mostly physicians and patients—who supported his claim that Umckaloabo was an efficacious treatment for tuberculosis. A chemist hired by Stevens compared Umckaloabo with krameria and kino, finding—contrary to the BMA's accusations—no evidence to suggest Stevens's medicine contained the two substances. A bacteriologist and pharmacist further confirmed this finding to the jury.

Among the witnesses providing testimony in support of Stevens was a medical doctor named Edward Ferdinand Grün. The *Medical Evidence* publication suggests that Grün had dealt "with a good deal of tuberculosis. He had written a book on Dr. Koch's treatment of tuberculosis."[8] After Grün learned of Umckaloabo, he obtained samples from Stevens. During the libel case, Grün described a variety of patients to whom he had administered the samples. "On the whole, he was of the opinion that the treatment had been extremely beneficial, and in any future cases he should have recommended its administration. He had used the mixture since 1908 and had noticed no difference in its outward appearance or in its taste."[9]

Anthropologists Margaret Lock and Vinh-Kim Nguyen assert that from the late nineteenth century onward, a more rational and systematic method of gathering and applying medical knowledge, particularly in the field of infectious diseases, has significantly enhanced the therapeutic effectiveness of biomedicine across a wide array of conditions.[10] The extent to which the appeal of this rational and systematic approach was ascendant in the early 1900s was visible in several regards during the libel case. This was evident from the manner in which Umckaloabo was chemically evaluated to the specific claims made about the biological workings of the medicine by its proponents, despite their general ignorance on this matter.

For example, in the cross-examination of Dr. Grün by the BMA's lawyer Mr. Holman Gregory, Grün repeatedly deployed a biomedical explanation of Umckaloabo's workings, centered specifically on the idea that the medicine targeted and killed tuberculosis, the disease agent. Considering Koch's postulates, it was the only explanation.

GREGORY: What effect do you suggest this medicine has upon the person, what is the work of it?

GRÜN: It appears to me to have a specific destructive influence on the Tubercle Bacillus in the same way that Quinine has upon Malaria.

GREGORY: Then it is a form of germicide, you think?

GRÜN: Yes, I think so.

GREGORY: Are you suggesting to my Lord and the Jury that Stevens' Mixture is a specific for Tuberculosis?

GRÜN: I am. I think it is a matter which requires further careful medical investigation, but as far as I have been able to form an opinion there is some ingredient in this drug which acts as a specific bacteriacide.

GREGORY: I put the words to you, "which will cure every case of Consumption or Tuberculosis." Do you say that?

GRÜN: I have not had sufficient experience of it to be able to say that.

GREGORY: Do you think it would?

GRÜN: No, I do not think it would: some cases would be too bad for cure.

GREGORY: You get in Tuberculosis a disease which is called, I think, external Tuberculosis?

GRÜN: Yes.

GREGORY: That is some breaking out perhaps in the joints?

GRÜN: Yes, or the skin.

GREGORY: It may take that form?

GRÜN: Yes.

GREGORY: Have you ever tried it in a case of that kind?

GRÜN: No, I have not had a case.

GREGORY: Would you prescribe this medicine for a case of that kind?

GRÜN: Certainly I would. I saw Dr. Koch use Tuberculin for the same purpose.[11]

A deadlocked jury forced the trial to continue until 1914. By that year, the BMA had improved its defense. The association hired a laboratory scientist to demonstrate that Umckaloabo did not kill tuberculosis's infectious bacilli in ten minutes as Stevens had claimed. Stevens was an easy target; neither he nor his witnesses understood the therapy and its workings.

Stevens's strategy of secrecy also backfired. His main medical supporter, a physician by the name of Bennett, had relocated to Australia during the case's proceedings. Stevens took a risk and hired an imposter to take the stand as Dr. Bennett. The imposter had a penchant for embellishment in his statements, however. At one point he claimed to be a Liberian commissioner with enough power "to hang you if you committed an offense."[12] Stevens lost credibility when the imposter was revealed to be not only a charlatan but also a petty criminal who had recently served three jail terms. Adding to Stevens's woes, the BMA's lawyers called attention to the fact that Stevens's bacteriologist, Dr. Lord, had recently been committed to a Church Army home for dipsomaniacs. Stevens lost the case and was forced to pay significant court fees to the BMA.

3 On Expansional Belonging and Ethnic Capture

During my fieldwork, I came to see that environmental laws in South Africa fostered business partnerships between chiefs and drug companies in a former homeland. The agreements signed between these groups allowed drug companies to obtain lucrative biological resources. The agreements were controversial because they defined "access-providing communities" in the contemporary Ciskei region as chiefdoms. Some rural groups contested this definition and complained that it allowed chiefs to capture and hoard pharmaceutical royalties.

In conventional benefit sharing, the key axis of entitlement to drug benefits "is not physical property claims (i.e., whose land is that plant on?) but the question of intellectual labor, and contributions to innovation."[1] However, the South African government's version of benefit sharing packaged plant-commodity trade and drug discovery together, a move that tilted this axis of entitlement. In this version, the identification of "proper" benefit recipients could pivot precisely on a version of the question *whose land is this plant on?* And by expanding the latitude of benefit sharing in this way, South Africa's laws did not merely expand the latitude of what companies bear responsibility to share their takings. They also expanded the latitude of *which people belong* in benefit-sharing agreements. In doing so, the laws fostered an emergent and hazardous politics of belonging.

In his book *The Perils of Belonging*, Peter Geschiere argues that, despite movements of groups, objects, and information around the globe, people are becoming more preoccupied with what are emphatically *local* attachments.[2] The preoccupation is not about wistful longing for the past. Nor does it reflect the desire to disconnect from a wider world. Instead, beliefs about located cultural difference concern how people position themselves "to benefit more fully from market ventures, citizenship, and the promises of modernity."[3] Expressions of autochthony or indigeneity, in particular, generate questions about the boundaries of localities and who belongs within them. According to much of the anthropological scholarship on the subject, such questions have tended to generate exclusionary answers. "The turn to the local," George Paul Meiu argues, is often accompanied by efforts to "close off certain autochthonous polities."[4] Closure restricts who can belong, restricting in turn who can materially benefit from locality derived capitalist resources or ventures. "What is at stake," Geschiere suggests, "is less a defense of the local than efforts to exclude others from access to the new circuits of riches and power."[5]

The locations and people may vary, but the pattern of boundary closure has appeared rather consistent. Alongside longer-standing citizenship rules, Native North American tribal governments increasingly require DNA tests to determine who can become a tribal member. Membership, some hope, will confer rights to casino royalties, free health care, housing, or education.[6] The intensification of resource exploitation across many parts of Africa has also contributed to deepening social differentiation. The definition of belonging has consequently tended to narrow. Conflicts over property like land and landed resources are also struggles over ever-stricter definitions concerning the legitimacy of those making claims.[7] Cultural differentiation in the context of South African mining on land controlled by chiefs is illustrative. The king of the Bafokeng Nation in South Africa sought to impose and defend ethnically defined boundaries of community to control wealth generated from platinum mining.[8] "In the past, entry and exit was fairly fluid and quite frequent," Comaroff and Comaroff argue, but "the borders of Bafokeng appear to be a matter of rising concern."[9]

At an early stage of my research, I contemplated the possibility that struggles for control over biotraffic in the Ciskei would play out to the abovementioned kinds of effects. Surely, I thought, with drug royalties in play, chieftaincies with benefit-sharing agreements would seek to restrict their sociopolitical boundaries, limit group membership, and thus shrink the number of potential royalty recipients. I initially anticipated such outcomes, but as my observations unfolded, it became clear that the reality was quite different. Defying the "overall tendency toward closure of the local group," I observed chieftaincies and a kingdom using representational claims to *expand* membership and *capture* people into their polities, in some cases growing their ranks of subjects.[10] As shown in chapter 5, sometimes agreements were kept effectively secret, meaning locals knew nothing of their absorption into chieftaincies for the sake of providing access and possibly accumulating benefits.

Chapter 1 described the Alice group's involvement in the challenge against Schwabe Pharmaceutical's pelargonium patents. This chapter picks up the story where it left off, documenting something the group and its NGO ally did not anticipate: their subsummation into a nearby chieftaincy via a benefit-sharing agreement between the chieftaincy and Schwabe. By situating the group's historical and contemporary experiences, we can begin to see how contests over the control of biotraffic are also contests over territory and subjects.

A MEETING BETWEEN ACB AND THE ALICE GROUP

In November 2011 the NGO ACB organized a meeting in a village in the Eastern Cape. The meeting was conducted in isiXhosa, and attending were villagers who had allied with ACB to challenge Schwabe's patents. Funeka Nkayi, a female leader of the villagers, stood before thirty-some people seated on wooden benches and began to speak. She introduced an ACB representative, a Xhosa man I call Mava, who was new to the villagers. Funeka nodded her head toward Mava. She said, "The brother next to me will introduce himself, as I'm also just meeting him for the first time." She then gestured across the room in my direction. "Chris is sitting over there. All of us know him. He's also attending the meeting." Funeka then proceeded to tell Mava about his audience that day: "Brother let me tell you briefly about us. As a community of about five villages who were former farm dwellers—mostly our parents—we were left by White farmers on this area of land. There was a time when a traditional medicinal plant that was growing abundantly here came to be commercialized. In other words, it was harvested extensively and sold to a certain middleman. We were then referred to and are currently assisted by ACB with regard to the pelargonium industry."

Eventually, Mava stood alone in front of the group. He spoke while pacing about in confident strides. His eyes slowly tracing the faces of the attendees, he seemed to eventually make brief eye contact with everyone in the room. After he introduced himself, he said: "It is wise in meetings of this nature to always be able to give, however little, a background of the issues at hand, like where and how the story began, so that we can all have one understanding (*ukuba nokuqonda okunye*)." He began handing out sheets of paper and pencils. "What I'd like to request from you," he said, "is that you kindly chat with the person next to you about what one can recall about the whole pelargonium issue. Then write down what you come up with."

The residents began talking in pairs. After ten minutes, Mava collected the papers and began reading aloud from them, attempting to arrange the events they described in chronological order. "Someone mentions Nomthunzi going overseas to Germany to the European Patent Office," he said. "This one speaks of selling the plant to a local middleman. And this other one is again that 'Nomthunzi went overseas and came back with the news that the case had been won by us.'" He continued to read aloud from the scraps of paper, then asked for additional comments from the residents. "Now you've heard all of the points read out we should also try to include others that may not have been mentioned." A resident spoke up: "The introduction of the botanist to the community. Upon their arrival, they recorded the registration details of the vehicle used by the middleman. After that, they introduced us to the NGO and others, to liaise and work with to challenge Schwabe."

Mava eventually arrived at the urgent matter the NGO had come to announce. He began speaking about South Africa's laws concerning drug discovery and plant trade. "Any foreign pharmaceutical company that has an interest in accessing medicinal plants must come to an agreement with those people of the area where the plant grows. The people of that area shall benefit from any kind of trade or selling of the plant," he said. "Can anyone remember when we held a workshop to explain this? We said that a company that has an interest in trading with you shall have to come to an agreement with you. Can anyone remember?" An attendee raised her hand and said, "I was present at that meeting." A few others concurred, lifting their hands also. Mava nodded his head and went on. He started speaking of a chiefdom located near the villagers. The chiefdom, called Imingcangathelo, was one of forty-two such entities that fell under the authority of a larger political structure, the Rharhabe kingdom, an Eastern Cape paramountcy that claimed tens of thousands of subjects. The leader of Imingcangathelo was a chieftainess who, after her husband's death, assumed the role of regent for her son, the prince, until he attained the age required to become chief. According to Mava:

> That last time we met, we had heard that Parceval and Schwabe had come to an agreement with a chieftaincy near here—the Imingcangathelo chieftaincy under its chieftainess, Tyali. Recall also that there were people from your community who indicated that they did not wish for chiefs to be involved in this trade. ACB then went and consulted Chieftainess Tyali. When asked if there was an agreement between Imingcangathelo and the companies, the answer was no. We explained then that if any agreement was to have been made, the parties concerned must advertise this publicly—that's according to law. We then wrote to the Minister [of Environmental Affairs], requesting that this be recognized and done accordingly.

The room was silent and still. Mava continued:

> After lengthy discussions a conclusion was arrived at that the companies would come to an agreement with the Imingcangathelo chieftaincy. The companies declared that they had met and consulted with the communities of the region through the kingdom and chiefs, and therefore their understanding is that the people have agreed to this deal. The chiefs themselves are situated on the land of the state. There are people like you who have your own allocated land, but no difference is made between you and the land under the chiefs. There is no mention made that those people like you, who have your own land, should also be approached [for informed consent and benefit sharing]. They simply use one blanket for all. The agreement states that the agreement was done with the traditional leadership on the principle that they were doing it on your behalf, as their subjects.

Like others who harvested pelargonium in the region, the villagers had long earned low wages and endured the erratic behavior of biotraders, who sometimes failed to show up as scheduled and visibly tampered with the scales used to weigh plants and pay collectors. But the involvement of the chieftaincy and kingdom presented a more recent difficulty. The villagers were located only a few miles from Chieftainess Tyali's Great Place, or homestead. Many of them told me that in 2010, Tyali had demanded the pelargonium they harvested be brought to her to be weighed and sold to a biotrader. There, Tyali would expropriate a percentage of the sale as a form of taxation, they learned. Finding the demand preposterous, most apparently refused her demand. Others may have acquiesced.[11]

The Imingcangathelo chieftaincy had previously claimed the villagers as its subjects. The chieftaincy had located in the area in the early 1980s, after the consolidation of the Ciskei homeland. Since that time, the chieftaincy's declarations of authority had been a source of discussion within the Alice group. Some residents seemingly embraced Tyali as their leader. Others identified a different chief as their leader. Some rejected chiefs altogether. Others combined elements of the abovementioned opinions.[12]

During a dialogue with me, Funeka, an elected leader of the Alice group, reinforced the complexity of the situation:

CHRIS: What is Imingcangathelo? And are you a part of it?
FUNEKA: It's the people who are under the chief, or Chieftainess Tyali to be specific—it's her people.
CHRIS: Are you under her authority?
FUNEKA: I'm not entirely sure how to answer that. Many of us don't want to be under the traditional leadership.
CHRIS: Would you say that most of the people here in this area are opposed to the Chieftainess being their leader?
FUNEKA: Yes, most of them are of that view or feeling.
CHRIS: How much does this opinion have to do with pelargonium and Imingcangethelo receiving royalties from plant trade?
FUNEKA: It's not even coming from that. The issue of the chiefs is such that even from way back the people were not having freedom from them. People were forced to toe the line of the chiefs, liking it or not. The people were obliged to abide by the chief and only do as he liked. They did not have much say or could not dispute or oppose the chiefs and their demands.

CHRIS: Can you give an example?

FUNEKA: An example would be that the wife of the chief would be pregnant and expecting. Upon the delivery of the baby, people were told to contribute money for things like diapers for the newborn baby. So these are some of the things that I don't think are right or in order.

CHRIS: And as of right now, you are under the authority of ...

FUNEKA: [Interjecting] We are under the authority of the municipality.

CHRIS: Under the municipality and not under Nosizwe [Chieftainess Tyali]?

FUNEKA: Yes, we are under the municipality. For all of our problems, we refer to the municipal councilor and not the traditional leadership. We have not referred any of our problems to her, we have our [ward] councilor [local government representative]. Instead of a headman we have a [village] chairperson.

CHRIS: So do you mean to say you have no chief over you?

FUNEKA: I would say that we don't take sides (*ukungathathi cala*). We are in "neutral-gear" (English) for Nosizwe. Yes of course, as for her, she'll relay messages to us, telling us what is to happen at the Great Place. But from our side there's nothing that she's ever provided to us—things like jobs and assistance with whatever, you see.

CHRIS: So the land you are settled on—who does it belong to, if there is an owner anyway?

FUNEKA: The land ... no it belongs to us, it is ours [laughing].

CHRIS: Would you mind sharing your view about traditional leaders in general?

FUNEKA: Eish, my brother, this issue of the traditional leaders, I simply blame the government for this. They are the ones who reinstated the headmen and chiefs without consulting the people on the ground. The government should have come and discussed with the people the reinstatement of the chiefs and what their authority would be over the people. Also, I believe that in this new dispensation the people should have the right to say or be able to choose who they should be ruled by. It's not that we don't recognize chiefs; after all they are the original traditional leadership from way back. It's just that we want to have a choice about which leadership we want to fall under and not be forced with them. That's where the mistake of the government occurred.

Reflecting what Steven Robins calls "the hybrid and situated subjectivities of postcolonial citizen-subjects," nearly everyone I spoke with expressed some respect for Tyali's ceremonial significance.[13] However, echoing many others in the former homelands, they equally rejected the government's imposition of any allegiance and any chief interfering with their livelihoods.[14]

Imingcangathelo's benefit-sharing agreement with drug companies appeared to signal such an imposition and interference. "There is nothing going right at all since the chiefs took control of the industry," one villager told me. "Before this, things were going well, when people were trading on their own. There is no partnership between us, the people, and the chieftainess." I asked what they meant by "partnership." "There's no development for the people whatsoever [from the royalties]. Nothing is coming from the side of the chieftaincy." Another resident articulated the problem this way: "I blame the government for this. Their officials don't ever come to communities to learn about our plight and to hear our side of the story about the chieftaincy. There's no follow-up from the government's side. And that is why the chiefs are having it easy in their misuse of what is meant for the people."

DESIRE FOR BENEFIT SHARING

In an analysis of benefit-sharing negotiations concerning a controversial pharmaceutical project in Peru, anthropologist Shane Greene highlights how pivotal NGOs can be in supporting Indigenous claims to intellectual property rights.[15] But despite their positive intentions, these NGOs can end up endorsing those Indigenous groups that most closely match their own institutional, political, and social agendas, as well as forms of expression that oppose corporate entities and drug discovery. NGOs often initiate such encounters "without ever confronting the complex political realities of local populations."[16]

ACB's activism both typified and complicated Greene's argument. The meeting led by Mava was illustrative. To be sure, the NGO had initially sought out a group that conformed to its anti-corporate position. Recall that ACB began its patent activism as an organization seemingly opposed to benefit sharing. But also recall from chapter 1 how the San lawyer Roger Chennells pondered the possibility that Nomthunzi and her neighbors might develop a different opinion. Chennells had been correct to wonder. By 2011, the position of some of the villagers appeared to have diverged from the NGO's.

I knew this was so from speaking with the villagers that year. Their aspirations tended to center on three things, each of which aligned with South Africa's laws that folded plant-commodity trade into benefit sharing. First, many of the villagers wished to establish plant nurseries and cultivate pelargonium on a large scale. Second, they wished for a means of direct export and sale to Schwabe and other European buyers and thus a means of cutting out biotraders. Third, they wanted their own benefit-sharing agreement with Schwabe or another drug company—an agreement that would not involve the Imingcangathelo chieftaincy or the Rharhabe kingdom.

A stumbling block to such arrangements was the villagers' reputation among industry players, interviewees told me. Numerous company representatives with knowledge of the patent challenge implied to me that the Alice group had become radioactive to potential business partners due to its association with what they saw as an aggressively anti-corporate NGO. Speaking to me about this impact on the Alice group, one South African scholar with knowledge of the patent challenge described ACB's activism as "global advocacy for a cause with an immediate impact." According to the scholar, the NGO's "global advocacy makes its mark. But it can also leave a stain on the community." As an organization, the scholar said, ACB was largely constituted by South Africans of Indian and European descent who tended to also be urbanites based in Johannesburg and Cape Town. What did they know of life in the rural Eastern Cape, the scholar asked. However, echoing Chennells's typology of activist NGOs, the scholar suggested that the matter ultimately boiled down to the meaning of activism. "What is it about? Is it watch-dogging? Is it community-based? What is the best approach when it comes to addressing biopiracy?" Nevertheless, every resident I interviewed expressed a positive view of the NGO, adding that ACB had reacted supportively to their new interests and had tried to help them accordingly.[17] In numerous conversations with representatives of ACB, they consistently evinced deep reflexivity when it came to their positionality concerning their activism.

But if the Alice group was opposed to the chieftaincy and kingdom, establishing any agreement that did not involve those parties looked unlikely. A DEA official told me as much when they said that they and other officials perceived "the Alice community" to be a "new collectivity" that had only recently congealed out of the EPO patent challenges. The collectivity was still in a state of becoming because it was only now asserting its independence. Per the official, the community had in fact long belonged to the Imingcangathelo chieftaincy, which had an established leadership structure under Tyali. What was now manifesting as "the Alice community," the official told me, had previously existed as merely an "area" of the larger "entity" of Imingcangathelo.

Who belonged where and to whom mattered a great deal. While the EPO challenge was unfolding, Schwabe rejected ACB's claim that the company unlawfully accessed pelargonium, without prior informed consent and material transfer agreements. It presented the EPO with a document—one that the company's opponents in the challenge weren't allowed to see—suggesting its access was lawful. What is more, the company said it had entered an initial, private benefit-sharing agreement with Imingcangathelo, and because "the Alice community" was ostensibly part of Imingcangathelo, they had been included in the agreement. Given this claim, Schwabe was able to make a case to the EPO and the DEA that they had complied with the national legislation and had not run afoul of the EPO's "public order" mandate. Apparently the company's lawful access had simply not yet been publicly disclosed.

Still, the national minister of environmental affairs was concerned enough about the confusion concerning the groups—and possibly its potential to sour the rollout of national drug discovery regulations—that in 2010 the DEA convened a meeting in the sleepy mountain town of Hogsback in the Eastern Cape. DEA officials traveled from Pretoria and expected to hold discussions with representatives of all the concerned parties. A representative of Imingcangathelo attended the meeting, but due to a miscommunication, a leader from the Alice group did not. Officials saw the meeting as a failure. Frustrated, they returned to Pretoria, where they remained uncertain about why members of the Alice group were pushing to set themselves apart from the chieftaincy.

"WE GREW UP UNDER DIFFERENT CIRCUMSTANCES"

Wanting to understand this push better, I spoke with Nomthunzi Api, the villager who had participated in ACB's patent challenge. I began to understand a history that challenged the view, seemingly so common among state and corporate actors, that the Alice group, by virtue of where they lived, were innate subjects of a chief. As Nomthunzi expressed it, "We grew up under different circumstances."

The contemporary landscape of people, land, and power in the area occupied by the Alice group has roots in a turbulent colonial history spanning over two centuries. At the core of this history lies the Eastern Cape frontier zone, the region where the British Empire and the Xhosa people frequently interacted and ultimately clashed during the Wars of Dispossession from the late 1700s through the late 1800s. Specifically, the area of the Alice group had belonged to a crucial strip of land nestled between two major rivers. In the 1820s colonial administrators called the strip the "Ceded Territory," but it could be more aptly termed the "Annexed Territory."[18] This land functioned as a supposed neutral buffer between the British Cape Colony and Xhosa territories. Highly coveted by all parties involved in the conflicts, it was nourished by the snows of the Amathole mountains and was prized as the finest of Xhosa pasturage. Xhosa groups held onto the hope that the British would eventually relinquish control of the territory. However, the aftermath of the seventh in the series of nine Wars of Dispossession, known as the War of the Axe, dashed these hopes by 1848. The British occupiers had no intention of forfeiting the territory; far from it, they were determined to extend their dominion, encroaching deeper into Xhosaland.[19]

The War of the Axe led to the displacement and deaths of thousands of Xhosa people, nullifying a signed treaty in the process. British forces seized swaths of land beyond the eastern border of the Ceded Territory, using the captured space to constitute a colony for Xhosa subjects known as British Kaffraria, a name derived from a racial slur. Following the war, the Ceded Territory was officially absorbed into the British Cape Colony, taking on the new title Victoria East District, a gesture to Queen Victoria. In this district, the village of Alice emerged as the administrative hub, its name honoring the queen's daughter. The British government then parceled out Victoria East's rich acreage to White settlers, who established farms. These settlers often employed Xhosa people as "farm dwellers"— laborers who were also permanent residents. The contemporary Alice group, known for assisting ACB, descended from families of farm dwellers.

These families resided on a series of nine adjacent cattle farms, allocated to White settlers in the Victoria East District during the 1850s.

Over a century later, when the apartheid regime began assembling the Ciskei homeland, it used pieces of Victoria East and what had been British Kaffraria. Even in 1982, when the Ciskei homeland was declared independent, the process of territorial amalgamation was still underway. The South African government embarked on a land acquisition drive, purchasing additional farm parcels within the Victoria East District to integrate them into the Ciskei homeland. This initiative included the acquisition of the nine farm parcels where the Alice group resided as permanent farmworkers. With the government's buyout, the White farm owners vacated, leaving the farm dwellers—the families of the Alice group—as the remaining inhabitants. As a result, from 1852 onward the farm dwellers and their descendants had been the only consistent occupants of the nine farms. As Nomthunzi stressed to me, "My parents were born on one of these farms, and it's where I was also born."[20]

This history also helps explain why members of the Alice group held different views about the Imingcangathelo chieftaincy and the Rharhabe kingdom under King Sandile. The colonial invention of tradition and "tribalism" in much of South Africa is well known. As in many other African contexts, indirect colonial rule distorted the powers of chiefs, centralizing their authority and eroding the processes of chiefly accountability and consultation that characterized the precolonial political order.[21] But as I outlined in this book's introduction, the region that became the Ciskei homeland did not follow this pattern—at least for a time. The Wars of Dispossession ravaged the Xhosa nation and its political order under chiefs. Xhosa chiefs were systematically targeted for capture or murder. Among those targeted were the ancestors of the chiefs who would later become involved in the pelargonium plant trade. Chief Mkrazuli Tyali (1798–1842) of Imgingcangathelo and Mgolombane Sandile (1820–1878), the senior Xhosa chief of the Cape frontier, had both fought heroically against the British and died during the Wars of Dispossession. The descendants of the anti-colonial chiefs found themselves pushed hundreds of kilometers eastward, into the Transkei, the region whose name meant "beyond the Kei River." In the aftermath, colonial officials opposed hereditary leaders in the Ciskei, casting aside the trappings of chiefly authority there and eventually governing the region via liberal common law. In non-White settlements, those chiefs who remained surrendered their powers to elected authorities called "headmen."[22]

The apartheid state thus faced a problem when it attempted to consolidate the Ciskei as a homeland and "retribalize" its system of government. When the area was established as an administrative region in 1961, there were no formally recognized Xhosa "tribal authorities" to appoint.

The newly sovereign Ciskei state reacted to this problem by establishing such authorities by giving the headmen new powers and retitling them "chiefs." The state also set about resuscitating Rharhabe authorities like Tyali and Sandile, retrieving their descendants from the Transkei or wholly fabricating others, jurisdictionally positioning them to uphold the homeland's legitimacy and its president, Lennox Sebe.[23]

And yet this process of resuscitation did not directly impact Nomthunzi's family and the other former farm dwellers. This was the case because within the Ciskei homeland's already different historical context, they were additionally unusual.

"What happened after the White farmers left, during the consolidation of the Ciskei?" I once asked Nomthunzi.

"The Ciskei homeland had a department of agriculture," Nomthunzi said. "That department began leasing the farms to a handful of Black cattle owners." The move reflected the government's view of the farms as commercial assets to be kept productive, much like the previous administration.[24] Consequently, after the White farm owners departed in 1982, the Ciskei homeland government elected to keep the land the farm dwellers occupied as working farms rather than incorporate it into any chiefly jurisdiction. What is more, the Black lessees rarely settled in the area permanently. Instead, they relied on the land's existing occupants, including Nomthunzi's family members, employing them as managers of their cattle. For a minimal fee, the government also permitted stockowners from nearby communal areas to use the state-owned farms for grazing. This arrangement provided many of Nomthunzi's neighbors with jobs as local stock rangers, employed by the Agriculture Department. Their responsibilities included safeguarding farm equipment from theft and vandalism, as well as preventing overuse of the land by additional families.

The former farm dwellers considered themselves fortunate; unlike those in overcrowded neighboring villages, their land was fertile and they benefited economically from employment opportunities. Their incomes allowed many to buy and breed their own livestock, which they sold locally. For these and other reasons, some residents on the farms looked back on the Ciskei era with nostalgia, recalling it as a time when "life was better," with more jobs and greater government support.[25] "Lennox Sebe looked after the people, at least when it came to jobs," one resident told me.

"But we faced other difficulties!" Nomthunzi insisted to me. "When those Black wealthy lessees came, they eventually claimed the land as theirs, telling us it all belonged to them now." They also started depriving the residents of access to things like cattle dipping sites. "They would lock up gates to those places, preventing us from dipping our own cattle as we had previously done." The government sold one of the farm plots to a private buyer. The residents started to fear eviction. What is more, people from the surrounding villages increasingly drove their cattle onto the farms. They did so in part because, unlike what they encountered in their overcrowded settlements, the fields were in prime condition for grazing. In 1992 tensions climaxed after those neighbors streamed onto the farms, began dismantling packing sheds and fences, and pushed scores of livestock onto cultivated areas.[26]

"Nelson Mandela was released from prison in 1990," Nomthunzi continued. "The Ciskei was eventually reintegrated into South Africa in 1994. It was only after these things happened that we felt we could speak openly about our challenges. That's when we began to stand up (*saqala ukuma ngenyawo*) and voice our concerns and complaints." Previously, the families on the farms had acted independently, never discussing or taking decisions collectively. They decided to change this pattern. They moved closer together and nearer to a main road to form small villages with better access to services. They began holding meetings. Soon thereafter, they registered themselves as a resident association called Masakhane, meaning "we build together."

From 1994 to 1996 they appealed to the newly established Eastern Cape provincial government to grant them ownership of some of the land they occupied. They hoped that title deeds would offer them statutory power to keep encroachers away. They also wished to receive access to basic services—like water and electricity—and perhaps even institutional support for their farming. In 2000 the residents learned that they had successfully used the Communal Property Associations (CPA) Act of 1996 to form two communal property associations (CPAs) to hold and manage their land. They named one Masakhane and the other Iqayiyalethu, meaning "our pride." The CPAs were set to receive title deeds to the nine farm parcels they occupied. The government also promised state funding for farm infrastructure like fencing and irrigation pipes.

But the transfer of title deeds never happened. The funding never arrived. The residents had found themselves waiting, hoping that their tenure on the land could still be secured. In the meantime, they insisted that continued confusion over the ownership status of their land had led the DEA to conflate their villages with the nearby Imingcangathelo chiefdom.

THE MISSING TITLE DEEDS

After learning this history from Nomthunzi and others in the middle of 2011, I visited the Deeds Registry Office in Qonce, looking for any trace of the CPAs and title deeds there. Digging through files in a thick, light brown binder that still bore the old colonial name Victoria East District, I located the records of all nine of the farms. The records detailed all sale activity regarding the properties from the 1850s until 1982, the year the farms had been purchased for incorporation into the Ciskei homeland. Troublingly, however, nothing in the documents indicated that the farms had been transferred since that time or that the farms had any link to CPAs.

Seeking more information, I started making inquiries at the provincial office of the Department of Rural Development and Land Reform (DRDLR) in the city of East London. I met with the official responsible for case files for the Masakhane and Iqayiyalethu CPAs and was immediately puzzled by the official's statements. The official recalled receiving a file concerning the CPAs from a colleague sometime in the mid-2000s. He understood the transfer of title deeds had been mismanaged. However, he insisted the file he had received was missing key documents, foremost among them a power of attorney authorizing the land transfer. I responded by telling the official that the CPAs themselves had most, if not all, of the documents in question.

The documents no longer mattered anyway, the official replied to me. This was so because while the official had been in the process of assembling the missing documents, a new minister had taken charge at the national DRDLR office. According to the official, the new minister, Gugile Nkwinti, had "issued a moratorium on the disposal of state assets to communities." The official was explicit: regardless of documentation and regardless of his personal wish that the CPAs secure ownership of the farms, the moratorium had made any transfer impossible.

The official proposed what he saw as a preferable alternative to ownership. He was attempting to establish a "caretaker agreement" for the CPAs, enabling them to lease the land rather than own it outright. As part of this plan, he was working on a "recapitalization" application to help the CPAs financially stimulate their farming activities. The farms needed to become as "productive" as possible, he insisted. To qualify, the CPAs would need to develop a "business plan" with the help of a farming mentor.

Aware of the significance of the official's claims, I wanted to get a sense of the Imingcangathelo chieftaincy's perspective concerning the CPAs, their land, and the benefit-sharing agreement involving pelargonium. I had started interacting with a representative of the chieftaincy, a Xhosa man I call Mr. Makeba.[27] "If they don't want to belong to the chief, that is their right," he explained to me about the CPAs. "And if they want to have the CPAs, that is also their right." It was understandable, he added, why the CPAs would "feel confused" about the land and the chieftaincy. "They long toiled under the White colonist farmers. They were separate from the chiefs all that time. They must be saying, 'We worked so hard, and now these White farmers have left. Why don't we grab the land that is left behind?'" He implied that the CPAs' members, like so many other South Africans, exemplified the identity and consciousness-altering impact of the colonial encounter. "I think that our people here, historically speaking, were disturbed by the intruders who came to take the land by force and introduced their system of government and their way of life." The perspective was understandable; in the words of historian Jeff Peires, the colonization of the Eastern Cape had long penetrated and undermined the national, cultural, and economic integrity of Xhosa people, immersing the mass of the population "in a world of which the chiefs and their cohorts knew nothing."[28]

Mr. Makeba stressed the impact of colonialism, both physical and mental, in our three English-language interviews. In our first meeting, he arrived with a pile of notes labeled "for interviews with UK journalists." Upon inquiry, he revealed his experience with numerous prior interviews. He told me his message to me would echo what he had shared with others: South Africa had suffered extensive extractive exploitation by colonizers. He said this status was changing, however, and companies like Schwabe were showing the way forward with benefit sharing. Beyond the monetary royalties to the chiefs, Schwabe was investing in local projects like a fruit-tree planting scheme, which began in 2010 at a local school but was expanding from there. "One reason why I respect them is that it was their decision to give us this fruit-tree project. It may look small at the beginning, but as it grows, and if people can look after these trees, it will make a difference." The trees would provide families with fruit they could eat and sell, he told me. They would also provide shade. "After ten years, when the trees have grown and are giving fruit to the people, those people will say, 'We are eating Schwabe.' Schwabe will have put its name in the hearts of people." (See figure 5.)

I asked about the money the chieftaincy had received from drug companies. What did they imagine doing with it?

"Let's say a village wants to start a project like a piggery, we could assist with that. But we don't want to impose projects on villages. They must decide what to do with this money. But the money from pelargonium will never be enough to sustain projects. We'll have to get support from elsewhere, from government and other businesses."

The spokesperson and I had never meaningfully discussed the CPAs until our third interaction. The time seemed right to ask: Did the leaders of Imingcangathelo support the Masakhane and Iqayiyalethu CPAs receiving title deeds?

"Even if they get their title deeds, if they remain under Tyali, we see no problem with that," Mr. Makeba said. "We know that they pay allegiance to Tyali; they know who their chief is. And because she is their chief, she is there to service them, to help them. We support their land claim."

"Would you say more about why you support it?"

"We feel that, if they want to develop, it's not easy to develop without land. They need that something—those title deeds—that can open

Figure 5. Imingcangathelo-area elementary school's bulletin board welcoming representatives of Schwabe (2011). The company had undertaken a benefit-sharing project with its South African supplier, Parceval, to plant fruit trees near the school. Also displayed are newspaper articles about the project. Photo by the author.

the doors for them for funding. Otherwise, without such documents, they will suffer."

Mr. Makeba's point about the CPAs receiving title deeds but remaining "under Tyali" seemed particularly important. I asked: "Wouldn't remaining under Tyali cause conflict when it comes to benefit sharing?"

He answered:

> I don't know if there will be conflict. People around here benefit in the sense that, if they go and harvest from the wild, they are filling their bags, and they sell those bags direct to a biotrader. The money they make that way, it goes into their pockets. That money does not go to the chief. That is one way they are benefitting. And the percentage that the drug companies will pay goes into an account of the national government. Then it goes to the provincial government and eventually to the kingdom. The kingdom will then pay a percentage into the trusts of individual chiefs.

CONCLUSION

As made clear in chapter 4, the Imingcangathelo chieftaincy's position stood in contrast to those of other chieftaincies—and even the national minister of DRDLR, Gugile Nkwinti—when it came to its support of CPAs. And yet when Mr. Makeba insisted to me that the chieftaincy would support the CPAs receiving title deeds, he also implied that such support hinged on the CPAs "remain[ing] under Tyali." If they remained so, there need not be any conflict over pelargonium, he indicated. Money from biotraders would go into the pockets of harvesters, he said, and chieftaincies would receive benefits, too. In this scenario, capital generation was less about a chiefdom directly controlling land; the Imingcangathelo chieftaincy appeared willing to acknowledge the sovereignty of the CPAs in this respect. It was thus more about a chiefdom's recognized authority over communities and laborers who occupied territory. The recasting of harvesters as chiefly subjects was expedient for traditional leaders, who were paid royalties under benefit sharing according to how much raw material was harvested from their jurisdictions. With pelargonium abundantly distributed across the province, and royalties associated with Indigenous knowledge of the resource not yet in play, a traditional leader like Tyali found little reason to limit membership within their "community." Rather, they sought to enroll as many subjects as possible to serve as laborers and help generate royalties. In this respect, as a means of accumulation, the chief's jurisdiction over *persons* was just as important as their jurisdiction over property.[29] Central to the operation of benefit sharing were the people constituting the Masakahane and Iqayiyalethu CPAs *belonging* to Imingcangathelo.

This situation reminds us that in access and benefit sharing, "community *is* as community *represents*."[30] As Cori Hayden remarks, this "requirement of representativity—suffused with notions of territoriality and identity but readily stripped down to an essential political functionality (the capacity to speak for)—is certainly one of the most striking aspects of benefit-sharing agreements and the intellectual property logics to which they are pegged."[31] But the situation also contrasts with what we often read about free-market approaches to conserving nature—namely, that such approaches lead to the spatial excision of people who live in areas where nature is to be conserved.

In line with initial theories about neoliberal capitalism, scholars originally understood neoliberal reforms in the 1980s and 1990s to be a kind of "ideological software" designed to weaken the regulatory capacity of governments.[32]

Before long, however, scholars better grasped these reforms to be acts of *reregulation*. Governments had not been enfeebled—they had instead been refashioned as instruments to privatize and commodify ever-broadening domains of life.[33] In the context of nature conservation, political ecologists have shown how reregulation entails the division and containment of space, or what Peter Vandergeest and Nancy Peluso term "territorialization."[34] By creating conservation parks, for example, states can enclose existing commons, eliminate competing property claims, and secure ownership for select (often private) parties. In their original formulation of territorialization, Vandergeest and Peluso argue that the process is "about *excluding or including* people within particular geographic boundaries, and about controlling what people do and their access to natural resources within those boundaries."[35] It strikes me, however, that a preponderance of research concerning conservation stresses spatial exclusions—that is, *human displacements* that are intended to create territorial binaries of nature and non-nature.[36] This emphasis is understandable given the violent manner through which such displacements have historically played out.[37]

Benefit sharing is an offspring of neoliberal conservation. But in contrast with most other forms of conservation, its territorializations cannot function without people-in-nature.[38] Biotraffic and its governance in South Africa reveal a nuanced pattern in the distribution of power and resources, one in which the expansion of community membership drove a form of territorialization that *includes people*, sometimes against their wishes.[39] In the next chapters I return to this topic of biotraffic's spatialities of power and subjection, but my analysis adds to the mix the themes of time and scale explored in chapter 2.

INTERLUDE

"The Doom of 150,000 People" (1915–1953)

> This treatment can be taken in one's home, no change of air or climate necessary; in fact, consumptive patients seem to get better in the East End of London just as fast as on the high plains of South Africa, or in the mountains of Switzerland.
>
> —Advertisement for Umckaloabo, 1927

Charles Henry Stevens's libel suit against the BMA had unintentionally put Stevens and his medicine Umckaloabo on trial. His loss to the BMA, however, had little impact on sales of Umckaloabo. Between 1915 and 1919 CH Stevens Co. continued to grow. With the onset of World War I, however, business slowed, and Stevens served with distinction in the Royal Flying Corps. The war changed him physically. He had crashed his fighter plane and broken his leg. After the broken bone was plated with three pieces of steel and seventeen screws, he had resumed his service, flying in France. By the war's end, he had climbed the military ranks to the position of major. His Umckaloabo business resumed shortly thereafter, and by 1931 Stevens's company had expanded to fifty employees who manufactured capsules, tinctures, and lozenges. Stevens continued to be accused of quackery, and medical associations across Europe persisted in attempting to identify the ingredients of the remedy.

In 1931 a person claiming to be an English physician and the medical correspondent for a prominent British newspaper published *Tuberculosis: Its Treatment and Cure with the Help of Umckaloabo (Stevens)*. The book recounts fifty-five case histories of tuberculosis-stricken patients receiving Umckaloabo. It claims that all of the patients had recovered, and all subsequently had been declared cured. None of the patients had been under the care of the author, however, and they had been assessed by means of a single visit with a doctor.[1]

The book presented Stevens as a notable case study of Umckaloabo's efficacy, suggesting that Stevens's good health, which misfortune had repeatedly tested, was the result of the medicine. Indeed, despite having contracted tuberculosis in the late 1800s and more recently having survived an airplane crash, Stevens lived on: "Now it does not matter in the slightest degree whether the accidental discoverer of any remedy is a cardinal or cobbler; it is only the value or worthlessness of the remedy that matters, *except in one respect*. Where the result in one individual in regard to subsequent and sustained and exceptional fitness is a remarkable one, not only will the confidence inspired in that individual be great, but the indisputable fact of sustained fitness over a period of thirty odd years is worthy of note."[2]

Perhaps most notable about *Tuberculosis: Its Treatment and Cure* is its promotion of Umckaloabo as an alternative to sanatoria. And indeed, in speculating about the medicine's continued popularity, we might consider how claims about it as a tuberculosis cure resonated with doubts surrounding sanatoria, particularly in light of the prevailing skepticism about use of sanatoria, which had been the predominant tuberculosis treatment method in England for many years.

Although the exact reasons remain a matter of debate, tuberculosis infections declined across Europe in the early twentieth century.[3] However, historians largely agree that isolating patients in state and private sanatoria, along with voluntary hospitals, was not particularly effective, especially for those with advanced infections, although it did provide some level of comfort.[4] But did this isolation work as a public health tactic? One historian says no, arguing that the proliferation of sanatoria in Britain not only failed to reduce the incidence of tuberculosis but also may have contributed to the disease's spread by promoting cross-infection and diverting resources from more promising medical strategies.[5]

What is clear is that by 1898 sanatoria, alongside public education campaigns and the eradication of tuberculosis in cattle, were viewed as the most effective interventions for tuberculosis by the BMA.[6] The BMA's position is evident in a comment about the island of Trinidad, made in the same 1905 issue of the *Lancet* that criticized Stevens: "It is satisfactory to find that in Trinidad an enlightened policy is being followed with respect to tuberculous diseases and that the Trinidad Association for the Prevention and Treatment of Tuberculosis is issuing leaflets for the instruction of the public in elementary hygiene. The objects of this association are (1) to disseminate information regarding the prevention of tuberculosis; (2) to establish in the town of Port-of-Spain a dispensary for the gratuitous treatment of tuberculous disease of the lungs; and (3) to establish a sanatorium for consumption."[7]

This preventive focus marked a general shift in tuberculosis treatment in the early 1900s, as "open-air treatment of tuberculosis became the treatment of tuberculosis in the open-air."[8] The shift, in other words, entailed movement away from noninstitutional access to "open air" to segregated, institutionalized settings that could provide, among other treatments, access to "open air." This transition reflected the belief that "it was the institutional regime and not the mystical properties of ozone or whatever" that became foundational for treatment.[9] Institutional isolation was a key component of the larger BMA-backed movement to thwart the "contingent contagionism" of the disease, or the idea that tuberculosis was infectious only where unsanitary behavior and conditions thrived. The BMA campaigned on the matter, attempting to educate the British citizenry about containing the disease. The problem was that the convolutions of "contingent contagionism" ended up being lost on the general public, "who increasingly saw the disease as very contagious, shunned the tuberculous and viewed sanatoria as dangerous places."[10]

The fear was justified, as growing evidence from Europe made clear. A physician named William Camac Wilkinson, for example, publicly called attention to the disturbing results of follow-up reports from thirty-one sanatoria in Germany: four years after their release from sanatoria, 80 percent of patients were either deceased or severely debilitated.[11]

The book *Tuberculosis: Its Treatment and Cure* took issue with the "prevention as treatment" model for tuberculosis, echoing Linda Bryder's later claims that a mainstream emphasis on sanatoria had precluded better interventions.[12] "This idea of prevention is still an *ideal* that must ever be set before us, but an ideal not yet attainable in this imperfect world. The ordinary man wants something *more practical and more immediate*. My own suggestion, whatever it may be worth, is that all this seeking for preventive measures against disease may be a *positive hindrance* to the discovery of a remedy or a cure for it."[13]

During Stevens's libel case against the BMA, his witness Dr. Grün suggested something similar to a BMA lawyer named Gregory:

GREGORY: It goes without saying that all the millions that are being spent on Sanatoria in England are wasted according to your idea?

GRÜN: I think Sanatoria are useful for putting patients in good hygienic conditions, but at the same time I think they could be dispensed with.[14]

In contrast, supporting witnesses for the BMA appeared unable to espouse anything but mainstream methods like sanatoria. In the following exchange during the libel hearings, Stevens's lawyer Atkinson asked one such BMA witness, a Dr. Price, about the sensibility behind testing a drug that showed promise against tuberculosis. Dr. Price refused to give Atkinson any satisfaction with his answer:

ATKINSON: If you find marked improvement in a tuberculosis patient after using an unknown drug, would you consider it worthy of further trial?

DR. PRICE: Not necessarily; you do get improvement without drugs.[15]

Supporters of Stevens documented the experience of consumptives in sanatoria and the improvement of their condition once they exited and began imbibing Umckaloabo.[16] Consider the stories of two men who spent months in the Royal National Sanatorium in Bournemouth during the 1930s. Howard Robins of New Malden, Surrey, was assessed by six doctors and placed on a creosote respirator. To keep his head immobile, he wore a specially prepared collar and slept with sandbags next to his ears. His doctors considered him incurable, but he recovered after exiting Royal National and drinking Umckaloabo. Three doctors confirmed the diagnosis of another man at Royal National, W. H. Davis of Buxton, Derbyshire. Davis had thought his tuberculosis was dormant when he departed but soon suffered numerous severe hemorrhages. Rather than return, he began taking Umckaloabo, reporting the following improvements:

1. Increased sputum.
2. Immediate increased appetite.

3. Reduction in cough.
4. Increase in weight.
5. Decrease in sputum.
6. Increased optimism.
7. Improved color and general appearance, causing comment by his doctor.
8. Maintained weight.

A radiograph indicated that lesions in Davis's lungs were healing, and a doctor at a tuberculosis clinic recommended he no longer be listed as consumptive.

Tuberculosis mortality was on the rise again after World War I. Stevens and his supporters sought to take advantage of persistent public skepticism about sanatoria and the perception that the BMA was biased against Umckaloabo. The book *The Doom of 150,000 People*, which was published in 1931 and contained letters from former tuberculosis patients and claimed to have been cured, accused British minister of health Arthur

Figure 6. Dust jacket of *The Doom of 150,000 People* (1931). Photo by the author.

Greenwood of having encouraged Umckaloabo to be condemned "without investigation." The book's dust jacket was cleverly designed to provoke readers' fears of sanatoria (see figure 6). It is unclear if it sold widely, but its publication did provoke significant discussion of Umckaloabo within the national government. It was a topic of conversation among officials considering an unpassed bill that would have more strictly regulated medicines like Umckaloabo. According to one historian, "Stevens was still selling in 1939 and in 1941 was again asking patients to lobby MPs against another threatened Government Bill. Since the cure was still being sold in 1953, this cannot have materialized—so, in the last analysis, he prevailed in his battle with *Secret Remedies*."[17]

4 Waiting

This chapter ties together themes from the previous two chapters, delving deeper into the consequential relationship between scale, time, and space in the context of biotraffic. Chapter 2 examined a stop-start trade in high volumes of pelargonium from the region that once constituted the Ciskei homeland. Chapter 3 homed in on the spatiality of biotraffic and its governance in that region, spotlighting the ability of a chieftaincy to expand its powers over territory and resources via claims to people. In the pages that follow, I continue the story of the Masakhane and Iqayiyalethu CPAs, revealing how the insecure status of their land tenure threatened both economic and noneconomic ways of life that the residents hoped to secure for the future. In the eyes of the residents, their clash with the nearby Imingcangathelo chieftaincy over pelargonium reflected merely *a symptom* of their tenure insecurity. But that clash, they would soon learn, actually reflected *a cause*; the department of the South African government that administered land had placed CPAs throughout the former homelands at risk. Paradoxically, and amid the complexity, the Masakhane and Iqayiyalethu CPAs once again began to pose a threat to Schwabe—a threat that arguably equaled, if not exceeded, the challenge to the company's pelargonium patents.

"WE WILL WAIT AS LONG IT TAKES"

During my research in 2011, I interviewed Anathi, a Xhosa woman in her mid-twenties and resident in a village belonging to the Masakhane and Iqayiyalethu CPAs. Anathi recalled taking part in the pelargonium industry when she was in her teens. She described the mid-2000s as the peak of the industry—a period when, as she put it, "almost everyone in the villages participated in collecting, including the youngsters like me."

She said that the area youth would come back from school each day and join the people who were already harvesting. "This, of course, was to the benefit of families who had children because they were adding income to their households."

Old and young took part in the parade to and from the forest, hauling coarse, woven plastic sacks with pelargonium tubers back to their houses.

"How long would it take to fill a single bag?" I asked Anathi.

"The young people had it easier with that. We could fill a bag in a few hours. As for the older people, by five o'clock in the afternoon, they would still not have filled a bag. They often had to continue the following day."

Anathi reflected upon the period with nostalgia. "No one needed any permit. We would dig as much as we could and then wait for the biotrader to appear."

This harvesting heyday proved relatively brief, however—at best a few years, Anathi estimated. Various factors contributed. The plant had become increasingly scarce near village areas. Also contributing were the provincial government's moratorium on harvesting and the fact that Schwabe had stopped buying; recall from chapter 2 that by 2011 the company said it had accumulated enough stock of the plant to continue producing medicines for the foreseeable future.

What had slowed to a trickle and then a halt for South Africans like Anathi had been a continuous surge for Schwabe. While the harvesters had ceased their collection, over in Schwabe's laboratories, the journey of the harvested plant material was progressing through intricate stages of pharmacological processing. Schwabe's revoked patent described the process the company used for producing Umckaloabo, a process that in pharmacology is called "extraction." The material that had been dried and shredded into small pieces had been shipped to Germany. In Schwabe's facilities, this material was ground to a pulp. This "mashing" broke down the plant's cell structure, releasing substances stored inside the cells and making them more accessible to the solvent that would be used in the next step. The pulpy mass was then introduced to *percolation*, where it was soaked in an ethanol-water mixture that worked its way through the pulp like rainwater infusing soil, leaching out various therapeutic elements. Alternatively, the plant material could go through a two-step *maceration* process. In this method, Schwabe's technicians soaked the plant material in a strong ethanol solution, then filtered out the liquid and subjected the remaining solid to a second, milder solvent. The liquids from both steps, each rich with the plant's properties, were subsequently combined.

The resulting extracts were then subjected to vacuum evaporation. Schwabe technicians carefully removed the solvents to leave behind a concentrated essence of the plant. This essence contained the key therapeutic compounds of the plant, including proanthocyanidins and coumarins, whose alleged antibacterial effects and antioxidant potential contribute to the plant's purported healing profile for gastrointestinal disorders and respiratory diseases. As part of the quality control process, this extract was put through rigorous testing. Schwabe's laboratories measured the levels of total phenols and coumarins, ensuring the extract had the desired potency and was safe for therapeutic use. These tests were important because the antioxidant properties of the extract, which may help in healing and preventing tissue damage during infections, depend largely on the total phenol content. The final phase in the journey of pelargonium's transformation involved converting the extract into various pharmaceutical forms. The extract was formulated into tablets, capsules, liquid tinctures, and syrups, each combined with pharmaceutical excipients to ensure the medicines were stable, effective, and convenient for users.

This juxtaposition of the pelargonium industry's operations in South Africa and Germany foregrounds the mixed temporalities and scales of biotraffic, highlighting differential experiences based on a person's position in the value chain. *Waiting* was a pervasive feature of such traffic, its temporalities reflecting, overlaying, or interacting with other temporal circumstances that stood in the way of local people attempting to plan and build a future.[1] When I asked Anathi about the pelargonium industry possibly returning to her area in the future, she was matter of fact. "Maybe it will come back and start again—we don't know. It's not something we can rely on." She said: "We care more about the land, the title deeds. We will wait as long as it takes."

As former farm dwellers, the villagers were among the most marginalized and tenure insecure in the country.[2] They were part of an expanding number of people in South Africa who were *un-titled*, living in situations that exist outside of the formally recognized land tenure system.[3] Their home, the land, had been one of the few continuities in their lives. They associated it with enduring material livelihoods. But the land was also a place to which they attached less tangible values. Without title deeds, they feared that everything was at risk—both their material and immaterial ways of life.

TEMPORAL DISPOSSESSION

In the early spring of 2011, I walked with Anathi and her mother near the CPAs' land. As we made our way closer to a river valley, an open savannah dotted with umbrella-shaped *Acacia natalitia* trees and *Tephrosia capensis* shrubs transitioned to a thicket of aloes and candelabra-like *Euphorbia* trees. We were nearing a forest of succulents.

The forest embodied a difficult past. The Eighth War of Dispossession, which unfolded between 1850 and 1853, was a period of great upheaval and resistance. The eighth war was the War of Mlanjeni, named after the Xhosa prophet Mlanjeni, a once sickly boy who became a charismatic spiritual and military leader during a time of intense conflict between British colonial forces and Xhosa resistance fighters.[4] Mlanjeni advocated a spiritual cleansing to empower the Xhosa army, and his influence had been deeply rooted in his connection to the land and waterways, earning him the moniker "Riverman." He was believed to possess the ability to control the rivers, a symbolic representation of his perceived power to cleanse and renew. His teachings resonated with chiefs, who sought his insights about military strategy. Their successes during the war had been crucially dependent on the terrain upon which they fought, and in 1851, Mlanjeni urged them to enter the river forest, where they gained a significant victory against the Queen's Regiment.[5]

Figure 7. Anathi revealing a pelargonium plant hidden in a shrub (2011). Photo by the author.

Having perceived the forest as an impenetrable hazard, British forces tried to set it ablaze, hoping to flush out Xhosa fighters. Yet the landscape had stood defiant. Its succulent vegetation, rich and moisture-laden, stubbornly resisted the flames, failing to ignite as the British had planned.[6] This act of nature, defying the colonial military strategy, became a powerful symbol of resilience. Still, Mlanjeni's prophesies did not come true; the British eventually triumphed in the Wars of Dispossession. The series of conflicts concluded with the Ninth Xhosa War, which ended in 1879, leading to the effective defeat of Xhosa groups and their eventual incorporation into the Cape Colony. Forced to confront their incorporation, many Xhosa people "took their places in the schools of Alice and the docks of Port Elizabeth to work out a new destiny inside the belly of the colonial beast."[7]

During our walk, Anathi eventually stopped and pointed to a pelargonium plant that had sprouted from under a shrub (figure 7). She had spotted its plush, heart-shaped foliage, she said. "*Uvendle* heals (*nyanyanga*)," she added, further describing the plant.

"I know about the plant from her," she said, gesturing at her mother. "But it's different for other people. A neighbor of mine says they know about it from a dream."

"What happened in their dream?" I asked.

"They said they found themselves standing on the bank of a river. A man appeared and showed them the plant. He told them to dig it up, take it home, and wash it. He said to mash it and then boil the pulped bulb."

"That's what you told me you do as well. To prepare it," I said to Anathi's mother.

"Yeah. Anathi had a terrible gastrointestinal illness (*ndandi nesisu segazi*). It left her weak. I prepared it, and after it had cooled, she drank a cupful. It helped her."

Like others, Anathi and her mother used the isiXhosa word *izifozonke* to describe the plant, likening it to a jack-of-all-trades, treats-all-diseases medicine whose therapeutic versatility was its strength. "We think of it as a 'booster' of the body, strengthening (*ukomeleza*) the immune system."

Anathi and her mother had grown up using the plant and others for ailments. The nearest medical clinic was a long walk from her village, and a veterinary clinic was even farther away. If they, a family member, or one of the family's cows were suffering from an upset stomach, they would enter the forest, searching the ground for the plant's foliage.

Pelargonium did not wish to be found, Anathi insisted. Like the individual plant we had come across, it often hid under bushes, and in a region with notoriously fitful rains, might not even sprout after a downpour. Furthermore, horticulturalists describe the plant as "low density," meaning its distribution is sparse, compelling harvesters like Anathi to traverse large distances for collection. It had not helped that she and others had collected extensively around village areas. Compounding these challenges, the part of the plant most valued, its lignotuber, grew deep in the hard soil, demanding considerable effort to extract. In a sense, the plant was defiant, not unlike the landscape of which it was part. Eventually, the plant seemed to become another representation of Anathi's stalled attempts at getting ahead.

In his book about the War of Mlajeni and the Xhosa cattle-killing movement, historian Jeff Peires emphasizes themes of waiting and postponement.[8] Facing immense pressure from colonial encroachment, Xhosa groups grasped for solutions to the existential threats they faced. The act of waiting for the fulfillment of prophesies became a communal experience for many, tied deeply to their hope for salvation and liberation. Some Xhosa believed the Riverman was possessed of the "secret of Eternity"—an ability to transcend temporal limits and conquer death itself.[9]

Wars can entail what anthropologist James Smith calls "temporal dispossession," referring to the ways in which people or communities are dispossessed not just of their land or physical resources, but also of their time and future.[10] It suggests a form of cultural and social disruption in which affected groups lose control over their temporal existence: their histories, their futures, and the progression of their cultural and social narratives.

Violence reverberates across time, space, and materialities, becoming generationally embodied.[11] The Wars of Dispossession were over. Apartheid had officially ended. Yet temporal dispossession seemed to remain a fixture of life for South Africans like Anathi. She was just one among many whose ability to plan, anticipate, or build a future seemed to be curtailed.[12] "Underlying the physical insecurities of everyday life and the kinds of survivalism they demand," Maxim Bolt and Dinah Rajak argue in the context of South Africa, "there is an existential insecurity that comes from radical uncertainty about the future."[13] In post–structural adjustment Africa more broadly, many people sense that "established ways of getting ahead and getting by were sabotaged, producing a sense of ruptured temporality and reversed or forestalled 'development.'"[14] A consequent inability to anticipate and plan one's future in an incremental way, according to Jane Guyer, means that "punctuated time," or "fateful moments and turning points," come to fill a "gap between an instantaneous present and an altogether different distant future."[15]

A NATIONAL TEST CASE

One such fateful moment occurred for Anathi a couple of weeks after our walk near the forest. I was away from the CPAs' villages at the time when I received a distressing phone call from Anathi. She was in a hospital in the city of East London, several hours away from her home. She had been transported to the hospital from her village after being severely beaten by a man in his early twenties who had been staying at her family's house.

I knew the man; he was one of four male workers overseeing a water pipe project in the larger area. To secure some extra income, Anathi's family had agreed to house the four young men for the duration of the project. The project entailed fifty or so villagers digging trenches and laying water pipes from a manifold near the town of Alice to the most remote of the villages in the area, a distance of nearly ten miles. The project was running months behind schedule, and over this period, Anathi and the other villagers came to feel they knew the men relatively well. On weekend—and increasingly weekday—nights they would drink and dance together until the early hours of the morning.

The men lived a transient life, moving from one water pipe project, and one rural village, to the next. This existence seemed to wear increasingly on them; they seemed to feel trapped. The fact that their employer forbade their using the one company vehicle on the weekends to leave the village contributed to this situation. Heavy drinking became a regular practice. According to Anathi, she had maintained a flirtatious relationship with one of the men over the past weeks, but during a night of drinking, he became upset with her and proceeded to strike her numerous times. Not wishing to face the law or local retribution, the man immediately fled the village that night on foot and never returned. Anathi was left stranded and alone at the hospital in East London. Without money, she called me to ask that I transfer funds via mobile phone for her return trip to her village.

The water pipe project had been plagued with problems from the outset. Housing unruly strangers was only tolerable for Anathi's parents in light of the extra money it provided them. Additionally, since local villages had themselves been entrusted with selecting which residents would be employed through the project, complaints about favoritism and exclusion were common, and in an area with few work opportunities, these complaints led to significant tensions. Moreover, the company running the project regularly failed to pay workers, who toiled in dirt trenches for ten hours a day. The lack of payment led many workers to strike, and a number, including Anathi, eventually quit. The situation had been lose-lose for Anathi and her family. Anathi's brother had just returned from a six-month contract in a city working for Eskom, the country's power utility. Her sister was set to return from a similar short-term contract in a nearby game reserve. The family would now only have welfare grants to make ends meet. Not only was Anathi not earning the $10 per day for digging trenches, but the family's gamble on housing four strangers had ended with Anathi in the hospital.

The incident proved a turning point for me as well. I recognized from my research in the villages in 2011 that what had occurred with the title deeds preoccupied the people there more than any other topic, including pelargonium. Indeed, what many of them wanted me to research—instead of plant trade—was the failed transfer of title deeds from eleven years prior. They hoped the outcome could be reversed, and that with title deeds they could qualify as formal CPAs and receive development grants. Spurred by the continued violence of insecurity that Anathi and her family's situation exemplified, I decided to start looking into the issue of the title deeds in earnest. I contacted scholars at a nearby university who had a history of advocating for the villagers, asking them for advice. They told me that if I wanted to understand the nuances of the land story and identify a path forward, I would need to speak to a land governance researcher named Rosalie Kingwill, who had also been instrumental in helping the villagers gain their status as CPAs. Kingwill happened to still live nearby. I telephoned her and she agreed to speak with me about the case. "It may even help illuminate why land reform is so complicated in South Africa," Kingwill told me during that initial phone call.

Kingwill recounted the story of the CPAs to me during numerous conversations and email exchanges over the latter months of 2011. According to Kingwill, her work with the villagers had been a national test case for occupational rights. It had all unfolded during the middle to late 1990s. At that time, Kingwill clarified, South Africa's Department of Land Affairs argued that people occupying "state land" were not regarded as "beneficial occupiers." "This meant that they would just be regarded as rightless squatters or farm workers, not occupiers with rights."

Understanding the government's definition of "state land" during this period means grasping the legacy of two past national laws and the colonial consolidation of the Ciskei homeland. The first of the old laws, the

Natives Land Act of 1913, sought to maintain an existing system of racially segregated land ownership and occupation—that is, ensuring that White and Black South Africans had differential rights concerning where they could live and what they could possess. That act also called for the possible expansion of existing "native reserves" for Black South Africans. The second law, the Native Trust and Land Act of 1936, set the expansion of reserves into motion and empowered a state "trust" to purchase land for such expansion. "The Trust and Land Act of 1936 stipulated that the Trust could buy up land from Whites (or whoever) all over South Africa," Kingwill told me. "But the effort to consolidate the Ciskei as a homeland entailed the Trust making particularly extensive purchases in the Ciskei region." After all, she clarified, "prior to the Ciskei becoming consolidated, it was bits and pieces, not one united 'territory.'"

This historical backdrop helped me understand what Kingwill clarified next. She said that the farms the state trust purchased from White settlers for incorporation into the Ciskei homeland were regarded as "state land," making them legally separate from the land historically occupied by Black groups. "It was a discrete category that the state kept control over." Portions of this category of land were sometimes allocated in small plots to new Black occupiers, and the system of tenure on such newly allocated plots was called "trust tenure." "It was similar to 'Permission to Occupy' certificates but less secure," Kingwill explained. "It was a very tightly controlled version of occupational rights where the state regarded itself as the owner and these people just tenants at will. Over time though, this kind of tenure came to resemble 'communal tenure.'"

Kingwill then arrived at the topic of villagers like Anathi. In contrast with those who had lived on land reserved for Black people and had fallen under the trust tenure system, families like Anathi's had lived on land owned by White settlers. They had been employed as farm dwellers and as such had been permanent residents. These residents, including Anathi's family, had consequently "been disconnected from communal tenure and traditional authorities [chiefs and headmen] for generations." After the consolidation of the Ciskei, the farms purchased from the White owners were leased out to Black commercial farmers and were never allocated as "trust plots" to occupiers. "They remained farm parcels, as surveyed for the White owners, under state leaseholds."

The situation exposed a flaw in national land policy. The new African National Congress–led government under Nelson Mandela had sought to legally recognize and secure the rights of people who were de facto occupiers of land. Such people enjoyed (insecure) tenure rights in practice but not yet in the law. The Interim Protection of Land Rights Act (IPILRA) of 1996 sought to protect these occupiers from eviction by introducing "beneficial occupation," a legal concept the act defined as "the occupation of land by a person, as if he or she is the owner, without force, openly and without the permission of the registered owner." The concept was powerful, but people like Anathi's family exposed a limitation because beneficial occupation did not apply to occupiers of "state land." It was this limitation that Kingwill—and eventually some of her colleagues—hoped to persuade the National Department of Land Affairs to change. As Kingwill explained it to me in an email, "I had to prove that the villagers were beneficial occupiers by showing that they were farming livestock independently of the new Black lessees. But most importantly for the definition of beneficial occupation, I had to argue that they had NOT been given permission to live and farm that land. If they HAD been given permission from former owners, or the state, or the new Black lessees, they would be regarded as under a contract to the owner, e.g., workers not occupiers. It was a complicated point of law."

Kingwill spent many months in the area observing the activities of the residents, including their participation at local stock fairs.[16] She also watched where and how the residents herded their animals. "I had to try to work out the respective distribution of land that we would ultimately recommend—why, for example, we would recommend x farms and not x farms. In other words, I tried to match their livelihood from livestock farming with the extent of land I thought they were entitled to." Some of the White former farm owners got involved, too, making statements and writing letters that attested to the former farm dwellers' skills.

The test case proved successful. In 1998 Kingwill submitted a memo to the Department of Land Affairs arguing that the former farm dwellers, having had effective use and occupation of the farms since 1982, should receive title deeds on the basis of beneficial occupation. That department eventually approved the application. On February 13, 2000, Minister of Land Affairs Thoko Didiza signed a power of attorney authorizing the transfer of nine portions of the farms. Having formed their CPAs to hold and manage the land, the villagers awaited the transfer. They had also qualified for development grants, including municipal support for farming totaling nearly $50,000.

Exuberant in the wake of their hard-fought victory, the residents organized a party and invited the Eastern Cape official tasked with transferring the land. Dressed in their best clothing, hundreds of people gathered and began celebrating, waiting for the official to arrive. But day soon turned to night and then to morning. The official never appeared. The land was never transferred, and the promised funding never arrived. They began a period of waiting that would last decades.

I interviewed numerous people with knowledge of the story. Some blamed "state incapacity" for the failed transfer. Others suggested that the provincial official had been bribed. For her part, Kingwill told me the reason "is probably way beyond what we could ever know." The institutional procedures for transferring land from the national to the local level are complicated, she explained, meaning "state incapacity" may have been partly to blame. But circumstances in the area were also "a political cauldron," she maintained. Cattle owners who had leased sections of the land since the 1990s had appeared to oppose the farmworkers getting any land, and they had "a thousand times more political clout than the CPAs."

"ASSOCIATIONS IN NAME ALONE"

The predicament of the CPAs prompted many questions. Foremost among them was: What was their legal status? The passing of the CPA act allowed for the variety of customary and local land tenure forms that exist in South Africa to receive legal recognition. The CPA was conceived as a legal vehicle for accommodating many of these forms.[17] But what of untitled CPAs? What rights did they maintain, if any?

In December 2011 I traveled to the national DRDLR office in Pretoria. My first aims in that office were to confirm the registration of the two CPAs and locate the complete files concerning the land transfers. With the help of a diligent administrator, I was able to do both in less than an hour. I made multiple copies of the documents and put them in my bag to bring back to the CPAs and Rosalie Kingwill. The administrator agreed to fax the documents to the director of the department's Eastern Cape bureau.

That afternoon, I also interviewed Sithembiso Gumbi, South Africa's CPA registrar. Mr. Gumbi spent nearly two hours with me answering my questions about the Masakhane and Iqayiyalethu CPAs. During our conversation, a colleague of Gumbi's who specialized in geographic information systems (GIS) happened to be in the process of printing out large maps of the provinces and the CPAs registered within them. I sensed anticipation from the two officials; they were looking forward to identifying the CPAs on the map of the Eastern Cape. "She is the queen of GIS," Gumbi said of his colleague. "She will have plotted the CPAs you are talking about."

Gumbi and I spoke while we waited for his colleague to reappear with the maps. "Let me start by taking you backward," he began. "When apartheid ended and after the elections of April 27, 1994, there was a new dispensation. We had a new, inclusive government. Among other things, our Constitution has Section 25, which is called the property clause. Everything we do in this office is based upon that section of the law." Gumbi zeroed in on subsections 5, 6, and 7 of the property clause, noting that each corresponded to a program managed by the DRDLR. Each was also tied to the formation of CPAs, he explained.

> The first is our restitution program, which deals with communities who lost land during colonization and apartheid. These communities can lodge claims against the state to receive land. The second program is redistribution. Anyone who is landless and needs assistance from the state—even if they do not have a restitution claim—can apply to receive a grant to help them buy land. And the third program is for people with precarious tenure— people who stay on someone else's property, like farm workers living on farms and in communal areas. This program is called tenure reform. The legislature—politicians—decided that, in each of these instances of receiving land, the administration of that land must be in the hands of a legal entity. Then, in 1996, Parliament passed the CPA Act. This law is administered by us at DRDLR, and currently, I'm the Registrar.

Gumbi cited two recent national-level developments that had undoubtedly informed the provincial Eastern Cape land office's decisions about the Masakhane and Iqayiyalethu CPAs. The first related to an important detail mentioned in chapter 3: the provincial official in charge of the CPAs' case had told me that he wanted to make the residents "caretakers" of their land, or lessees rather than owners. Gumbi outlined the national strategy informing the provincial official's plan. "We have what is called the Proactive Land Acquisition Strategy [PLAS]. The state buys up land and then waits for people to come and say, 'We're looking for a farm.' We don't give these people title deeds. We give them five-year leases, which they can renew after they demonstrate that they are committed to farming." Gumbi explained that the rationale behind the strategy was to stimulate farm productivity. "With some of the land that we purchased, the previous White owners had been producing food. But after the land was given to Black communities, no more food production was happening. Recently, government decided that this was not okay, and the new strategy emerged."

The second national development Gumbi mentioned concerned what the provincial official had described to me as a "moratorium on the disposal of state assets to communities." "Yes, there is a moratorium," Gumbi told me. He became more specific, recounting what DRDLR minister Gugile Nkwinti had internally communicated to department officials. "The Minister has said that, where there are traditional leaders, we must tread cautiously when forming CPAs. In fact, we must not encourage communities to form CPAs where there are chiefs."

"Why the moratorium? Why 'tread cautiously' when it comes to CPAs in areas where chiefs are present?" I asked.

"The CPAs and the chiefs are at loggerheads," he replied.[18] "The chiefs think that the CPA committees have taken over their functions and powers as traditional leaders. It's a problem throughout much of the country—in North West Province, in Limpopo, KwaZulu-Natal, and the Eastern Cape." Gumbi insisted the moratorium was not permanent; high-level officials at the DRDLR were actively "discussing and debating" its future.

When I asked Gumbi his opinion about the future of relations between CPAs and chiefs in the country, his response was measured. He asked me: "Have you heard of Mandla Mandela, the grandson of Nelson Mandela?" I nodded. He said that Mandela, in addition to being a chief, was a member of parliament and a member of the DRDLR's portfolio committee. When Gumbi presented his annual CPA report to the latter committee in June 2011, Mandela listened with great interest. He told Gumbi and others in attendance that he knew of a CPA and a traditional leader in the Eastern Cape who were working harmoniously with one another to stimulate rural development. Mandela said he hoped that such relationships would become more common. "We have a few such examples," Gumbi told me. "In KwaZulu-Natal, two CPAs and two chiefs get along very well." He paused. "But in the majority of cases, there's polarization."

At this point in our conversation, Gumbi's colleague entered the room carrying large, printed maps of locations and names of the country's CPAs. Gumbi's face brightened. "I'm so happy," he said. He looked at his colleague, adding, "It's like I was telling you the other day, you should become a chief director." The colleague smiled. "I have differentiated the CPAs on the maps," she told us. "Those marked with blue are restitution cases. When you see a CPA marked with red, you know it was a land-reform case."

We scanned the impressively detailed map of the Eastern Cape province together. Alas, we could not find any plots for the Masakhane and Iqayiyalethu CPAs. The room turned quiet for a minute, then Gumbi's colleague looked up at me, her brow furrowing in puzzlement. "I think I heard you say that the land was not given to them. Is it possible that they are not CPAs then?" Gumbi told her that I had confirmed the CPAs' registrations that very day in the same building. A discussion ensued between Gumbi and his colleague. Visibly perplexed, Gumbi said he planned to have the CPAs added to the next round of maps they printed.

We returned to the topic of the current minister's moratorium and the Masakhane and Iqayiyalethu CPAs. "Look, these CPAs were formed prior to the moratorium," Gumbi protested. He pointed at the two CPAs' entries in the CPA registry on his desk. "When we register CPAs—all of them that you see here in this registry—their land is supposed to be private. The land should go to those people. It's not affected by the moratorium. It does not apply to them." He swung his neck and began looking at the ceiling of his office, shaking his head in turn. "As to why CPAs were registered in 2000 but the land did not transfer, it boggles the mind."

His tone became more somber. To that date, some fourteen hundred CPAs had been registered in the country, he said. In truth, however, hundreds of them were what he called "dysfunctional." "There are complaints that the CPA committees don't perform their duties. They don't call meetings. They aren't accountable." He then implied that CPAs without title deeds would fall into the category of dysfunctional. "Some CPAs that we registered in good faith have not received their land. Maybe the original landowners withdrew their offer to sell. Or they asked for more money, and it became too costly to buy."

What Gumbi said next revealed the ideological connection between the minister's moratorium and the state's fixation on the productivity of farmland. It also gave credence to the increasingly widespread anxiety among rural people that the DRDLR intended to take land away from debilitated or unproductive CPAs.[19] Gumbi put it this way: "Parliament is asking me: 'How are the CPAs using the land?' If a group has a CPA, but they don't have a title deed, it's difficult for me to report on how they are using the land." He said a CPA without a title deed is "an association in name alone." "The purpose of the CPA is to hold the land in common. They must have ownership." He finally came to a point he had seemed to delay articulating to me. The department was in the process of a "cleaning-up exercise," he declared. "CPAs that are in the books but have not yet received land are going to be deregistered." He said he would be thoughtful about the process; he would collect evidence before proceeding. But it was clear the Masakhane and Iqayiyalethu CPAs were at risk.

NOMBLE IN THE FOREST

Gumbi had been left especially perplexed by the inaction of the provincial land official who administered the Masakhane and Iqayiyalethu CPAs. Why hadn't that official effected the transfer before Minister Nkwinti's moratorium? In effect, the official had unilaterally forced the CPAs into the country's Proactive Land Acquisition Strategy (PLAS), thereby requiring them to prove, once again, that they met the state's definition of "productive" farmers.

As South African scholar Ruth Hall has observed, the narrow focus of the PLAS on "production discipline" reactivates an ideology of "proper farming" that gestated under colonialism and apartheid.[20] This reactivation "has blinkered policy thinking about the rich situations, needs, and possibilities to which land and agrarian reform can respond, and the profound structural changes it could bring about."[21] The measure of the strategy's success is technocratically centered on the number of farms purchased by the state, while the actual impact of the farms on the redistribution of wealth or property remains a secondary concern. In the meantime, rural South Africans typically wait years for the approval of business plans and recapitalization applications, which now precede secure land rights.[22]

I shared my opinion with a sympathetic Mr. Gumbi that to focus solely on the productivity of the Masakhane and Iqayiyalethu farms would be myopic and unjust. The residents' activities as farmers had been foundational in the successful beneficial occupation case, and they continue to farm productively today. Over many months, I had observed this firsthand: watching them manage their livestock and sell their cattle to buyers, some of whom were immigrant business owners living in Alice, who purchased whole animals directly from the farm to oversee their slaughter for religious reasons. Just a week before, I had woken up in a village to the sound of my host softly conversing with his cows as he milked them in his kraal. Yet without their promised state support, the farms were beginning to show signs of neglect. The residents had themselves expressed concerns to me about the deteriorating fencing systems and the pernicious problem of soil erosion.

But the residents' connection to their farms—and their interest in protecting those farms—transcended economic productivity. Nomble, a man in his late twenties who lived in the CPAs' villages, was a case in point. Like other residents, Nomble had once harvested pelargonium. But with that industry on hold, he had been picking up odd jobs around the villages to earn money. Like others, he also "tapped"*Aloe ferox*. To tap the plant, he cut and positioned the aloe leaves in a rosette-like pattern, mirroring their natural arrangement but with their severed ends pointing toward the center. This configuration allowed tappers like Nomble to drain the plant's "juice." The sap from the fleshy leaves dripped down onto a plastic sheet placed at the base of the rosette. After waiting a period of days for the leaves to fully drain, Nomble would return, pouring the tapped juice into five-gallon buckets and eventually selling those containers to a biotrader.

Nomble had found himself frequently waiting on the juice, but he was rarely bored. He consequently seemed different from Luthando, the young man I introduced in chapter 2 who had also harvested pelargonium in the region. Recall that Luthando had told me how his inability to secure a job in the Eastern Cape had left him feeling bored, with each day passing seemingly more sluggishly than the last. His situation was not unlike young male Ethiopians described by anthropologist Daniel Mains (2007). Framing such temporal problems as a kind of overaccumulation of unstructured time, these young Ethiopians, who were often unemployed, saw migration as a spatial solution to incrementally actualizing their life goals.

Luthando and Nomble's long-term plans had similarly entailed a spatial solution to their problems of future economic viability. Luthando did ultimately find a secure job in Cape Town. Nomble had hoped to achieve the same outcome in the Western Cape city of Knysna. But he eventually landed back home on the farms. Nevertheless, the land that surrounded Nomble seemed to serve as a solution to his problems of time. He told me he wasn't actualizing the financial future he had planned, but he also insisted that he preferred rural life over city life because he had the forest at his feet.

It was in the nearby thicket of vegetation known locally as *ihlathi lesiXhosa* (Xhosa forest) that Nomble said he found his greatest solace and sustenance. He hunted small kudu with two dogs he had spent months training. And though this activity was scrutinized and often illegal in the eyes of conservation authorities, Nomble only occasionally managed to kill an animal. The hunt was what interested him, rather than the kill. If he did succeed, his dogs would pursue the prey. Once his dogs had cornered that prey, Nomble would approach and deal a fatal blow with a ditch bank blade.

During my research, Nomble and his dogs had unintentionally encountered a black-backed jackal in the forest. The dogs and jackal engaged in a violent scrap before Nomble could extricate his hunting companions. The jackal had apparently carried the distemper virus, as the dogs began to suffer from the bites the jackal had inflicted. Over the next weeks, we watched as the dogs became increasingly frail and emaciated. One of the two, still quite young, appeared to be the worst affected. Nomble had not been able to afford to vaccinate his dogs against canine distemper. We placed the quivering animals in the backseat of my car and drove to a veterinary clinic in a nearby town, inquiring if a belated vaccine could be of any help. Upon learning that a vaccine would be ineffective, we purchased antibiotics and cans of the most calorie-rich dog food we could find, hoping these would help the dogs recover. Days later, the puppy died, but the older dog survived. A few months later, Nomble acquired another dog to serve as a second hunting companion, and together, they continued to hunt kudu.

Nomble regularly used that same ditch bank blade to collect wood for various purposes. He sought out wild olive wood and fashioned the branches into walking sticks. He often carried one when leaving his house, especially when going to socially drink home-brewed beer or the mead he had crafted using honey from the forest's beehives. Nomble also enjoyed collecting larger quantities of dead wood and was always in a jovial mood when he arrived at his house with a full wheelbarrow. He used some of this wood to create fires on a sheet of corrugated metal in his family's living room during the winter months. He also used it to make fires for cooking, especially during important weekend gatherings, such as weddings and rituals honoring ancestors. Later in the year, he gathered wood for a bonfire to celebrate the young men who were undergoing initiation near his village. The wild olive and sneezewood he collected were also used to construct seclusion lodges for those initiates. He and other men would shape and entangle the branches to construct large dome structures (*ibhoma*), which they then protected from the elements with a patchwork of tarps, garbage bags, and leaves.

Over the years, residents from neighboring peri-urban settlements had driven their livestock onto the CPAs' farms in search of better pastures. In those settlements, uncontrolled grazing and browsing by domestic livestock had transformed the thicket into an open shrubland. "Their soil is thin [*umhlaba wabo ubhityile*]," Nomble told me. In contrast, the CPAs' had been advantaged by the historical exceptionalism of their land. But they feared the impact of continued incursions on their farms, worrying that their thicket would soon disappear too. But without title deeds, they also feared they lacked the statutory authority to do much about it.

South African scholars Michelle Cocks, Anthony Dold, and Susi Vetter argue that "conservation is not merely a matter of appropriate conservation technologies and management processes. It is a process that is inextricably bound up with people's values and world views on nature."[23]

Nomble's and his fellow residents' interactions with the forest reflected an approach to conservation that contrasted with Western norms, emphasizing more-than-human exchanges and values. These practices represented a form of productivity that extended beyond the narrow definitions of the state or the Western conservation models, suggesting that true productivity includes not only economic output but also the maintenance and fostering of cultural and ecological well-being. This broader conception of productivity seemed crucial for understanding the multifaceted roles that farms can play in rural South African communities, calling into question the prevailing perspective on what constituted a productive farm in South Africa.

A LAND DISPUTE

Recall from chapter 3 that when the NGO ACB held a meeting in one of the CPA villages in 2011, the ACB employee Mava had informed the villagers in attendance of a benefit-sharing agreement between Schwabe and the Imingcangathelo chieftaincy—an agreement that, according to the NGO, had subsumed the villagers under the authority of that chieftaincy. Toward the conclusion of the meeting, Mava stood before the attendees with plaintive eyes. He said the NGO saw it as unfair that the residents had been kept in the dark about the benefit-sharing agreement. The parties involved in the agreement did not appear to care about the CPAs and their claims to the land. "We took it up with the relevant government offices to complain that this deal had not been done correctly," Mava told the group. "We submitted a letter of complaint to the Minister's [of environmental affairs] office. It has been a long time, and unfortunately, there has been no response from the government."

But it turned out the government had eventually started listening to ACB. I learned how and to what effect after my year of research had concluded and I had returned home to Colorado. In a conversation I had in late 2012 with a Schwabe executive via telephone, I discussed the challenges the company faced in obtaining a national permit to access pelargonium from South Africa. To my surprise, the executive seemed to attribute these challenges primarily to a land dispute involving Imingcangathelo and the CPAs. The permit was apparently on hold until that dispute could be resolved.

As I previously explained, Schwabe did not require an approved permit; the DEA had granted the company and others "amnesty" to continue their activities in South Africa (as long as they had successfully submitted permit applications). Despite this, the quest for a formal permit was of clear importance to the company. From its perspective, the crux of the issue was the need for security and predictable regulations in a provider country like South Africa. The executive expressed concerns about potential criticism from NGOs, which could question the legality of their operations due to the prolonged permit approval process. This uncertainty was seen as detrimental, potentially impacting consumer trust and the company's reputation.

During our dialogue, the executive mentioned a recent meeting in Brussels focused on the Nagoya Protocol, which seemed to underscore that while international regulations could be navigated by companies like Schwabe, establishing a coherent, consistent governance system within the source countries was the larger issue. Schwabe had invested substantially in research to demonstrate the abundance of pelargonium in South Africa. The company provided large amounts of data to the DEA as part of the efforts. Yet these efforts, as conveyed to me, had not facilitated the permit application process.

The executive shared their personal view, which seemed to resonate with a sense of inevitability, that the permit application would likely stall due to political caution and fear of renewed NGO criticism. Furthermore, an expert group had convened to assess the status of pelargonium and make recommendations to the government. The group had supported Schwabe's proposed approach in its permit application, but the backing had not appeared to advance the process because the land dispute remained unresolved. The situation, as I interpreted it, had left Schwabe in a state of limbo regarding its activities in South Africa.

At the time of the phone interview, I was preparing to present my research about the dispute at a March 2013 conference in Cape Town called "Land Divided." The conference was organized by universities but included speakers from the South African government. The first plenary of the conference included the highest-level land official in South Africa, then minister of the DRDLR Nkwinti. At that plenary, I listened and took notes in a large lecture hall as Nkwinti delivered remarks about the future of land reform in the country. After Nkwinti finished speaking, a question-and-answer exchange ensued. A member of the audience spoke out against the DRDLR and implied that chiefs were wrongly interfering with CPAs in the former homelands. The audience member asked Nkwinti to speak to the matter directly. Nkwinti responded by saying that "it is an exaggeration to say that only traditional leaders have problems with the CPA. It's not entirely correct." Nkwinti said the CPA was "the wrong model introduced by us as government" because it creates a "communal area within a communal area," implying that the associations conflicted with communities already established under the authority of chiefs. He suggested that, beyond the current moratorium on land transfers, he had organized a legal team to look into retroactively dissolving existing CPAs located in former homelands.[24]

At the Land Divided conference, Rosalie Kingwill and I shared the documentation we had collected concerning the CPAs with scholar-activists engaged in land advocacy work. In 2014 a South African organization called Legal Resource Center sent a letter to Minister Nkwinti and the minister-general of the DRDLR detailing the failed transfer of the land to the Masakhane and Iqayiyalethu CPAs. Legal Resource Center demanded the DRDLR issue title deeds to the CPAs, threatening legal proceedings if the department refused to comply. Receiving no response, Legal Resource Center initiated litigation.

In 2016 the national government relented, agreeing to transfer the land. And yet once again, the transfer stalled. Neither DRDLR nor the local municipality would agree to pay the thousands of dollars required for rate clearance certificates, leaving the title deeds suspended.

Seeking insight into the complexities of the case, I consulted with a South African lawyer familiar with such land cases. I inquired whether it was typical for the state to struggle with providing adequate compensation in these types of land transfers. The lawyer noted the general rarity of such transfers and implied that this might contribute to the challenges faced. Budgetary constraints could certainly be a factor, but they believed that something even more fundamental was to blame: a lack of will to transfer land to CPAs.

The lawyer found it baffling, given South Africa's constitutional commitment to fair land redistribution and securing land tenure for its citizens. They felt that transferring land to CPAs represented a straightforward task for the government, one that would significantly advance the constitution's objectives. I then referenced public statements made by the minister at a conference regarding the stance on CPAs, questioning if DRDLR's apparent opposition to CPAs was still as overt.

Leaders of the department remain resolutely opposed, the lawyer suggested, but by 2018, they no longer bothered to announce or debate the topic publicly. "They have gone silent on the matter of chiefs," the lawyer told me.

CONCLUSION

While visiting South Africa in 2018, I visited with Funeka to check in about the status of the title deeds. Surrounded by lively young grandchildren coming and going from the room, Funeka said there was nothing new to report. But she proceeded to tell me something I had not expected. Before finally securing its national permit in 2015, Funeka told me that Schwabe approached the CPAs to propose a benefit-sharing agreement involving pelargonium. After numerous meetings about the topic, the CPAs had decided to decline the offer.

The decision appeared to have been significant in ways she had not expected. She recalled to me how the DEA and the Imingcangathelo chieftaincy had called a meeting to discuss the CPAs' decision. She said that at the meeting, representatives from Imingcangathelo voiced their displeasure about the refusal of the CPAs to sign agreements. She was made to feel that by contesting the chief and disputing who controlled the land, the CPAs had hindered the chieftaincy's involvement in the industry. I was unable to corroborate Funeka's claims about Schwabe's approach and the meeting with the DEA. Nor could I confirm any details about the Imingcangathelo chieftaincy's participation in the pelargonium industry in 2018. However, some interviewees intimated to me that Schwabe had quietly moved on and was no longer procuring plants from the area. One person claiming to have knowledge said the money the chieftaincy had received from Schwabe had "dried up."

According to Funeka, at the meeting a DEA official had politely questioned her about her resistance to benefit sharing, expressing disbelief that the CPAs would refuse such an opportunity. At the same time, that official also appeared to acknowledge the CPAs as their own entities, independent of chiefs. "You are a young community," the official said to her. "Why have you refused the companies? You could benefit from this industry. What would you like to see happen with it?" Funeka told me she answered this way: "We are unemployed. Our families are dependent on social grants. We want to send our children to school and help the neediest of our families. However, we are interested in trading plants only if no middleman or chiefs are involved. If the state or a drug company wants to help us, they would be welcome to visit us and discuss a way forward (*indlela eya phambili*)."

If Funeka and her neighbors were awaiting such an outcome, patience was familiar to them. For over two decades, they had been waiting for title deeds. The wait was worth it, as Anathi often reminded me. The deeds promised something enduring: a secure home with ties to the forest—ties that went beyond mere economic value. In contrast, biotraffic was erratic, unlikely to forge any lasting link between present and future.

INTERLUDE

The Red List (1920–2024)

The significance and implications of a cough were markedly heightened by the emergence of the COVID-19 pandemic. Yet even before that global health crisis began, coughs were a prevalent concern, spurring high numbers of health-care visits. For instance, shortly before the pandemic, approximately thirty million Americans sought medical attention for cough each year, highlighting its status as a common health complaint. The quest for relief has also fueled a substantial market for cough medicines, with Americans spending over $600 million annually on these over-the-counter remedies. However, despite this financial expenditure and frequent medical consultations, empirical evidence supporting the efficacy of such medicines remains elusive. The pandemic has further complicated the narrative surrounding coughs, intertwining it with fears of a life-threatening viral infection and necessitating a more nuanced understanding of its societal and medical ramifications. This complexity in understanding and treating respiratory illnesses has deep historical roots, with medical professionals and researchers exploring various treatments and approaches over time.

In this historical context, the work of Swiss physician Adrien Sechehaye is noteworthy. He was a firm believer in the efficacy of Umckaloabo for treating tuberculosis and contributed to advancing its biomedical legitimacy outside of England in the early 1900s. While initially skeptical, Sechehaye grew interested and eventually obtained a sample of the medicine. In 1920 he prescribed it to a twenty-one-year-old parlor maid who was wasting away due to severe tuberculosis of the bone. She also had a "knobby and painful swelling" around her pelvis, indicating tuberculosis adenitis in her iliac glands.[1] The medicine improved her condition swiftly, motivating Sechehaye to obtain a regular supply from a local pharmacy in Geneva, which itself procured materials from Stevens.

Sechehaye also tested the medicine's safety on himself. He injected the fluid extract into his thigh muscle, causing what he described as sharp pain and a fever that rendered him immobile for a day. The fluid was similarly problematic when he administered it intravascularly to guinea pigs and rabbits. And yet Sechehaye said he found ingesting the medicine was harmless. He subsequently dispensed Umckaloabo to some eight hundred patients between 1920 and 1929. He documented the results and summarized them in his 1931 book *The Treatment of Tuberculosis with Umckaloabo (Stevens' Cure)*.

In the book, Sechehaye makes clear that Umckaloabo's therapeutic results were uneven. He nevertheless considered the medicine a significant development in the treatment of tuberculosis. Importantly, and in contrast with Stevens and his physician supporters in England, Sechehaye did not claim that Umckaloabo killed tuberculosis bacilli. He thought it more likely acted as an immune stimulant that helped the body limit infection. He presented case studies to Swiss medical societies and traveled to London to promote the medicine.

Upon its release, Stevens flooded England with advertisements for Sechehaye's book, a move that was intended to circumvent the efforts of the BMA and the British Advertising Agency to halt all direct promotion of Umckaloabo in the country's newspapers.[2] "This advertiser is very persistent," the general secretary of the Advertising Association complained in a letter to the British Medical Association. "Finding the way barred for straight advertisements of his remedy, he has adopted this method of advertising a book which in turn advertises the remedy."[3] The Advertising Agency "spent a whole Saturday morning telephoning the papers urging them not to accept the advertisements."[4]

But Stevens was gaining allies in the newspaper business. Some periodicals had started to side with him against the BMA. A columnist for the *Sunday Pictorial* named Candide promoted Umckaloabo and implied "that organized medicine is antagonistic to new medicines." Alfred Cox, the medical secretary of the BMA, grumbled that

> the temptation to have a shot at the General Medical Council has evidently been too strong for the "Sunday Pictorial," as it always is for the "Daily Mirror" for example, and one or two other papers who carefully foster the idea that the body which governs the medical profession is composed of hidebound persons who have a strong objection to progress in medicine and a determination to put down heterodoxy at any cost.[5]

Stevens was reaching patients in India and Australia. He offered his medicine to Canadian soldiers who had served in World War I. In 1933 Umckaloabo started appearing in historical records in Germany. That year, a distribution company called Umckaloabo Stevens Corp. was established in Freiburg. The company was run by a German noble named Irene Von Bojanowski, who had obtained Umckaloabo supplies from CH Stevens Co. In 1935 the German National Formulary, also called the Red List (*die Rote Liste*), described the drug as a powder-form preparation treating tuberculosis. In 1939 the last formulary before World War II showed Von Bojanowski having transformed her Umckaloabo medicine into a tincture, which is the version of the medicine most consumers encounter today. The formulary records indicate that Von Bojanowski had transferred the production of the tincture to the German pharmaceutical company JSO Werks Regensburg.

After World War II erupted, Stevens found his supply routes from South Africa and across the English Channel disrupted. Business slowed to a halt. Stevens suffered an injury in a bicycle accident and developed a staphylococcal infection. He died on December 5, 1942, at the Royal Sussex Hospital in Brighton, aged sixty-two.

Stevens's son took control of CH Stevens Co. and soon resumed circulating Umckaloabo around Europe. In 1947 the company offered enough supplies to treat one hundred tuberculosis sufferers in Coventry City for six months. Learning of public interest in the offer, one local tuberculosis doctor wrote to the BMA requesting a copy of *Secret Remedies*. The doctor had lost his copy when an air raid destroyed his house, and he could not recall what the book had specified about the medicine.[6]

The Red List reappeared in 1949 but did not include Umckaloabo. This changed in 1952, although by this point the medicine was no longer manufactured and distributed by Von Bojanowski but rather by JSO Werks Regensburg of Germany. Indications for the medicine had expanded by 1957 to include scrofulosis and bronchitis. The year thus marked the first time the product became linked—in Germany, at least—to its contemporary indication: the common cold.

JSO Werks Regensburg eventually lost or became disenchanted with the Stevens family's supply chain. Wishing to establish its own sourcing, the company commissioned a University of Munich pharmacy student named Sabina Bladt to identify the plant contents of Umckaloabo. Bladt completed her dissertation on the topic in 1974, identifying two plants endemic to Lesotho and South Africa: *Pelargonium sidoides* and *Pelargonium reniform*.[7]

In 1987 Schwabe Pharmaceuticals of Germany acquired JSO Werks. In an interview with me, a Schwabe executive emphasized that the company did not purchase JSO Werks for Umckaloabo specifically but rather for its broad range of medicinal products. When Schwabe chemists examined Umckaloabo more carefully, however, they concluded that it was "a highly active substance"—one worthy of clinical tests, the executive told me.

German drug laws enacted in 1976 required pharmaceutical companies like Schwabe to submit quality, efficacy, and safety information about drugs marketed in the country. According to the Schwabe executive, the company spent in excess of €30 million to carry out observational studies and clinical trials. It prepared scientific data on the plant compounds and their mechanisms of action for the formal registration of the drug. Most of the trials tested safety and efficacy for acute bronchitis, and all reported some efficacy. Having submitted sufficient information to the national authorities, Schwabe formally registered Umckaloabo with the German drug regulatory agency in 2005, at which time the product received full market authorization.[8]

Schwabe initially used JSO Werks's supply chain, which was linked to Lesotho. According to the Schwabe executive I interviewed, however, the supplier proved to be noncompliant with Schwabe's quality and transparency criteria. Schwabe established two new chains. By the mid-1990s, wildcrafted pelargonium was arriving from a new Lesotho biotrader, and cultivated pelargonium was arriving from a Western Cape plantation. Public awareness of Schwabe's clinical trial results (the outcome of a modest marketing campaign, the Schwabe representative argued) grew in the early 2000s, and Schwabe found itself poorly positioned to respond to exploding market demand in Germany. Lesotho was proving a difficult country from which to source, Schwabe representatives implied to me. Its high altitudes, mountainous landscape, and generally poor infrastructure were contributing factors. One industry expert I spoke with likened obtaining pelargonium from Lesotho to the arduous and romantic quest for an Edelweiss in the Alps, undertaken out of love. This endeavor was not only a reflection of the seeker's determination but also served as a kind of sacred journey that symbolized the depth of their devotion. Schwabe had found the pursuit less romantic than unprofitable, and in the early 2000s the company pivoted its focus toward wildcrafted materials from communal areas in the Eastern Cape. This strategic shift not only fortified Schwabe's supply chain but also birthed a new alliance with biotraders from the province, showcasing the company's agile adaptation in a turbulent context of global supply and demand.

5 Royal Pharmaceuticals

"Bantustans are dead—long live the Bantustans" reads a 2014 headline from the *Mail & Guardian* newspaper. The authors argue that "the spatial and institutional legacies of Bantustans live on in contemporary South Africa."[1] It's a contention that an examination of the pelargonium trade in the Ciskei supports in important respects. Colonial legacies clearly matter, but their often obscured or submerged nature raises important questions about how they function, become entangled with contemporary governance practices, and produce varying effects.[2] The authors suggest that "new dynamics have emerged as to how traditional leaders engage with struggles for control over local economic resources." They note that "in many cases, this has led to the revival of the ethnic affiliations that colonialism and apartheid sought to promote, which manifest themselves through renewed chieftaincy disputes and competing claims over land by different traditional communities."[3]

Scholars of South African history and politics have critiqued "the uniform view of the homelands," which assumes all homelands experienced dispossession and its consequences in the same way.[4] They argue that this view overlooks "the internal dynamics inside the homelands and the differences between them."[5] I suggest these past differences matter because they draw attention to how contemporary governance policies, such as access and benefit-sharing regulations, are making these regions more alike in terms of the role and influence of traditional leaders. This is evident when we examine how and why multinational pharmaceutical companies, biotraders, and select traditional leaders have established partnerships with one another in the former Ciskei and Transkei, despite their distinct histories. The Ciskei's tenure was brief, and it had "absolutely no basis in any ethnic, cultural or linguistic fact whatsoever."[6] Traditional leaders historically enjoyed less meaningful power there compared to the Transkei. However, the realities of biotraffic and its governance have blurred these distinctions.

In this chapter, I explore the spatial, temporal, and scalar dynamics of biotraffic to demonstrate how these factors are reshaping the role and influence of traditional leaders in the former Ciskei and Transkei. This process is shaped not only by contemporary factors such as new governance policies but also by the adaptability of chiefs and their circumstantial relations with actors like biotraders. Through an analysis of these interactions, I argue that chiefly political authority in this context depends less on apartheid-era sociopolitical structures, which were weaker in the Ciskei, and more on the ability to navigate and leverage new postapartheid opportunities. This perspective challenges narratives that conflate customary order with chiefly power, revealing instead a complex interplay of historical legacies and present-day factors in the making of traditional leadership.[7]

INDIGENOUS COLLECTIVES AND BENEFIT SHARING

During my fieldwork in 2011, I attended a meeting about pelargonium at Mngqesha, the Rharhabe kingdom's Great Place (headquarters) in the Eastern Cape.[8] There, I sat beside Rharhabe chiefs, provincial environmental affairs officials, and industry biotraders at a long wooden conference table. They discussed a proposed pelargonium agreement between the Rharhabe paramountcy's business arm, the King Sandile Development Trust, and the dominant biotrader, who maintained business ties with a number of South African and foreign pharmaceutical companies.

Chief Langa Mavuso, the secretary and CEO of the kingdom's trust, led the meeting. I recorded his introductory comments, which included the following statement:

> My dear chiefs, at the trust, I was given the task of leadership in dealing with pelargonium. Upon discussion with the Department of Environmental Affairs, we could detect that harvesting and selling of these plants was not going accordingly. Now the situation is such that it involves a bioprospecting legislation, which regulates how things should be done. According to the legislation, the *Indigenous communities* in these areas where the plants are available should also benefit from this commercial industry. It is stipulated that such communities should benefit through a portion of 5 percent. *This means that this is the benefit that should go to the chiefs of these areas with the Indigenous communities.* I can also categorically state that we have already begun receiving this 5 percent shared profit from Parceval Pharmaceuticals, amounting so far to 120,000 rands [$9,400] for the paramountcy's trust and 50,000 rands [$4,000] for the Imingcangathelo chieftaincy. Thus I'm trying to show you the potential of business from this venture if *we* can handle it well. Currently, there are about three pharmaceutical companies interested in doing business with *us*, and *we* are one of only three areas in southern Africa where pelargonium is available—Free State Province, Lesotho, and *us*. As such, the various pharmaceutical companies are in such a rush to work with *us* (emphasis added).

To grasp the claims of representative authority in this quotation—claims welding traditional authority to "Indigenous community" and biogenetic resource rights—I once again direct attention to the CBD, a legally binding framework that transfers control over genetic resources from the global commons to national jurisdictions. Alongside its supplementary Nagoya Protocol, the CBD outlines a "grand bargain" between resource "users," who want to access resources and knowledge for the development and commercialization of pharmaceutical products, and resource "providers," who seek compensation for facilitating this access.[9] The responsibility of equitably legislating and enforcing this arrangement falls to CBD signatory states.

The CBD and Nagoya Protocol are legal focal points for a number of rationalities. I focus here on four. First, the frameworks reframe nature as "biodiversity," an entity characterized by its inherent economic value and subsequent compatibility "with ideas of industrial and economic management and intervention."[10] Second, they couple conservation with the trope of economic incentivization, arguing that "the fair and equitable sharing of [biodiversity's] economic value with the custodians of biodiversity are key incentives for the conservation of biological diversity and the sustainable use of its components."[11] Third, they discursively triangulate inclusionary participation with the market and the conservation of biodiversity, internalizing distinctive kinds of people—"Indigenous communities"—into the production of biodiversity's value.[12] Fourth, they position sovereign states as facilitators in this triangle's center, tasking them with administering benefit sharing and identifying claimant communities.

The inclusionary shift described here, which understands nature as "a resource that comes with (new kinds of) potential claimants attached," has proved problematic for signatory states.[13] Ambiguities abound: Who are the appropriate claimants? How and to what extent shall they be compensated? Who decides? In the wake of this proprietary and participatory reframing of nature, rights-based claims have proliferated, wildly generating both expectations and expressions of entitlement.

In such claims, *indigeneity* is a key idiom.[14] International frameworks have expanded the meaning of this idiom by adding different but related categories, including the International Labor Organization's use of "indigenous and tribal peoples" in its Convention 169 (1989). Such frameworks have informed the ways African groups seek recognition; while few on the continent claim to be "first people," they nevertheless "share a similar structural position vis-a-vis their nation-states as indigenous peoples in the Americas and Australia."[15] The development has contributed to *indigeneity* becoming a hotly disputed category of belonging across Africa, where "defining which groups may count as indigenous is . . . problematic and controversial, as there are long and ongoing histories of migration, assimilation, and conquest."[16] After all, the descendants of original populations like the Khoi and the San are not the only people to whom the term *indigene* applies. As anthropologist Pauline Peters reminds us, *Indigenous* is also a relative status in the sense of prior occupation, aspired to by "nonoriginal" groups competing over land and landed resources.[17] Traditional leaders in the former homelands of the Eastern Cape tend to be indigenes in this latter sense.

The phrase "indigenous and local communities" is visible throughout the Nagoya Protocol, casting a broad net regarding who can claim resource rights, including people who "are not comfortably described as indigenous but are local."[18] South Africa's laws are similarly inclusive regarding relative indigenes. The country's regulations define "indigenous community" as "any community of people living or having rights or interests in a distinct geographical area within the Republic of South Africa with a *leadership* structure" (emphasis added).[19]

Beyond communal territoriality, the definition's emphasis on leadership points to the representational issue at the heart of the signatory state's task—that is, producing "a centralized structure of representative authority . . . with which external actors can negotiate."[20] This matter of which voices—or "leaders"—to privilege over others is fundamental to the state's efforts at administering agreements between corporations and collectivities.[21] In this sense, benefit sharing is "a crucial site of struggle over what will count as a collective, as representation, and as a 'legitimate' form of political sociality."[22] And with traditional leaders being but one among a number of actors vying for representative authority across a pluralized governance landscape, benefit sharing foregrounds a central problem with frameworks like the CBD. They reflect a supranational interest in shaping national policies on what are exceedingly complex cultural matters.[23] Such matters "have not historically been the responsibility of [the South African DEA] and arguably do not belong in [its] mandate."[24] What is more, the DEA is programmatically overburdened and lacks resources and knowledge regarding benefit sharing.[25]

DEA officials themselves told me as much, often stressing that their capacity to monitor and police benefit sharing is limited. The trade in pelargonium was growing, they argued, and chiefs provided the kind of broad geographic and sociopolitical jurisdiction that DEA officials felt they lacked in the Ciskei. This jurisdiction was especially crucial, they insisted, to operationalizing benefit sharing and surveilling the industry. One provincial official summarized a common refrain: "The chiefs will be our eyes and ears on the ground." Other officials, echoing the CBD's far-resonating call for the market-based, incentive-oriented management of nature, similarly expressed the hope that chiefs would act as rational business actors and thus as environmental custodians.

Reflecting the DEA's ambivalence about benefit sharing is the lack of interest in the biodiversity legislation it crafted in vesting the state with ownership of biological and genetic resources. Rather than initiating agreements between the state and pharmaceutical companies, the legislation's modus operandi for securing benefit-sharing rights hinged on bilateral agreements between such companies and claimant communities.[26] This move outsourced the task of identifying access providers to permit applicants, which is what occurred with pelargonium. Indeed, the DEA appeared to merely ratify partnerships that pharmaceutical companies and biotraders had already established with Rharhabe chiefs.

Such moves typify widespread trends in regulatory governance, with state sovereignty increasingly decentralized and oriented toward shaping constellations or forums of governance.[27] African states in particular have frequently reverted to modes of administration akin to indirect rule, or the maintenance of "nested territorial jurisdictions."[28] Aninka Claassens notes how such nesting enables power-sharing deals between central governments and local actors.[29] Yet such jurisdictions, like quasi–gatekeeper states sitting astride "the interface between a territory and the rest of the world" that desires its resources, additionally depended on financial and political support from foreign corporate entities—in this case drug companies.[30]

"THE BIG CHIEF COMBO": CHIEFS AS AFROMODERN CAPITALIST COSMOPOLITANS

How does "leadership" in the biodiversity legislation's definition of *Indigenous community* come to be understood as traditional authority? How do "distinct geographic areas" in this same definition come to be demarcated through apartheid-associated "tribal" boundaries? Given the contingent politics of representation and recognition that are invited by CBD and Nagoya Protocol rationalities, it is unsurprising that authorized forms of indigeneity in benefit-sharing agreements assume a local character, depending on alliances forged between actors.[31] Yet understanding why some groups have prominence over others in such alliances—indeed, to use Noel Castree's words, "how different indigenous peoples step onto the political stage locally and regionally while others are marginalized or silenced"—requires a consideration of other factors as well.[32] It requires asking how the political history of a country shapes the translation of rights that get adopted there.[33]

After the dismantling and reintegration of the homelands into the new South Africa in 1994, chiefs in the former Ciskei region found themselves once again on the margins of governance plans. The new ruling party, the African National Congress (ANC), established decentralized tiers of government in the form of provinces and municipalities. In response, traditional leaders who had ascended during the apartheid era loudly complained about being marginalized.[34] They waged a juridical campaign for their authority to be recognized, claiming to be closer to the people and using idioms of cultural and human rights. Their appropriation of "the global mood" surrounding Indigenous rights and their ability to "redefine [this mood] to suit their needs" has proved especially productive.[35] Indeed, the capacity for malleability is a hallmark of traditional leadership worldwide.[36]

This malleability was personified by the secretary of the Rharhabe kingdom's trust, Chief Mavuso. After a month of trying to secure an interview with him, I met him in 2011 at the local Spur Steak Ranches restaurant, where he often holds business lunches. Like all Spur Steak Ranches locations across Southern Africa, Mavuso's haunt is daubed in kitschy Native North American iconography. Menu items include the "Eat Like a Chief Special." But the towering Mavuso did not need the menu; with great earnestness, he ordered his usual, the Big Chief Combo, a meal consisting of pork ribs, a quarter chicken, a lamb chop, heaping portions of onion rings and fries, and unlimited soft drink refills. A few booths over, an acquaintance waved at Mavuso. Her children, tangled in a playful wrestling match, sported the restaurant's cardboard Native American–styled headdresses.

Embodying "Afromodern capitalist cosmopolitanism," the Spur Steak Ranches restaurant was a ritual space where indigenous aesthetics emanating from the United States undergirded Mavuso's performance of royalty.[37] The encounter illustrated how "African traditional leaders look to the geographic, economic, and discursive West for capital, credibility, and consumption of goods and services."[38] It also affirmed that traditional leaders invoked "a notion of 'tradition' that is not only distinctively modern and plural but is actively being created and negotiated within the wider national and sub-Saharan political audience and with their 'own' presumed subjects."[39]

During our meal, Mavuso spoke of the business opportunities afforded by traditional leaders' increased political and legal recognition in the new South Africa. These opportunities included travel and tourism, with the Rharhabe Great Place serving as a hotel and conference center, its website imploring tourists to "visit the forested land of Xhosa kings." In my notebook, Mavuso drew a chart of the trust's other ventures, listing citrus orchards, cattle farms, a biosphere project, water bottling, and finally pelargonium, around which he penciled a circle. He described how, at an early 2011 meeting, he had persuaded the state to organize the pelargonium industry and its benefit-sharing arrangements through the paramountcy's trust rather than through individual Rharhabe chiefdoms (as had previously been the case). Under that new arrangement, the trust had kept a percentage of the royalties and was responsible for distributing the remainder to participating chieftaincies (based on volume of material harvested).[40] Mavuso's declaration to me that he was above all "a politician" seemed apt, since he had endeavored to bring chiefdoms like Imingcangathelo into line with the paramountcy's interests. The task was "hectic," Mavuso said, with some chiefs unhappy about losing money to the kingdom.

The kingdom's ability to assert this kind of broad representative authority seemed under threat, however. In 2010 the Nhlapo Commission, which was established by South Africa's national government to investigate the legitimacy of kingdoms in the country, had ruled that the Rharhabe paramountcy was not in fact a kingship. Citing the "irregular appointment" of Sandile as king under Sebe, the commission relegated Sandile to "senior traditional leader," or mere chief.[41] Although Sandile was allowed to retain his ceremonial status as king until his death, this grace period proved brief. Two days before I met with Mavuso at the Spur Steak Ranch in 2011, Sandile died of renal failure. According to Mavuso, the kingdom's status in the pelargonium industry wasn't at risk. And anyway, he was far more preoccupied with a legal challenge against the ruling, led by Sandile's widowed queen, Noloyiso Sandile, daughter of a Zulu monarch.[42]

At first glance, it appeared odd that the DEA would organize such controversial, potentially profitable agreements through an authority structure that a national commission had deemed illegitimate. At least one provincial DEA official I interviewed saw the situation this way. "[The DEA is] going to have to call in Mandela on this one [to sort matters out]," this official told me in 2011. But a member of the Nhlapo Commission I interviewed disagreed. The ruling meant little in terms of the trust's legitimacy in the pelargonium industry, the commissioner insisted, because the Rharhabe paramountcy's trust was one of the most organized traditional-corporate entities in the province. Moreover, the commissioner argued, the Rharhabe kingdom appeared better at generating authoritative consent from its subjects than many of the paramountcies that the commission considered legitimate. And in the end, Mavuso and other Rharhabe advocates' efforts to reverse the Nhlapo ruling eventually paid off. The ruling was set aside in 2016. Tragically, however, the queen died from COVID-19 in 2020, and her son's ascension to the throne was announced at her funeral. In 2021, South African president Cyril Ramaphosa officially recognized Rharhabe as a kingdom again.

Taken together, the patterns outlined here echo the findings of scholars who argue that corporatization can serve as a mode of legitimation for traditional leaders in contemporary South Africa.[43] Along these same lines, the King Sandile Development Trust's line of pharmaceutical products was yet another frontier of possibility. Medicine of Rharhabe (Amayeza Akwa Rharhabe), a brand conceived by Mavuso and Parceval, included a pelargonium-derived medicine called Ukhohlokhohlo.[44] Alongside Mavuso, a number of Rharhabe chiefs saw themselves as the culturally legitimate owners of the traditional medical knowledge associated with pelargonium. They were thus at the forefront of an emerging identity economy linking Rharhabe culture and ethnicity with a biological resource—a development echoing other case studies of culture being commodified under neoliberal conditions.[45] And although there was no explicit link made in existing agreements between any commercial product and the acknowledged traditional knowledge associated with pelargonium, Mavuso told me the trust wanted "to move things in this direction." A high-level official told me that any state decision regarding the traditional medical knowledge of pelargonium would "conclude with kings and chiefs."

OF WARRIOR CHIEFS AND MAFIOSOS

The South African Constitution contains an independent chapter on traditional leaders that affords them a role in "local communities," creates a house for them in Parliament, and reserves them seats on provincial councils.[46] These gains have been foundational to a collection of traditional-leadership laws introduced by South Africa's Parliament in the new millennium. The laws legislate state salaries for chiefs and strive to invest them and their "traditional councils" with statutory powers concerning land administration, welfare allocation, the administration of justice in traditional courts, safety and security, economic development, and the governance of natural resources.[47] Yet not all traditional leaders maintain such powers. Only a select few were involved in benefit sharing in the Ciskei and Transkei. In fact, in constructing benefit-sharing agreements, biotraders, drug companies, and DEA officials attempted to order a political landscape across which the status of traditional leaders was deeply uneven and contested, even within the institution of traditional leadership itself.

According to some chiefs who were not involved in plant trade, the Rharhabe paramountcy gained its prominence in the region by acquiring territorial jurisdiction and political capital under apartheid—acquisitions, they insisted, that have made the paramountcy disproportionately powerful and exclusionary in the post-1994 period. This was how a chieftaincy I encountered while attending a small Heritage Day festival in 2011 saw the paramountcy. The festival took place at Ntaba kaNdoda, the erstwhile national temple of the Ciskei, located in the region's wooded hills (see figure 8). Under apartheid, one of the homeland's presidents, Lennox Sebe, had hoped that constructing the temple would bolster the link between his ideology of ethnic nationalism and a precolonial, royal past.[48] Sebe's government even repatriated and interred at the temple's graveyard—known as the Heroes' Acre—the remains of the region's most famous warrior chief, who had died in imperial confinement on Robben Island in 1873. But the burial event and the memory of the warrior chief ultimately contrasted a genuine chief's anticolonial legacy with Sebe's clearly manufactured one. As a result, Sebe's government stripped the warrior chief's descendant of his authority and exiled him from the homeland.[49]

Figure 8. Ntaba kaNdoda, the erstwhile national temple of the Ciskei homeland, on the day of the Heritage Day festival (2011). Photo by the author.

At the time of my research, the temple sat derelict. Its graveyard had succumbed to weeds. Locals had dismantled the full-sized statue of Sebe years before, and the eighteen-thousand-seat arena was a potholed pitch. At the Heritage Day festival, a group of men gathered alone at the temple's graveyard. Standing before the gravestone of the warrior chief, they began a eulogy. One man, dressed humbly in a worn woolen army jacket, claimed to be the deceased warrior's heir.

A council member of this heir, having initially taken me to be a journalist covering the festival, invited me to spend the afternoon with the group. He became visibly frustrated, however, when I told him about my research concerning pelargonium. He had never heard of the trade in the plant, and this seemed to confirm to him his chieftaincy's continued marginality. In explaining this marginalization, the council member recounted facts that are familiar to historians of the region. Among them, he emphasized not only the resurrection of the Sandile lineage under Sebe but also the apartheid-era positioning of the family of current Rharhabe trust secretary and "CEO"

Mavuso.[50] The Mavusos are not ethnically Xhosa, the council member insisted, and therefore lack any historically supported claim to a position within the traditionally Xhosa Rharhabe kingdom. As a result of the political emplacement of these figures, the council member maintained,

> Sandile is getting more money from the government. Sandile is getting more money from business. And that money, he is controlling it alone. In South Africa today, if you are not politically connected, you are going nowhere. Even in the rural sector, at the Sandile kingdom, or their trust, if you are not connected to the right people, nothing will ever be channeled to you. You'll never have access. You'll never have information. If I can give you an appropriate term, one that you will understand better, Mavuso and the Rharhabe kingdom are like the *mafiosos*. Those people will do whatever is in their power to keep you out of the circle.

The signs of Mavuso's status were everywhere and went far beyond pelargonium, the spokesperson suggested. For example, that same day, hundreds of miles from the decaying temple and its overgrown graveyard, Mavuso was attending a much larger, media-covered festival in a major Eastern Cape city. In his critique of Mavuso and Sandile, however, the spokesperson failed to mention that many in the region do not recognize his own leader as the genuine heir of the warrior chief—a revelation that could have exposed his group's presence at the graveyard as yet another instance of historical appropriation.

What these examples showed was that representational legitimacy and its recognition by the federal government and multinational corporations need not pivot on primordial birthright. It need not find substance in symbols of the past, either. In the context of benefit sharing, "a collective that 'works' in political terms" emerges from the entanglement of the performative, the historical-political, and the circumstantial, with corporate and state interests often seeking out paths of least resistance to establish alliances and contracts.[51] This was especially reflected in the news that by 2014 individual Rharhabe chiefdoms had wrested control over the governance of pelargonium benefit sharing from their kingdom, excluding Mavuso and the paramountcy from agreements. The untimely death of King Sandile played a central role, officials told me. Undoubtedly the legal challenge of the Nhlapo Commission ruling had also reordered the kingdom's priorities.

BIOTRADERS AND BENEFIT SHARING

At the 2011 meeting convened at the Rharhabe kingdom's base in the Eastern Cape, one chief had looked fixedly at Schwabe's biotrader and proclaimed, "We don't want the middleman." After all, they continued, "I will not get the same amount of money I would have received directly from [pharmaceutical companies located in and near] Cape Town." Despite this sentiment, biotraders had been instrumental in enabling chiefs to participate in and accumulate from benefit sharing. Indeed, the functioning of the industry—and thus benefit sharing—under chiefs was built on material and social infrastructure provided by biotraders. Their mobility and ability to cause confusion for local law enforcement had additionally aided chiefs and further exposed differentiation within "the state" concerning power over and knowledge of the industry. Recognizing their importance, Chief Mavuso rejected his fellow chief's criticism of the biotrader. The biotrader possessed equipment and know-how that traditional leaders lacked, Mavuso insisted.

A long-standing and well-developed literature concerning community-based natural resource management describes how the devolution of control over resources from centralized states to local actors can have unintended consequences.[52] For example, in instances where high-value resources coexist with low institutional accountability, local elites and private companies may assert control of resource allocation and capture resulting benefits.[53] Moreover, to assert control, these actors may claim to represent local communities and their interests.[54] *Community* is thus identified as a site of both material and discursive contestation, with the delineation of membership and jurisdictional boundaries being of paramount importance.[55] The frequently overlapping nature of jurisdiction and membership in a given geographic space complicates this delineation, shaping in turn the localized idioms of authority, rights, and ethnicity used to stake claims.[56]

In the former homelands of South Africa, traditional leaders have frequently invoked "custom" in their efforts to delineate such community boundaries and assert control over land, resources, and people (Cousins 2008). Their interpretation of custom, which articulated with past colonial and apartheid distortions of unilateral chiefly power, was endorsed by a series of laws enacted by parliament since 2003. According to Aninka Claassens, the laws "envisage a totally separate realm of customary law that is restricted to the boundaries of the former Bantustans and is coterminous with chiefly authority over both land and people."[57] Beyond the elite capture of benefits from resources by traditional leaders, the laws "additionally lock 16.5 million people into ascribed tribal identities, and simultaneously attempt to lock alternative institutions such as Communal Property Associations out."[58]

Scholars have noted the differential impact of the abovementioned laws in the Eastern Cape, due especially to historical disparities in the power of chiefs in the former Ciskei and Transkei.[59] Indeed, in contrast with the Transkei, where long-standing powers over land allocation have helped traditional leaders remain "the main institutions of authority," many rural groups in the Ciskei had successfully established their own land and resource management entities in the form of CPAs.[60] As one scholar has justifiably noted, "Particularly in the former Ciskei homeland, traditional authorities have been thoroughly discredited."[61] And yet during my research I saw that benefit sharing had become a means by which some traditional leaders were changing this pattern.

Biotraders had apparently helped on this front, too, expanding their impact beyond the material and social infrastructure I mentioned earlier. The biotrader was a case in point. I first interviewed him on a rainy winter day in 2011. We met at his office, which at the time was an add-on to a house in an Eastern Cape town. A retired colonel in the South African Defense Reserves, he sat at a desk strewn with various curios, jars of nuts and bolts, and a large, ornate "sword of command," given to him in recognition of his service, which lay on a wooden frame. Hanging conspicuously on a haphazardly decorated wall was a newspaper photo of him in full military regalia, posing with the British Countess of Wessex during her visit to South Africa in the early 2000s.

In my discussions with the biotrader, I gathered that early in his operations, he had engaged directly with local chiefs to discuss the potential for harvesting medicinal plants, leading to initial verbal agreements on benefit sharing which were later formalized in writing. He emphasized his commitment to boosting employment in the Eastern Cape by localizing initial production phases, suggesting he aimed to contribute to community employment and economic development.

The approach the biotrader described to me involved not only the establishment of commercial relationships but also a deep integration with community structures, aiming to ensure sustainable harvesting practices. This was an effort to engage with traditional leaders in the pelargonium trade, a point that seemed to be acknowledged by Schwabe representatives, who indicated to me that internal community dealings had been managed not by them, but by the biotrader and local leadership.

The structure of these agreements, the biotrader explained, involved a collaboration with numerous chiefdoms within the Rharhabe kingdom, though not all had access to pelargonium. The process evolved to include formal agreements ratified by national officials, involving the King Sandile Development Trust in the revenue distribution to ensure a fair share reached the local communities involved. From what he shared with me, the biotrader appeared to view traditional leaders as playing a crucial role in ensuring the orderly and sustainable harvesting of resources, also facilitating an effective distribution of benefits. The biotrader highlighted that the regulatory framework adopted for both drug discovery and plant trade later seemed to recognize and incorporate the control measures he had initially established, with coordinators from each chiefdom playing a key role in the system of control.

By 2013, however, the biotrader seemed to express doubts to me about this control. The biotrader feared his chiefly partners were not distributing benefits to their communities. His Alice-based coordinator, who during the 2000s had held a position within the Imingcangathelo chieftaincy but by 2010 no longer maintained ties with it or the biotrader, made similar claims to me:

> [The Imingcangathelo chieftaincy doesn't] make a report for the benefit sharing [funds intended for communities], or about how it has been spent. They elected me to the [Imingcangathelo chieftaincy's] trust, but I was working in darkness. They didn't tell me where to fetch the funds, or how much they have got. And I learned that they were using my signature for their benefit, so I moved out. I'm no longer in the trust and I'm not interested until it is fair, or until they open up to the community. That money is for the people. And up until now, nothing has been spent to uplift the community. Look, I'm just saying, Parceval has stated that they have enough [pelargonium], and that was 200,000 kilos at 35rand if [Parceval] got it from [the biotrader]. So there should be a lot of money here. But only the chief and the chairperson of the trust know what's there.

A STACK OF HANDWRITTEN ACCESS AGREEMENTS

A key objective of the national environmental management plan for pelargonium was "to ensure wild collection is based upon adaptive, practical, participatory and transparent management practices." Yet the plan did not state how participation and transparency for harvesters would be established or maintained. Such matters were crucial—the material harvesters sold was, by virtue of benefit-sharing agreements arranged by the national government, set to generate benefits that would be funneled to chieftaincies. Harvesters and other locals hoped the benefits would reach their villages, but many insisted to me that no one had informed them how benefits would be allocated.

I returned to the Eastern Cape in 2018 and spoke with provincial officials about matters of participation and transparency. They indicated that an insufficiency of information from chiefs and the national office had impacted their department, compounding existing provincial capacity problems and contributing to confusion in the pelargonium trade. "This benefit sharing is a daunting task," one of them told me. "It's a national regulation, and we don't fully know how it's implemented. Yet we still have to adhere to it." By the time provincial officials became aware of a benefit-sharing partnership, another official said, "a chief has already signed the agreement and we don't know what was involved in the negotiations. It's strictly between the national office and the pharmaceutical companies." The officials had the impression the national office wanted provincial officials like them to help facilitate agreements between industry actors and chiefs, but otherwise, to avoid getting in the way.

To illustrate some of the challenges the officials identified, I need to rewind the story somewhat. In 2013 the DEA ended Parceval and Schwabe's apparent duopoly by issuing national drug discovery/commodity-trade and export permits to two Eastern Cape companies, one of which belonged to the biotrader. The biotrader proceeded to sign benefit-sharing agreements with three chieftaincies in the Ciskei and Transkei regions. For their part, Schwabe and Parceval recommenced their activities in the mid-2010s. The companies signed a benefit-sharing agreement in 2015 with a chieftaincy near the town of Whittlesea, which is located some one hundred kilometers north of Alice but still within the former Ciskei region.

During my trip in 2018, I came to sense that the biotrader and Schwabe had not necessarily outrun the controversies they had previously encountered near Alice. Indeed, not unlike Imingcangathelo, the chiefdoms that became partners to the companies appeared to be mired in their own conflicts over land and subjects. That winter of 2018, I saw that these conflicts were generating headlines in South African newspapers. They were also the focus of nationally televised investigative reports.

In the case of Schwabe's new chiefly partner, the conflict dealt with the politics of representational legitimacy. In the years preceding 2018, two successive Eastern Cape premiers had sought to dethrone the chief. They had done so on the grounds that his father and predecessor, a man who allegedly tried to prevent locals from gaining control of land and notoriously played apartheid patronage politics, had been illegitimately installed by his brother-in-law, the then Ciskei president Lennox Sebe.[62] Despite a government commission's previous recommendation that the chief be removed, the Constitutional Court ruled in the winter of 2018 that he retain his position.

The story of one of the biotrader's new benefit-sharing partners, the Tshatshu chieftaincy, was different. In contrast, the legitimacy of the Tshatshu chieftaincy's lineage was not what was generating headlines in 2018. Rather, it was a situation that strongly paralleled that of the Masakhane and Iqayiyalethu CPAs, only on a far larger scale because it involved some seventy-seven farms on nearly forty thousand hectares of land. An area now known informally as Gwatyu in the Eastern Cape was historically part of a larger Tshatshu polity under the leadership of a chief named Gungubele. In the 1850s, a colonial governor sought to wholly annihilate this polity for the sake of creating a new administrative district. The Tshatshu people who managed to survive—including the descendants of Chief Gungubele—ended up scattered across great distances.[63] The governor allocated the land as farms to White settlers, who employed Black laborers, most of whom lived on-site as farm dwellers. Over one hundred years later, in the 1970s, the apartheid state purchased the farms from the White owners and transferred them to the Transkei government, whose president, Kaiser Matanzima, leased them to political allies. With the White farmers gone and the new Black lessees rarely visiting or utilizing the farms, the former farm dwellers remained and became independent farmers. In the early 1980s the Gungubele lineage resettled in the area, and the senior male became leader of the new "tribal authority" structure established by Kaiser Matanzima as part of a larger project of "retribalization."

The situation had been ripe for conflict. Tenure arrangements in the area were complex, farm infrastructure was rapidly deteriorating, and the farm dwellers had no prior experience living under the authority of a chief.[64] After the homeland phase ended and the Republic of South Africa emerged in 1994, the former farm dwellers unsuccessfully sought security of tenure on the farms on the basis of beneficial occupation. Some of them eventually relocated to a formally declared township within the Gwatyu area. In 2009 Chief Gungubele installed a headman to administer that township, and the headman allegedly began a campaign against those who opposed his authority, confiscating sites already belonging to township residents for the benefit of his followers.[65] A few years later, residents who remained on the farms sought to form a CPA and in doing so also found themselves in conflict with the Tschatshu chieftaincy. In reaction, the chieftaincy lodged an official claim to the land, thus impeding a transfer of title to the CPA. During this period, allegations also arose that the government had started advertising for sale—and indeed allocating—upwards of forty Gwatyu farm parcels.[66]

While in the Eastern Cape in 2018, I visited Chief Gungubele at his Great Place in Gwatyu to introduce myself and inquire about formally interviewing him in the future. But I arrived unaware that only a week before my visit, the South African Broadcasting Corporation (SABC) had nationally televised an investigative report titled "The Other Side of Eden" that described the clash between the chieftaincy and the CPA. Speaking to the chief, I explained that my research primarily concerned the trade in pelargonium. But when I described my related curiosity concerning land politics in the Eastern Cape, he became understandably frustrated. Clearly aware that he had become of a figure of national interest in the wake of the SABC report, he speculated aloud that I was withholding my true identity as a journalist.

According to the provincial officials with whom I spoke in 2018, the relationships between chiefs like Gungubele and biotraders were central challenges their offices faced when it came to benefit sharing. With Schwabe and Parceval no longer working with their old biotrader, they hired a new intermediary to access plants from the jurisdiction of their chiefly partner. But problematically, this "new biotrader" they employed quickly expanded his collection activities north and eastward, into the former Transkei and beyond what the officials saw as the jurisdiction of the chieftaincy with whom Schwabe and Parceval maintained their access and benefit-sharing agreement. After residents reported the new biotrader's unauthorized activities, the Green Scorpions confronted him. An official told me the new biotrader "then ran to the chief [of a new area from which he was buying pelargonium] to arrange a letter [granting him permission to access the plant]." This letter and a small stack of others arranged by the new biotrader—all handwritten and submitted to the government by the councils of chiefdoms—had accumulated in a manila file folder in a provincial office.

One agreement the new biotrader presented to the provincial office came from the Tshatshu traditional council under the authority of Chief Gungubele. It read: "This letter confirms that [the new biotrader] has collected the perlagonium [sic] plant for the past five months from the above-mentioned council [the leadership structure of the chieftaincy]." The document bore a red-ink stamp from the chiefdom's traditional council. The stamp's "date" section had been left blank, however, leaving officials uncertain about the time frame of collection. The document and another (see figure 9) from the same council were also noteworthy to provincial officials because the Tshatshu chieftaincy already maintained a national-approved benefit-sharing agreement with the former biotrader. The upshot, officials concluded, was that the new biotrader had expanded his operations such that they now overlapped with his competitor biotrader, whom officials saw as law-abiding and likely unaware that his chiefly partner was supplying Schwabe and Parceval with pelargonium.

What did the letters signify? Were chiefs themselves confused about the national regulations? Were "benefits" taking the form of bribes paid by the new biotrader to select chiefs? Were benefits being lopsidedly distributed to the one chieftaincy with a state-approved agreement? For their part, provincial officials told me they saw the letters as evidence that provincial officials and likely local residents were equally in the dark about unofficial and official agreements. "There's confusion," one of the officials said. This was especially the case when it came to access sites possibly

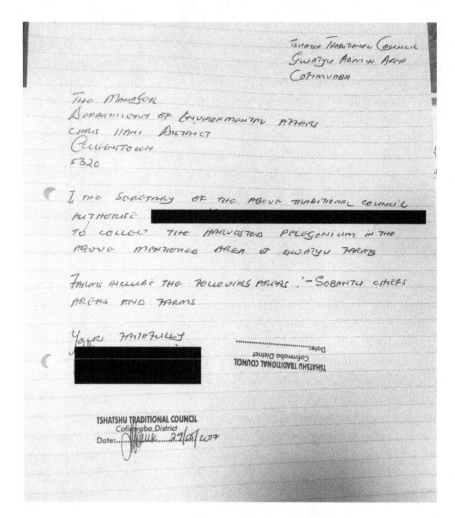

Figure 9. Handwritten access agreement (2018). Photo by the author.

overlapping. "One doesn't know who fits where, and who [which chief] is superior to whom," an official suggested. "We have colleagues from rural areas here in the Eastern Cape, and it doesn't make sense even to them." To try to control the new biotrader, the provincial offices had resorted to fining him when possible. But mostly they tried to track his movements, which they said had taken him farther north toward the Lesotho border.

CONCLUSION: SEGREGATION AND SUBJECTION

"Implicit in the question of who benefits from the Wealth of the Ethnonation," Comaroff and Comaroff contend, "is the prior one of who belongs to it."[67] Much of the anthropological scholarship exploring this question has thus far centered on the exclusionary and excisional potential of ethnic boundary construction in claims to culture as property. In places like the Ciskei, however, a dangerous politics of forced membership is the flip side of the coin. Critics of the laws supporting ethnonations like Rharhabe argue that they reentrench the boundaries established in the Bantu Authorities Act of 1951. According to Aninka Claassens, being located in a former homeland currently preempts "rural people's ability to constitute or organize themselves on any other basis than as tribal subjects."[68]

The laws were only one manifestation of contemporary segregationism. In the Eastern Cape especially, a spatial perspective dominated economic development planning as well. Strategic areas (mostly cities, or "industrial development zones") received investment in public resources, while residents in nonstrategic areas (rural spaces in former homelands) were "governed by custom, tradition, and welfare."[69] And as rural constituents increasingly mistrusted promises of material transformation, the ruling ANC faced its own crisis of legitimacy.[70] The institution of the chieftaincy is highly adaptable, as I have suggested, and the political agency of chiefs should not be understated.[71] Yet it is within an instrumental context that many scholars also situated state alliances (and amalgamations) with traditional leaders, alliances in which mobilizing electoral support is paramount.[72] This mobilization relied increasingly on hegemonic tactics, or the shaping of attitudes, values, and perceptions among residents in the former homelands.[73] Thus, the project of building consensus on an ANC-led future included discursively promoting abstractions like tradition and custom. According to Clifton Crais, the ruling party, although resolute in its objections to traditional authority in the preliberation period, came to co-opt it in the uncertain present.[74]

Segregationism suffused thinking about benefit sharing in South Africa. Encounters with elite actors revealed this throughout my fieldwork. In some instances, interviewees used race as a category to articulate cultural differences between homeland residents and other South Africans.

In other interviews, stakeholders took a different but no less problematic view. For many, geography, rather than race, was the relevant factor. As a provincial official told me, urban Blacks rely on municipalities when they access goods and services. Rural Blacks, by comparison, abide by their customs and get what they need through their traditional leaders. A conversation with a pharmaceutical company representative implied something similar. When I asked about democratic alternatives to unelected traditional leaders in benefit-sharing agreements, the executive reproached me for ethnocentrism. Speaking of the Ciskei's uniqueness, he said, "One must be very careful with this advanced democratic viewpoint that there need be options to get rid of people. Of course, with our [Euro-American] history," he continued, "it is very important to have those systems in place. But it is very much dependent on the historical and cultural background."

The insinuation that former homelands like the Ciskei and Transkei were containers of (traditional) culture mirrors the apartheid vision of homelands as ethnically and spatially coterminous. It also recalls part of the representational self-critique that anthropologists undertook in the 1990s and early 2000s. Beyond a spatial incarceration of the subaltern, one could also read these comments as manifestations of allocronism or as a flawed distinction between rural and urban worlds.[75] Raymond Williams showed how the process of urbanization in Europe was facilitated in part through an experiential segregation, fed by perceptions among urbanites about the life of the rural Other.[76] In Zambia, James Ferguson considered how such imaginings were disrupted by the intrusion of rural life into cities, with migration and semi-immigration between country and city being quite common.[77] The history of migration between homeland residents and cities equally problematizes the provincial official's distinction. "The assumed isomorphism of space, place, and culture," Akhil Gupta and James Ferguson write, "results in some significant problems."[78] One such problem, seen in policies and actions concerning biotraffic, concerns how discourses about difference in the former homelands were bound up with the production of particular knowledges, subjectivities, and legitimacies.

Such factors informed the decision of provincial officials to hold onto the handwritten access agreements between a biotrader and chiefs. The officials were unsure about the future of a national environmental policy but aware that they might need to present the documents to superiors—including high-level DEA officials—to justify their decision-making. The filing of the agreements in their office turned them into "parallel, practical contracts of recognition," in which rights and authority became functional and effective, despite their actually faint connection to official law and norms.[79] For the new biotrader, they functioned by helping him leverage bureaucratic formalities to his advantage, allowing him to manipulate space, time, and scale in ways that, as Jane Guyer might observe, generate economic gains through the strategic use of documentation and temporal gaps in enforcement.[80] The temporal lags in policing the agreements engendered allowed the biotrader to "buy time" to expand his operations, adding chiefly jurisdictions as access zones and thus allowing him to collect more plant material.

Throughout my fieldwork, I noted that the kind of political subjectivity these dynamics evinced was quite circumscribed. And at the heart of contestation over what would count as a subject and polity was the relationship between liberal, modern, rights-bearing citizenship and an accommodation of centralized chiefly authority. Yet the actual nature of this relationship had less to do with an inherent tension between static poles of rights and custom, or individual and community, than with historically situated struggles over the actual status and content of these volatile abstractions.[81] Clearly isomorphism, familiarity, and mutuality characterized the contemporary collision of such abstractions as much as tension does. One example was the chiefs' increasing capacity to link their local authority with global capital and international rights discourses. Another was the shared (and ultimately convenient) elision of diverse interests and identities by traditional leaders, national officials, and pharmaceutical company representatives. "Indigeneity" featured prominently in both, and the fact that the concept's deployment accorded with segregationist thinking about stakeholders in former homeland regions was likely not coincidental. "The UN concept of 'indigeneity,'" Sarah Ives provocatively argues, "is notably analogous to South African apartheid-era ideologies that called for maintaining and reproducing 'distinctive' peoples and cultures in separate environments and through (ostensibly) separate systems of governance."[82]

Conclusion

OLD BOUNDARIES, NEW EXTRACTIONS

Over centuries and across great distances, trade in plants entangled empires and fueled contests over territories and populations. The companies whose ships' bowels were distended with foreign botanicals and other resources were progenitors to modern multinationals. In the 1600s, the Dutch East India Company toppled the fortifications of competitors, roused insurrections against its competitors' rule, and signed commercial contracts with local elites, all to gain a foothold in Asian resource markets. The company shipped resources like China root (*Smilax china*) from East and Southeast Asia to Amsterdam's apothecaries, where consumers sought the plant to treat paralysis, venereal afflictions, and other chronic afflictions.[1] During this same period, French, Spanish, Turkish, and Russian consumers valued *Sassafras* trees for their antifebrile powers. Bulk shipments of wild-harvested tree roots from colonized lands in the Americas met the demand.[2] These are but a few examples. What is certain is that such trade nurtured both an appetite for raw materials for medicines and the creation of lucrative, hybrid medical knowledge that Europeans later assembled, packaged, and claimed as their own modern scientific expertise.[3]

Movements of biological resources are not new, nor are entwinements of their im/material forms. But if such movements persist as "problems" of environmental conservation, is benefit sharing a solution? No, many scholars increasingly suggest. In an article titled "Rethink the Expansion of Access and Benefit Sharing," Laird and colleagues argue that since the rollout of benefit sharing, commercial interest in genetic resources has proved insufficient to spur meaningful conservation.[4] And the agreements made under the CBD haven't yet delivered significant benefits for conservation, they add. Frequently, domestic political goals have steered benefit-sharing initiatives toward limited economic growth rather than conservation. Despite its central mention in policy language surrounding benefit sharing, conservation has steadily receded in actual practice, now seemingly relegated to a minor concern. "After almost 30 years, innumerable national [access and benefit-sharing] measures, and tens of millions of dollars spent discussing and developing these policies," Laird and colleagues write, "there is relatively little to show in the way of conservation, technology transfer, capacity-building, or other monetary or nonmonetary benefits."[5] And while many wait for the tide to possibly turn, critics will ask what that thirty-year promotion of market approaches to conservation across the world has accomplished. If anything, our current era has witnessed an acceleration of ecological devastation, with roughly one million plant and animal species on the verge of extinction due to human activity, according to the United Nations.[6]

And yet the policy approach of benefit sharing has only experienced expansion in recent years.[7] The CBD boasts membership of 196 countries, with 138 having ratified its supplementary agreement, the Nagoya Protocol, including a significant representation from 48 African nations. This widespread ratification has led to the creation of numerous national regulations aligned with these international standards. In the European Union, for instance, member countries are mandated to adhere to regulations governing the utilization of genetic resources and the traditional knowledge associated with them, particularly in the context of research and development activities. Consequently, it has become a standard practice for European businesses to require a benefit-sharing permit as a prerequisite for engaging in the commercial trade of plant-based products and other biological materials. Likewise, various government entities are increasingly stringent about enforcing benefit-sharing laws, leading to the restriction or shutdown of operations that fail to comply with such regulations.

As in South Africa, persistent concerns about "biopiracy" have played a role in this expansion. When *biopiracy* emerged as a term in the 1990s, it served predominantly as a rallying cry among activists.[8] It has since transcended quotation marks in media and ascended to the forefront of many governments' regulatory priorities. Consider what happened in March 2022, when a conference center in Geneva buzzed with urgency. Representatives from 164 countries had gathered in the Swiss city for a UN biodiversity summit. Often working late into the night, the representatives sought to reach a consensus on the targets for the post-2020 global biodiversity framework (GBF), which was set for adoption at the United Nations Biodiversity Convention (COP15) later that year.

From my home in Northern Virginia, I followed news about the Geneva summit, wondering if the meeting would yield expanded definitions and terms in the realm of benefit sharing. As the two-week talks neared their conclusion, a significant clash over "biopiracy" surfaced. The *Guardian* summed up the situation this way: "A standoff over biopiracy is threatening to derail a global agreement to halt the loss of nature, with developing countries demanding they are paid for drug discoveries and other commercial products based on their biodiversity." The talks wrapped without a resolution. Nevertheless, I noted the United Nations' official summit report. Its provisional language on GBF targets underscored a commitment to "prevent and eliminate biopiracy." But despite the more radical inclusion of the term *biopiracy*, the report's proposed solution struck me as conventional: to "substantially increase the fair and equitable sharing of benefits arising from the utilization of genetic resources in all forms."

To craft the GBF, negotiators from nearly every nation-state met in a Montreal convention center for two weeks in late 2022. What measures, asked the negotiators, could the roughly 190 countries that are party to the CBD collectively take to halt biodiversity loss? If measures could be agreed upon, what timeline was necessary to realize them? Shortly before Christmas of 2022, the negotiators proclaimed success—they had approved twenty-three targets, the most prominent of which would place 30 percent of the world's land and oceans under protection by 2030. Crucially, the framework reinforced the importance of benefit sharing, elevating it as a core strategy to propel the sustainable development agenda forward.

For its part, the NGO ACB has criticized the GBF and its predecessor, the CBD, for perpetuating business as usual through "embedding the commodification, separation, and ownership of nature and knowledge and incentivizing a focus on technological, privatized market-based mechanisms to solve underlying systemic, geopolitical and geo-economic issues and inequalities."[9] ACB expressed particular concern that a flawed GBF could worsen continental Africa's plight, but that the South African government showed signs of a different path, offering a "glimmer of hope." The country's draft 2023 "White Paper on Biodiversity Conservation and Sustainable Use," according to ACB, offers a progressive alignment with the constitutional right to a healthy environment and African philosophy of well-being. The proposed policy continues with the expanded scope of benefit sharing, aiming for "benefits [to be] derived and shared from the use and development of South Africa's genetic *and biological* resources" (emphasis added).[10] The policy also links this approach with Ubuntu, valuing "interdependent, respectful relationships among humans, nature, and the spiritual realm, promoting dignity and community."[11] However, as I read through the white paper, I noted something striking. Directly beneath a bullet-pointed goal about "adopt[ing] an integrated conservation approach in line with Ubuntu" was a related goal: "Institutionalize biodiversity conservation within Traditional Authorities."[12] By discursively hitching Ubuntu to traditional authorities in the context of biodiversity conservation, the government seemed certain to attract criticism.[13]

"Operation Phakisa" was the "hurry up" strategy South Africa unveiled to supercharge the biodiversity economy and funnel billions of dollars toward national development priorities with the help of market-based mechanisms like benefit sharing. But according to South African scholar Rachel Wynberg, *slowing down* this process might be a better option, "to enable genuine inclusion, to bring in a diversity of voices, to set in place appropriate governance mechanisms, to identify local development and conservation priorities, and, importantly, to challenge current trade and intellectual property models."[14] Wynberg's fear is that governments react to the complexities of resource exploitation and to the imperatives of frameworks like the Nagoya Protocol and the CBD "by entangling themselves in unworkable laws and by adopting a somewhat mechanical 'tick-box approach' that aims to ensure regulatory compliance rather than creating a climate that is conducive to ensuring social justice and stimulating economic development."[15]

As I write this conclusion, there are signs that departments of the South African government may be slowing down and even contemplating a reimagining of benefit sharing concerning pelargonium. Such a reimagining won't be simple.[16] When I raised the possibility of organizing access and benefit sharing through government municipalities, residents and policymakers alike suggested to me that, in a context where the state is frequently viewed as corrupt, incompetent, or intransigent, the state becoming the recipient of benefits would be an unwelcome outcome. And what of cultivation? As part of the biodiversity economic strategy, the national and provincial governments began in recent years to establish large-scale farm sites for pelargonium. Beyond moving beyond trade alone, the impulse behind the effort is to ensure that profitable value-adding is more likely to occur on South African soil. But national officials admitted to me that land available for such cultivation in the Eastern Cape is largely in the communal areas. The pelargonium cultivation site I described in chapter 2 was supported by funding from the local government and a South African drug company, yet the site appeared to be largely administered by the Imingcangathelo chieftaincy, leading to complaints from locals who opposed the involvement of traditional leaders in such matters. In the meantime, the state continued to confront a seemingly "illicit" industry. "Discrepancies between export and imported quantities suggest [the] need to investigate possible illegal trade," a 2020 resource assessment report proclaimed.[17]

What is certain is that the existing approach ensnares drug development with land politics, making that silver-bullet approach even less likely to achieve equity. As South African land-governance scholar Rosalie Kingwill argues, "Technical or bureaucratic solutions cannot instantly leapfrog over socio-cultural realities."[18] Taking these perspectives together, one implication of this book is that, should the South African government persist with its benefit-sharing model, meaningful rights concerning biological resources will only begin with the meaningful clarification of authority, land rights, and citizenship in former homelands like the Ciskei and Transkei. For their part, the Masakhane and Iqayiyaletu CPAs continue to wait for such a clarification. As of this writing, they continue to wait for title deeds to their land.

South Africa has materialized as a leader in market-driven environmental policy. Its efforts to govern biological resource movements have been labeled "rigorous" and "strict," and circumstances in the country have been described as "the mother" and "testing ground" of benefit sharing.[19] Undoubtedly, other governments are watching. Though well-intentioned, South Africa's approach has propelled these issues into new sociopolitical realms and with precarious outcomes. Attending closely to the politics of land in the Eastern Cape, for example, I have sought to show how efforts to control biotraffic via benefit sharing have become entangled with the re/constitution of illiberal political power in postcolonial South Africa. Indeed, in a context in which communal jurisdictions constituted ideal zones of resource extraction—especially given their reserves of underemployed laborers and legally accessible geographic expanses—resource rights became instruments of subjection and thus an important mode of accumulation for traditional leaders. It is in this sense that benefit sharing seemed to act alongside parliamentary laws and spatial planning schemes to entrench homeland boundaries.

To examine such entanglements, this book focused on the territorialization of biotraffic and its governance as an *extractive* phenomenon. Ethnographic interest in extractive capitalism has tended to center on mining and oil, and the characteristics of these industries consequently suffuse theorizations about extraction.[20] An examination of the large-scale and work-intensive removal of medicinal plants from the wild revealed shared features with mining and oil. It highlighted, for example, an economy characterized by considerable temporal uncertainty and rupture—qualities that shaped local laborers' experiences of time and their strategies to secure more predictable futures.[21] It showed how the production of biodiverse regions as extractive zones involves a series of contortions—legal, political, economic, and discursive—that can selectively appropriate and elide the interests of Indigenous occupants in such regions.[22] It additionally illustrated how extractive theaters, while very much about land and landed resources, are also sites of dizzying cultural production. Indeed, like scholars who have studied African chiefdoms involved in platinum and gold mining, I described chiefdoms involved in plant trade who have incorporated themselves as traditional-commercial entities seeking to monetize ethnic difference.

At the same time, the industry I explored opens possibilities for understanding different dimensions of capitalist extraction. Like timber, but unlike metals and minerals, wild medicinal plants are considered renewable resources that live, grow, and reproduce. This view informs the ways that wild plants, even if collected on a large scale, can be enlisted in ambitions for sustainable, and therefore limitless, commercial growth. Of course, to imply that access zones in the former Ciskei are "wild" would be to radically misapprehend their historical and contemporary production. Human activity has long altered the landscape; its forests and soils are archives of human life, anti-colonial resistance, and the evisceration of both during European conquest and apartheid rule.[23] Nevertheless, human design is always in question when it comes to control over living matter. Ecological and climatic factors greatly impact the distribution and availability of plants, their physiological character, and their perceived medicinal qualities. Those factors, alongside the unique habits of plant species themselves, can frustrate human intentions. In the case of harvesters seeking pelargonium, the plant's slow regrowth (which as noted allegedly lasts between four and fifteen years) could severely limit opportunities for return harvest, thus limiting the duration of their participation in the trade.

The organizational implications for the industry were significant. At stake in these spatiotemporal dynamics was who could profit from the trade and for how long. Some chieftaincies in the Ciskei lacked pelargonium within their jurisdictions entirely. But even those with the plant in their vicinity might not have been able to participate in harvesting for long. If the resource became exhausted, a lengthy wait ensued for plants to regenerate from the tuber bits harvesters left in the ground, intentionally or otherwise. Plants were meaningful agents in this sense, contributing to a more-than-human territoriality of plant access zones and their ephemerality.[24] Such zones materialized and dissolved. They were "mixed spatiotemporal assemblages" that drug firms could stitch together with the help of the highly mobile biotraders and access agreements with chiefs.[25] This was one reason chiefs saw themselves at a disadvantage when compared to biotraders and drug companies. Both of the latter could create continuities across geography and time. "They are mobile with their trucks," a chief once told me. "We are like pedestrians in comparison. We want everyone to eat (*atye*) from this business, but not the way some people are eating."

But if such continuities were hard to come by for access providers like chiefs, this was not for want of trying. I described the Rharhabe kingdom and its corporate arm managing to claim multiple access zones under an umbrella-like, temporally stable governing structure. However, an umbrella of such broad coverage proved difficult to maintain, and it eventually collapsed. Of course, such continuities were impossible for harvesters, who, due to high levels of social and economic insecurity in the former homelands, were nevertheless willing laborers in a toilsome industry. Harvesters tended to lack transportation and were thus anchored to village areas, contributing to overharvest.

Taken together, these qualities call into question any essentializing notion that, under extractive capitalism, corporations must omnipotently command the milieus in which they operate.[26] Or that they must themselves physically operate at all within such milieus. The biotraffic I have depicted in this book relied upon supply-chain capitalism: processes through which firms amass capital without having to manage (but in turn lack mastery over) the initial conditions that produce commodities. I emphasized the lack of interest by firms in disciplining resources via cultivation. But those firms similarly relinquished control of labor, and to consequential effect. Intermediaries like biotraders often defied their company partners, mixing infrastructural muscle with mercuriality as industry players. Harvesters presented different challenges. Still, those firms reduced their costs when *mastery of inventory* was their singular aim.[27]

Supply-chain capitalism usually begins with collection from common domains (rather than private ones), a fact that shaped how pelargonium access zones became bound up in property regimes and political order. In a series of works about such regimes and order, Christian Lund and Catherine Boone develop an important theoretical lens through which we can view biotraffic and its governance. In the former homelands of the Eastern Cape, state officials understood access zones to be "commons" in the sense that they were "communal areas" where the ownership status of land and resources was unresolved. Spatial control was a matter of rule rather than a matter of outright ownership.[28] Said differently, access zones were not the property of chiefs; they were the state-recognized territories of chiefs. As such, they were indirectly governed spaces that included resources and people. According to Lund and Boone, it follows that land control is a multidimensional and relational process whereby different kinds of *jurisdictions* overlap and compound as fields of political authority in the making.[29] In many parts of Africa, including the former homelands, chiefs exercise authority to define and enforce customary rights, "promoting a notion that land ultimately belongs to the 'community' of which they are the stewards."[30] Recognition of *jurisdiction over space* can thus be tied to—or enabled by—the recognition of *jurisdiction over people*. And this latter kind of jurisdiction could beget the representational authority to speak on behalf of people, augmenting the ability of leaders to define and enforce both rights of access to important resources and rights to community membership.[31]

I drew upon this backdrop of jurisdictional and representational politics to apprehend expansional patterns of belonging. If, as I mentioned earlier, conventional access and benefit sharing hinges on a tripartite formula of coterminous plants, people, and knowledge, South Africa's version of the instrument came built with an option to edit knowledge (and knowledge holders, consequently) out of the mix. The aim of this option, I reiterate, reflected a good-faith effort to bolster the capacity of benefit sharing to create equity in the context of both drug discovery and plant-commodity trade (or the two entwined). With knowledge seemingly removed from the equation, the volume of benefits a group could receive became tied to the material volume of uprooted plants. Nevertheless, with benefit sharing in this model still filtered through the logic of intellectual property, plants had to remain bundled with people, triggering the requirement that a representative authority be identified to speak for and negotiate on behalf of a collectivity.

Indeed, I suggested that, to the extent that chiefs could parlay representational authority over people into the de facto control over land and landed resources, they could also exercise leverage in national and international markets in ways that ordinary residents could not.[32] They could use this leverage to realize a variety of aims, like enhancing their status and influence, positioning themselves as good-faith promoters of rural development, or capturing drug royalties (or some combination of these). Whatever the case, well-positioned elites could collect more benefits by collecting more bundled plants and people. The dynamics I described were far from stable on the ground, with different communities rotating in and out of an industry that moved across ecologically and politically vulnerable landscapes. Together, these developments suggested that, while international and national frameworks concerning biological and genetic resources are intended to expand the rights of marginalized groups, their situational materialization could do precisely the opposite.

Beyond a story about local actors scrambling for treasure, the South African state's endorsement of chiefs in benefit-sharing agreements raises broader questions about the generative interface between local configurations of power and a global context of Indigenous rights and neoliberal capitalism.[33] I explored this interface, analyzing in further depth what material form commitments to international biological resource rights take when, through their translation to local circumstances, they encounter particular interests and histories. What, specifically, do such rights *do* in a former apartheid homeland where aspirations for benefit sharing meet chiefly demands for control over resources and subjects?

Liberal-democratic rights are empirically contingent.[34] They are not immutable concepts imposed wholesale on local conditions. Rather, they are abstractions with a capacity for translation and distortion, as Harri Englund demonstrates in his study of human rights discourses in Malawi.[35] Insisting that "human rights acquire significance situationally," Englund invites scholars to investigate the social and historical contexts in which rights discourses take concrete form.[36] Relatedly, Anna Tsing shows how rights discourses, as "engaged universals," mobilize and invite both powerful and marginalized actors to appropriate them, often with conjunctural effects.[37] Both Englund and Tsing note that such effects include depoliticization, as the ostensible universalism of rights may occlude the actual grounded dynamics of power.[38] The case of pelargonium illustrates how the translation of biological resource rights to a former homeland depoliticized the construction of rural residents as customary subjects. Specifically, in an effort to produce communities amenable to biodiversity conservation, the South African state constructed benefit-sharing agreements that elided complex, historically wrought subjectivities in favor of essentialist renderings of life under centralized chieftaincy. In a region where the centralization of traditional leadership was especially contentious, benefit-sharing agreements also *expanded* chiefly jurisdictions, at least as they concerned control over a valuable resource and the distribution of benefits associated with its trade. In doing so, benefit sharing fostered a politics of forced membership that many local residents opposed.

Examinations of Indigenous rights have shown that centralizing the Indigenous and the customary is often fundamental to decentralizing government under postcolonial state formation and widespread economic restructuring.[39] The ostensible desirability of providing access to rights, explicit in a global preoccupation with "good governance" and the rule of law, often depoliticizes, if not occludes, processes through which modern states devolve forms of authority to other power structures.[40] One outcome is the emergence of what some have called a "global conjuncture of belonging," or increasing concern with cultural identity and group classification at local, national, and transnational scales of power.[41] Much of the scholarship on this conjuncture has justifiably emphasized boundary closure, displacement, and exclusion in the contemporary construction of Indigenous collective belonging. Yet as a point of articulation between Indigenous political legitimization and the interests of global capital, access and benefit sharing highlights a different trend. I suggest that, beyond closure and the deepening of lines of distinction between groups, the strategic expansion of Indigenous group membership—a politics of ethnic capture—can be equally integral as a mode of capitalist, extraction-oriented accumulation.

Notes

PROLOGUE: TWO WEDDINGS AND A FUNERAL

1. The company's legal name is Dr. Willmar Schwabe GmbH & Co. KG. The other drug company representative at the wedding worked for Parceval Pharmaceuticals of South Africa.

2. The isiXhosa name *ikhubalo* is also used.

3. I was unable to corroborate the villagers' assertions regarding the chieftaincy's alleged hoarding of royalties from pharmaceutical companies.

INTRODUCTION

1. African Center for Biosafety is now named African Center for Biodiversity. I have kept the original name here for the sake of consistency when citing the NGO's publications.

2. Miller (2002). The *Pelargonium* and *Geranium* genera were historically confused—a mix-up that predates Carl Linnaeus's 1753 classification, which mistakenly grouped them into a single *Geranium* genus. Despite their later separation into distinct genera, conflation persists. Most "geraniums" sold globally are actually *Pelargonium* species (Lis-Balchin 2002). According to Lis-Balchin (2002), numerous publications perpetuate this error, employing "Geraniums" in titles when discussing *Pelargonium*. Genuine *Geraniums*,

which are capable of withstanding European climates, are sometimes labeled "Hardy Geraniums."

3. See Brendler and van Wyk (2008).

4. Brendler and van Wyk (2008, 421) and Street and Prinsloo (2013, 8).

5. The medicine is also known as Umcka in the United States and Umkalor in Ukraine, Russia, and Latvia.

6. McKune (2010).

7. Deutsche Welle (2010).

8. Deutsche Welle (2010).

9. African Center for Biosafety (2010c).

10. The focus on plant trade and the notion of "biopiracy beyond the patent system" initially left me perplexed. Most discussions about "biopiracy" position patents at their core. When Canadian environmentalist Pat Mooney and the NGO he helped establish in the early 1990s coined the term, they integrally tied it to patents. That NGO still characterizes "biopiracy" as "the appropriation of the knowledge and genetic resources of farming and indigenous communities by individuals or institutions aiming for exclusive monopoly control, be it patents or intellectual property." Arguably the most famous book about biopiracy, activist Vandana Shiva's 1997 *Biopiracy: The Plunder of Nature and Knowledge*, aptly kicks off with an introduction titled "Piracy through Patents."

11. André and Baux (2011).

12. Van Niekerk and Wynberg (2012).

13. See for example Careddu and Pettenazzo (2018). Researchers subsequently considered Umckaloabo's therapeutic potential against novel coronaviruses in the wake of the COVID-19 pandemic (Keck et al. 2021).

14. Here and throughout, my use of "drug discovery" refers to what is conventionally called "biodiscovery" or "bioprospecting."

15. Rachel Wynberg (2017a, 207) describes the controversial case of research and development concerning rooibos tea (*Aspalathus linearis*) and another Indigenous tea called honeybush (*Cyclopia* spp.) this way: "In this case, the food giant Nestlé secured rooibos and honeybush plant material from a local South African processor, did research on extracts and filed patents, but without the requisite agreements in place. Although the material was obtained from a local processor, it could equally have been purchased off the shelves of any European supermarket, raising questions about the challenges of regulating research and development on commodities such as rooibos tea that are already commercially available."

16. Commodity trade in biological resources like plants is commonly known as "biotrade," which the UN hopes to transform into "BioTrade," or "the collection, production, transformation, and commercialization of goods and services derived from native biodiversity under the criteria of environmental, social and economic sustainability" (UN Trade and Development n.d.). As a commodity,

Pelargonium sidoides also falls under the category of "non-timber forest product," or NTFP.

17. Mayor (2011). Much of the recent scholarship about links between Indigenous medicinal resources and the pharmaceutical industry has hinged on a central idea: advances in biotechnology over the past century have transformed the "discovery" and production of plant-derived drugs. Laboratory scientists now require only a limited amount of plant material to rapidly assess a plant's cells or genetics and set the production of a drug into perpetual motion. Contrasting this present-day use of genetic resources with a bygone era of imperial galleons loaded with botanical matter, Margaret Lock and Vinh-Kim Nguyen argue, "We have come a long way from the seventeenth century.... It is not now necessary, as was formerly the case, to import enormous quantities of materials for conversion into medicinals" (2018, 176). Examples like *Taxus contorta* and paclitaxel complicate such claims, however. Paclitaxel is used to halt the spread of various cancers by inhibiting cell division. Numerous pharmaceutical companies produce the compound without accessing bark from yew trees. An example is Bristol-Myers Squibb, which manufactures the drug, commercially known as Taxol, using a *Taxus* cell line in large fermenters. Nonetheless, some manufacturers, particularly in India and China, have continued to extract the substance directly from the tree. The International Union for Conservation of Nature added the tree to its "red list" of endangered species in 2011.

18. Neimark and Schroeder (2009, 46). Neimark (2012) describes a situation similar to that of *Taxus contorta*: when research recognized the *Prunus Africana* tree's potential for treating prostate inflammation, extensive collection in Madagascar followed, compelling the government in that country to classify the tree as a threatened species.

19. If the convergence of commodity trade and drug discovery is a "problem," should we call it "biopiracy," or perhaps a subset thereof? This book is unconcerned with delineating such boundaries. The term "biopiracy" possesses an ambiguity—potentially by design—and its polemical status can work to overshadow subtleties and critical distinctions. Robinson (2010) offers a commendable analysis of "biopiracy," and the phenomenon explored in this book might well fit within his characterization of the concept. While biopiracy typically emphasizes patent injustices, Robinson writes, the unauthorized or uncompensated use of biological materials and traditional knowledge can also evoke comparable injustices, deserving similar scrutiny.

20. If, according to Eva Hemmungs Wirtén (2008), biopiracy signals the degree to which material and immaterial forms of propertization can converge, biotraffic can foreground articulations between these things occurring at wholly different orders of magnitude.

21. Foster (2017, 10). Such articulations are the subject of Laura Foster's *Reinventing Hoodia*, which examines another southern African plant, *Hoodia*

gordonii, as both a molecule and a cultivated botanical. Foster focuses on the multiscalar dimensions of the plant's exploitation to understand how power operates across them, (re)producing profound inequalities between plant scientists, growers, and knowledge holders. Pelargonium, a plant that is more commercially successful than *Hoodia gordonii* but has received far less scholarly consideration, similarly demands attention to power across scales. However, its status as a wild—rather than cultivated—commodity from common domains yields different insights concerning power.

22. I am inspired here in part by Harris Solomon's conceptualization of "traffic" and the idea that, more than signifying relationality, movements produce relationality (2022, 18). Solomon builds on the work of Erin Manning, who describes movement as "the activation of a new field of relation" (2016, 18).

23. Escobar (2008).

24. Drahos and Braithwaite (2002).

25. See Cooper (2008).

26. Hayden (2003a).

27. Gollin (1993, 191).

28. In 1999, for example, the Indian government successfully challenged a patent obtained by American researchers to use turmeric for wound healing. Soon afterward, it joined a coalition of NGOs and Indian farmers—who were among those protesting the worldwide expansion of intellectual property laws—seeking to overturn a US agro-industrial company's patent on the neem tree as a biopesticide. The patent was eventually revoked, but members of the above-mentioned coalition interpreted the result variously, revealing a spectrum of political positions among stakeholders in such cases. The Indian state viewed the case as proof that mechanisms provided in the WTO's multilateral frameworks worked: Southern countries could successfully challenge patents (see Sunder Rajan 2006).

29. Brush (2004).

30. See Mgbeoji (2006) and Robinson (2010).

31. Bagley (2017).

32. Greene, Condrau, and Watkins (2016).

33. A prominent example is Harding (2011).

34. Pollock (2019).

35. Laird et al. (2020).

36. Berlant (2011, 5).

37. DST (2007, 4).

38. South African Department of Environmental Affairs (2015, 6).

39. The access and benefit-sharing provisions of South Africa's National Environmental Management: Biodiversity Act of 2004 outline the country's obligations to the CBD. In 2008 the Department of Environmental Affairs (DEA) gave effect to these provisions through the Bioprospecting Access and Benefit

Sharing (BABS) regulations. South Africa ratified the Nagoya Protocol in January 2013.

40. *Hoodia gordonii*, a plant commercialized internationally as an appetite suppressant, is one of the more famous of South Africa's biological resources. Unlike *Pelargonium sidoides*, *Hoodia* has received significant scholarly attention (Comaroff and Comaroff 2009; Foster 2017; Robins 2008; Vermeylen 2007).

41. Beinart and Wotshela (2011).

42. Oberthür and Rosendal (2014).

43. Laird and Wynberg (2021, 46) list the following benefits that companies and other entities with access and benefit-sharing agreements are expected to achieve (at least one; ideally more): "Conservation of the indigenous genetic and biological resources; support for further research on indigenous genetic and biological resources and TK [Indigenous knowledge]; enhancement of the scientific knowledge and technical capacity to conserve, use and develop indigenous genetic and biological resources; any other activity that promotes the conservation, sustainable use and development of indigenous biological resources for the benefit of South Africa; or improving livelihoods of the communities and enhancement of technical capacity of the communities or individuals involved."

44. Hayden (2003b).

45. Hayden (2003b, 362).

46. See Osseo-Assare (2014) and Wynberg (2017b). The notion that Indigenous knowledge "can be attributed exclusively to a people and a place" encounters both conceptual and practical challenges; conceptual because "knowledge evolves, hybridizes, and adapts over time to events and circumstances," and practical because "origin" of knowledge is often impossible to prove—it may not exist, it may be so historically distant that it becomes difficult to trace, or it may have become shared among various groups of people (Dutfield et al. 2020, 1). Osseo-Assare (2014) has relatedly argued that benefit sharing overemphasizes "local priority," consequently disregarding the fact that Indigenous medical knowledge tends to be widespread in distribution (among different groups of people). Roger Chennells, a prominent South African lawyer and scholar, likens such knowledge to a family's secret recipe. Cases like pelargonium present a "complicated situation," he argues, because "the secret has been 'out' in the public domain for many decades, and the issue of who should be the beneficiary or traditional knowledge holder has become far from a simple matter" (2013, 171).

47. Wynberg (2017b, 303).

48. Coombe (2005).

49. Biko (1987, 83). What resulted was one of the most notorious projects of racial segregation ever carried out. Each homeland was established to contain and isolate a government-designated ethnic group: Xhosa people in the Transkei and Ciskei, Zulu people in KwaZulu, Tswana people in Bophuthatswana, and so on.

50. Biko (1987, 82).

51. Oomen (2005).

52. See Jensen and Zenker (2015) for a discussion of the "homelands" as zones of contemporary contestation over the future of all of South Africa (rather than regions that empire made permanently marginal).

53. Jensen and Zenker (2015).

54. Beinart (2012, 5).

55. Ramutsindela (2007).

56. Simmel (2009).

57. Listening to Dabula's laughter, I was reminded of anthropologist Donna Goldstein's insights about humor as politics. Such a seemingly paradoxical emotional aesthetic could be understood as "a living example of the interconnectedness between comedy, on the one hand, and suffering and tragedy, on the other" (Goldstein 2003, 37).

58. SAB, K.20, Archives of the Secretary of the Commission of Inquiry into the Socio-Economic Development of the Bantu Areas, vol. 47, 4174, evidence of J. M. Brink, cited in Mager (1995).

59. See Desmond (1971).

60. Peires (1989a).

61. Peires (1989a).

62. Mager (1995).

63. Manona (1980).

64. Evans (2014).

65. Ntsebeza (2011).

66. See Hebinck and Shackleton (2011) and Phillips and Chipkin (2014).

67. Claassens (2014).

68. Westaway (2012, 116).

69. Berry (2018, 79).

70. In other words, I wish to avoid producing "an arbitrarily mapped-out and confined Africa" (Nyamnjoh 2012, 68).

71. See Beinart, Kingwill, and Capps (2021).

72. Much of this scholarship has focused on platinum mining in the South African provinces of KwaZulu-Natal and North West. See Oomen (2005), Williams (2010), Comaroff and Comaroff (2009), Cook (2011), Cook and Hardin (2013), Manson (2013), and Mnwana (2014, 2021). For an example concerning chiefs and gold mining in Ghana, see Rosen (2020).

73. Stoler (2016).

74. I borrow the term "policy intellectuals" from James Ferguson (2015, xiii), who describes these people as "sophisticated thinkers engaged with pragmatic issues of social policy." In my case, such persons included government officials in the Departments of Environmental Affairs, Science and Technology, Trade and Industry, and Health; the South African National Biodiversity Institute; the Medical Research Council; the Medicines Control Council; and the Technology

Innovation Agency, as well as corporate actors in the biotech sector, journalists, and a number of intellectual property and traditional knowledge experts, such as representatives of the South African San Council and various other intellectual property lawyers.

75. This section of ethnographies is formulaic to the point of being passé. At least this is what anthropology students I have taught at US universities have occasionally told me. I can appreciate their perspective. The criticism centers less on an ethnographer's use of the section to describe methods, sites, and interlocutors, and more on their use of it to interrogate their own positionality—a move that, while informed by a desire for reflexivity, can come across as performative. It can also serve to unduly amplify the ethnographer's presence in the story they wish to tell. Seasoned practitioners of anthropology sometimes level the same complaint: the representational and identity politics of ethnography are important, but they should not overshadow the topic spelled out in an ethnography's title (see Olivier de Sardan 2015). But the issue was never so straightforward to my South African interlocutors.

76. I established an affiliation at the University of KwaZulu-Natal. During the month I spent visiting the university's Howard College, students regularly protested on campus, often prompting administrators to close the campus. The protesters sought, above all, better financial support for their studies.

77. The protests unfolded in 2015 and 2016, and at a local level sought to decouple the university from the British imperialist and White supremacist Cecil Rhodes. The protests had been long in the making, but traces of them arguably helped animate the panel and the discussion it generated.

78. Vice (2011).

79. Mulligan (1999).

80. See Cantero (2017). Like Cantero, I find Derrida's (2006) idea of "hauntology" relevant to the problems of knowledge production plaguing anthropology.

81. Davis (2005, 373).

82. My framing here is inspired by Hayden (2003a), who recognizes the expectations readers may have when it comes to a book about biodiscovery, a practice with many dimensions.

83. A rich vein of anthropological literature extends beyond the purview of this book, challenging the conventional dichotomies between "bio" and "cultural" realms and exploring alternative relational modes with the vegetal, as exemplified in the works of scholars such as Descola (2014), Ingold (1987), and Laplant (2015), among others. This literature often transcends simplified narratives surrounding human-plant relations and delves into more nuanced engagements that defy mere commodification, a critical discourse slightly touched upon but not thoroughly explored in this work. This long-standing anthropological work surrounding nature-culture divides offers a myriad of perspectives that challenge rigid boundaries often assumed between humans and more-than-human worlds.

84. I have in mind here the work of scholars like Ferguson (1994), Sharma and Gupta (2006), and Li (2007b).

85. Li (2007b, 7).

INTERLUDE: "MY BOY, YOU ARE IN FOR IT" (1897)

1. Worboys (1992).
2. Daniel (2006).
3. Koch (1890).
4. Worboys (1992, 48).
5. Worboys (1992).
6. Bynum (2012).
7. Flint (2008).
8. Bladt and Wagner (2007) argue that Kijitse was ethnically Zulu. Crouch and Wolfson (2009) argue that this is certainly plausible, as Basutoland neighbored the region in which ethnic Zulus have historically resided. "It is not inconceivable that such a Zulu healer would live in Lesotho," they add, "and either learn from Lesotho nationals about the use of *Pelargonium sidoides* for treating tuberculosis, or independently discover this application whilst working there with the plant" (Crouch and Wolfson 2009, 5). In their argument, Crouch and Wolfson (2009) cite the work of Wood and Franks (1911), who wrote of a long-established international exchange of medicinal materials between Basotho and Zulu peoples.
9. Sechehaye (1930, 2).
10. Sechehaye (1930, 2).

CHAPTER 1: PATENT PROBLEMS

1. During interviews, Nomthunzi recounted to me her experience and these reactions.
2. Groenewald (2010).
3. Groenewald (2010).
4. Groenewald (2010).
5. Traugott (2010).
6. Traugott (2010).
7. Bethge, von Bredow, and Schwägerl (2008).
8. Bethge, von Bredow, and Schwägerl (2008).
9. Frein and Meyer (2008). I have translated the original title—*Die Biopiraten: Milliardengeschäfte der Pharmaindustrie mit dem Bauplan der Natur*—from the German.

10. Anders (2009, 2).
11. Frein and Meyer (2008, 144).
12. Frein and Meyer (2008, 144)..
13. In the original German, the ad reads "*unaussprechlich, aber ausgesprochen gut.*"
14. Mazzarella (2003).
15. Mazzarella (2003, 21).
16. Mazzarella (2004, 355).
17. More recent advertisements depict a roaring lion and the phrasing, "Strong Against Respiratory Infections" [*Stark Gegen den Atemwegs Infekt*].
18. This book admittedly fails to explore this history and Schwabe's role in it. For such engagement, see, for example, Baschin (2014); Hoffmann and Riha (2015); and Friedrich, Meyer, and Seyfang (2016).
19. This was another claim I heard anecdotally from German contacts. For example, after a German friend of mine became the director of a small biotech firm, he became frustrated with a lack of financial support for the firm's research. "The willingness of investors to provide money for innovations in medical biotech is very poor in Germany," he wrote me in an email. "This is how new inventions that could produce cancer drugs or other therapies simply disappear in the drawer [*verschwinden in der Schublade*]."
20. Theil (2009).
21. See Schippmann, Leaman, and Cunningham (2006).
22. Jenkins, Timoshyna, and Cornthwaite (2018).
23. Van Niekerk and Wynberg (2012).
24. In 2019. the department was renamed Department of Forestry, Fisheries and the Environment.
25. Crouch et al. (2008, 355).
26. In 2017, the DEA invited public comment on the amnesty provision. The fate of such a provision remains uncertain. Republic of South Africa, "National Environmental Management: Biodiversity Act (10/2004): Proposed Period of Amnesty to Facilitate Compliance with the Provisions of Chapter 6 of the Act and the Bioprospecting, Access and Benefit Sharing Regulations," *Government Gazette* no. 41220, November 1, 2017, Pretoria.
27. See Laird and Wynberg (2013).
28. Article 53(a) of the European Patent Convention specifically states that "European patents shall not be granted in respect of inventions the commercial exploitation of which would be contrary to 'ordre public' or morality." Referring to the Umckaloabo patent specifically, ACB (2008, 8) framed its opposition thus:

> We have argued that Articles 1, 8(j), 15, and 16 of CBD demands that when accessing biological resources and its associated traditional knowledge, prior informed consent be obtained from the traditional knowledge holders or provider countries. This means that Schwabe was in the first instance, required to reveal the purpose of

accessing the resources, namely for commercialization of a medicinal product as well as for patenting the invention based on traditional knowledge. Second, it was required to obtain permission for such commercialization and utilization of the resources. Third, it was required to share the commercial and other benefits with the providers of the resources and knowledge on mutually agreed terms. Since there is no evidence that Schwabe has done any of this, the patent contravenes Article 53 of European Patent Convention, which excludes patents that are *contra boni mores* or contrary to ethics and public morals or order.

29. The NGOs were assisted by a Swiss lawyer named Fritz Dolder, who was experienced in patent challenges, having played a major role in a ten-year campaign to cancel an agrochemical patent on a fungicide made from the neem tree. That case, which concluded in 2005 and had also unfolded at the Munich EPO, had achieved a kind of landmark status among anti-patent activist groups. Reflecting on the significance of the neem case, Dolder (2008, 583) argued that the EPO had "revoked for the first time a patent whose subject matter and claims were based essentially on traditional knowledge originating in a biodiversity country [India]" (2008, 583).

30. Frein and Meyer (2008, 220).

31. Stories about the origins of patent protections and their expansion are exhaustively recounted elsewhere (see Mgbeoji 2006).

32. Shiva (1997, 2).

33. Shiva (1997, 3).

34. Marx (1977, 874).

35. The continued enclosure of property can serve to reduce input costs, a crucial means by which companies can sustain (and grow) rates of profit in the face of troublesome surpluses in capital and workers. Building upon Rosa Luxemburg's work *The Accumulation of Capital* (2003), David Harvey (2005) calls this contemporary and ongoing process of enclosure "accumulation by dispossession."

36. Thompson (2009, 308).

37. ACB (2008, 10). The NGO specifically argued

> that if the effects of a patent amounts to the patenting of plant and plant varieties (which is prohibited in terms of Article 53 of the European Patent Convention), the patent claims which achieves this effect should not be allowed either. It stands to reason that if a letter bomb is clearly unacceptable, how could the process for making it be acceptable? In other words, if the patent of the main extraction method of the Pelargonium species amounts to the monopoly of the Pelargonium species, it should not be allowed, since it has the same effect as patenting of plant varieties themselves. The patent allows Schwabe to control the entire trade with the roots of the two Pelargonium species, as well as all extracts, tinctures, etc. because no one else would be allowed to make Pelargonium tinctures or extracts in the same way (ACB 2008, 9–10).

38. Mgbeoji (2006). The Conference of the Parties to the CBD expressed such a concern, noting that "intellectual property rights might, under certain

circumstances, constrain access to and use of genetic resources and scientific research" (2006, 118).

39. Mgbeoji (2006).
40. See Ritchie, Dawkins, and Vallianatos (1996).
41. ACB (2010a, 3).
42. ACB (2010a, 3).
43. ACB (2010b).
44. Myburgh (2011, 848).
45. Myburgh (2010, 7).
46. Koyama (2008, 7).
47. Alice may be best known as the location of the University of Fort Hare, where political heavyweights like Nelson Mandela, Julius Neyere, and Robert Mugabe attended courses.
48. ACB (2010a, 4).
49. Wiersum et al. (2006).
50. Dold (2009).
51. See Cocks (1997).
52. Academic recognition of Indigenous medicine has sometimes limited its effectiveness to the sociopolitical realm (see Flint 2008). The practitioners I interviewed viewed their expertise as encompassing these areas of healing, with some distinguishing their healing techniques from conventional biomedical methods for treating "disease" (Ngubane 1977). These practitioners often engage in "boundary work," adopting scientific language to frame their medical practices as a form of technoscientific work capable of addressing what is conventionally understood as "disease" in biomedicine (Gieryn 1983; see also Morris 2017). They aim to gain acknowledgment for their medical knowledge and techniques within the more narrowly defined biomedical parameters of health, as opposed to the broader definition of "illness" typically used in medical anthropology (Wreford 2005). This process of creating and valuing knowledge, increasingly encouraged and directed by state institutions in South Africa, involves some practitioners striving to define and limit the effective areas of Indigenous medicine. Anthropologist Susan Levine observes that healers not only sought formal recognition as practitioners but also viewed the testing of their herbs in clinical trials less problematically than some anthropologists (Levine 2012). Moreover, they saw the translation of their medical knowledge into state-sanctioned practices not as a detrimental process but rather as an opportunity for adaptation and innovative responses to socioeconomic disparities and poverty.
53. Comaroff and Comaroff (2009, 54).
54. See Coombe (2005, 2017).
55. Coombe (2016).
56. Goodale (2017).

57. Coombe (2016).

58. Mertz (1994, 1246).

59. Seuss (1961).

60. My use of the Dr. Seuss analogy is partly intended to capture the potential limitations of thinking about the law as a machinery of cultural production. Britta Rutert (2020) challenges the use of anthropological terms such as "lawfare" and "the commodification of culture," questioning these concepts for their deterministic and simplistic nature. Processes enabling group empowerment are more collaborative and dynamic than previously suggested. Indeed, while Indigenous groups do adjust to the legal frameworks and economic systems imposed upon them, they do not necessarily forgo their inherent noncommercial values. On the contrary, Rutert contends, it is often the case that emotional and cultural considerations take precedence over those driven by market forces.

61. Hirsch (2010).

62. Greene (2004, 212).

63. See Igoe (2006) and Fisher (1994).

64. Unlike pelargonium, *Hoodia* has received significant scholarly attention (see Comaroff and Comaroff 2009; Foster 2017; Robins 2008; Vermeylen 2007; Wynberg and Van Niekerk 2014; Wynberg, Schroeder, and Chennells 2009).

65. Comaroff and Comaroff (2009, 89).

66. Comaroff and Comaroff (2009, 92).

67. Coombe (1998, 34).

68. On the topic of strategic essentialism, see Robins (2008).

69. Coombe (1998, 35).

70. Wynberg (2017b).

71. The San Council disagreed, but this did not deter one NGO from later contesting recognition of the CSIR patent in Europe. That NGO's name was the Berne Declaration (Foster 2017).

72. Foster (2017, 158).

73. ACB (2008).

74. ACB (2011, 15).

75. André and Baux (2011). Few activists would find ACB's position surprising. Lorenzo Muelas Hurtado, an Indigenous Colombian activist and former senator, memorably condemned drug discovery outright, arguing that UN frameworks like the CBD were merely about creating a "negotiating arena" in which the extraction of Indigenous wealth and knowledge could be legitimated (quoted in Hayden 2003a, 41). In a different case, an NGO disputing the corporate patenting of Ayahuasca in Mexico insisted that no mechanism—including the CBD—was sufficient when it comes to protecting the rights and interests of local communities. The NGO considered "all bioprospecting agreements to be biopiracy" (Brown 2003, 122).

76. Chennells (2013, 173).

77. Chennells (2013, 174).
78. ACB (2010b).
79. Myburgh (2010, 5)
80. Myburgh (2010).
81. Myburgh (2010, 5).
82. Myburgh (2010).
83. Quoted from Myburgh (2010, 6).
84. ACB (2010c).
85. ACB (2010d, 6).

INTERLUDE: A "SECRET REMEDY" (1901–1909)

1. Packard (1989).
2. Sechehaye (1930, 3).
3. *Lancet* (1905a, 264)
4. *Lancet* (1905a, 264; emphasis in original).
5. *Lancet* (1905c, 640).
6. British Medical Association (1909, 31).
7. Newsom (2002, 464).
8. British Medical Association (1909, v).
9. British Medical Association (1909, 22).
10. British Medical Association (1909, 22).
11. Masco (2002, 451).
12. Simmel (1906, 462).
13. British Medical Association (1909, v).
14. British Medical Association (1909, 20).
15. British Medical Association (1909, 22).
16. British Medical Association (1909, 22).
17. British Medical Association (1908, 23). In a letter to the British Imperial Economic Committee, dated 1936, the deputy medical secretary of the British Medical Association wrote: "The attention of the Medical Secretary has been drawn to a paragraph in the Morning Post of August 15th which suggests that the Imperial Economic Committee is interested in "native medicinal plants" and is compiling an index of such products. I am therefore writing to you to ask if you can kindly give us, in confidence, some information about an African root called Umckaloabo which is said to be imported into this country and used in the manufacture of a secret remedy for tuberculosis." The committee replied that it could locate no reference to Umckaloabo in its *Index of the Minor Forest Products of the British Empire*.
18. British Medical Association (1909, 32).
19. Helmstädter (1996).

CHAPTER 2: A "HOMELAND'S" HARVEST

1. Cousins and Witkowski (2017) argue that demand for cycads as ornamental plants has placed them at high risk from illegal trade. According to Brummitt et al. (2015), cycads are currently the world's most endangered plant group.

2. Schwabe had temporarily ceased purchasing pelargonium during this period, and the official was therefore not referring to that company's activities in this instance.

3. Shackleton and Shackleton (2004).

4. Margulies et al. (2019). "With the exception of the illegal trade in timber," Margulies et al. (2019, 173) argue, "plants are absent from much emerging scholarship, and receive scant attention by US and UK funding agencies often driving global efforts to address illegal wildlife trade, despite the high levels of threat many plants face." Wandersee and Schussler (1999) first described the idea of "plant blindness."

5. Jenkins, Timoshyna, and Cornthwaite (2018).

6. Khwezi is a pseudonym.

7. Shackleton and Shackleton (2004).

8. See Wynberg et al. (2015).

9. Mostert (1992, xviii).

10. See van Niekerk and Wynberg (2012). Limited market connections, which also tend to be controlled by biotraders, also contribute to poor bargaining power (see Sunderlin et al. 2005).

11. Stiglitz (2013). I learned of this concept from Smith (2015).

12. Tom and Kenneth are pseudonyms.

13. Shackleton et al. (2009, 229).

14. Gerardy (2002).

15. Gerardy (2002; emphasis added).

16. ACB (2010a).

17. Bisseker (2002).

18. Van Niekerk (2009).

19. ACB (2011).

20. Wynberg and van Niekerk (2014).

21. ACB (2011, 16).

22. Republic of South Africa, "National Environmental Management: Biodiversity Act (10/2004) Proposed Period of Amnesty to Facilitate Compliance with the Provisions of Chapter 6 of the Act and the Bioprospecting, Access and Benefit Sharing Regulations," *Government Gazette* no. 41220, November 1, 2017, Pretoria.

23. This "illicit" trade was reported at a pelargonium stakeholder meeting in November 2010. Republic of South Africa, "National Environmental Management: Biodiversity Act (10/2004) Biodiversity Management Plan for *Pelargonium*

Sidoides in South Africa," *Government Gazette* no. 36411, April 13, 2013, Pretoria. A Schwabe representative indicated to me the company had stopped buying due to a drop in sales due to claims in Europe about Umckaloabo causing liver damage. A European study suggesting pelargonium is potentially hepatoxic led the Drug Commission of the German Medical Association to issue warnings about consumption of Umckaloabo. See European Medicines Agency (2011).

24. Khwezi described his escape from the mine this way:

> So what one would do was to secretly take one's belongings to the township in Soweto. One would try and hide everything that made a person look like a mineworker. You see, there were no cellphones and also our money was not accessible with bankcards. It was unavoidable then; one would have to go into the township. There, activities for the struggle [against apartheid] were taking place. We, as mineworkers who belonged to a trade union were recognized as political fighters and as such, we were hosted in people's homes. We would then be able to visit the trade union offices in town, bearing one's membership card, of course. Our union was NUM [the National Union of Mineworkers]. It was in these offices that that it would be arranged. We would get some pocket money and return tickets to go home.

25. Luthando is a pseudonym.

26. See Mains (2007).

27. "Money is like food ready to eat" [*Imali ikuKutya oku vuthiweyo*] is a common Xhosa expression.

28. See Bourdieu (1981).

29. Lodge (2003) and Pickard (2006).

30. Webster (2006).

31. Barchiesi (2011, 6).

32. Ruiters (2011). According to Jason Robinson, the Eastern Cape "has consistently been one of the worst-performing provincial administrations in post-apartheid South Africa and . . . has become a byword for inefficiency and mismanagement" (2015, 962).

33. Trade and Industrial Policy Strategies (2016).

34. Eastern Cape Department of Economic Development, Environmental Affairs, and Tourism (2014, 76).

35. Eastern Cape Department of Economic Development, Environmental Affairs, and Tourism (2014, 76)

36. Westaway (2012).

37. Westaway (2012, 116).

38. Chris Hani Municipality, "Draft Integrated Development Plan, 2008-9" (unpublished municipal document, Border Rural Committee Resource Centre, East London), 48.

39. Westaway (2012, 117).

40. Westaway (2012, 117).

41. "National Environmental Management: Biodiversity Act (10/2004): Publication of Lists of Species That Are Threatened or Protected, Activities That Are

Prohibited and Exemption from Restriction," *Government Gazette* no. 38600, March 31, 2015, Pretoria.

42. Shackleton et al. (2009, 231).

43. See Neumann and Hirsch (2000) and van Niekerk and Wynberg (2012).

44. South African National Biodiversity Institute (2010).

45. TRAFFIC, which has offices in South Africa, is a member of World Wildlife Federation and the IUCN and has advised the DEA on pelargonium-related matters.

46. Republic of South Africa, "National Environmental Management: Biodiversity Act (10/2004) Biodiversity Management Plan for *Pelargonium Sidoides* in South Africa," *Government Gazette* no. 36411, April 13, 2013, Pretoria, 11.

47. See Feiter (2018) and Normand et al. (2021).

48. Republic of South Africa, "National Environmental Management: Biodiversity Act (10/2004) Biodiversity Management Plan for *Pelargonium Sidoides* in South Africa," *Government Gazette* no. 36411, April 13, 2013, Pretoria.

49. White, Davies-Coleman, and Ripley (2008) and Moyo et al. (2013).

50. Yousefian et al. (2023).

51. Van Niekerk and Wynberg (2012).

52. Motjotji (2011, ii).

53. Van Niekerk and Wynberg (2012).

54. Van Niekerk and Wynberg (2012, 544).

55. Van Niekerk and Wynberg (2012).

56. Republic of South Africa, "National Environmental Management: Biodiversity Act (10/2004) Biodiversity Management Plan for *Pelargonium Sidoides* in South Africa," *Government Gazette* no. 36411, April 13, 2013, Pretoria, 16.

57. Republic of South Africa, "National Environmental Management: Biodiversity Act (10/2004) Biodiversity Management Plan for *Pelargonium Sidoides* in South Africa," *Government Gazette* no. 36411, April 13, 2013, Pretoria, 13.

58. De Castro, Vlok, and McLellan (2010, 18). This was a broadly recognized trend acknowledged by the provincial government (Eastern Cape Department of Environmental Affairs and Tourism 2004, ch. 12). High stocking rates in the Great Fish River Reserve Complex—where villages involved in harvesting are densely populated—has historically driven competition and conflict over resources, undermining in turn community-based natural resource management initiatives (Cocks, Dold, and Grundy 2001).

59. See Shackleton and Shackleton (2004).

60. Glewwe and Hall (1998) and Shackleton et al. (2009).

61. Given this mandate, it is noteworthy that state administrators have elected, among other things, to not invoke Section 92 of NEMBA, which allows national and provincial authorities to exercise their powers jointly and issue a single, integrated permit.

62. Moore (1998, 379).

63. Ruiters (2011, 5).

INTERLUDE: "MOUNTAINS OF PREJUDICE"
(1909–1914)

1. Brendler and van Wyk (2008).
2. "Exposure of a Quack" (1910, 872).
3. British Medical Association (1909, 31).
4. British Medical Association (1909, 30).
5. Flint (2008, 187).
6. British Medical Association (1909, 30).
7. Stevens (1912, 8).
8. Stevens (1912, 13).
9. Stevens (1912, 15).
10. Lock and Nguyen (2018, 34–35).
11. Stevens (1912, 17–19).
12. Newsom (2002, 465).

CHAPTER 3: ON EXPANSIONAL BELONGING
AND ETHNIC CAPTURE

1. Hayden (2003a, 37).
2. Geschiere (2009).
3. Meiu (2019, 148).
4. Meiu (2019, 150).
5. Geschiere (2009, 26). Meiu (2019, 148) makes a similar point, arguing that "some people now seek a sense of permanence in trying to close off social worlds, to 'return to their roots,' as it were, and to claim rights and resources through identities they see as immutable."
6. TallBear (2013).
7. Peters (2004).
8. Susan Cook (n.d., cited in Comaroff and Comaroff 2009).
9. Comaroff and Comaroff (2009, 111).
10. Geschiere (2018, 30).
11. One illustrative exchange I had with a resident about this topic went as follows:

    CHRIS: What did you make of the arrangement through which you would harvest pelargonium and then have to bring it to the Chieftainess's Great Place?
    RESIDENT: We did not like it at all, because there at the Great Place there are no harvesters. It would only be us who would dig and forward it there.
    CHRIS: Was there a tax on the materials you brought there?
    RESIDENT: Yes, that was obvious. We would receive far less money than usual. This did not go down well with us. The chiefs shouldn't be involved in the pelargonium industry. It's like taking bread from the poor.

12. "Yes, we are under Nosizwe's (Chieftainess Tyali's) jurisdiction," one middle-aged resident confirmed to me. "And as such we are part of Imingcangathelo." A woman in her seventies brought up a more extended history. "Before the Ciskei, it was Zulu," she recounted, referencing a chief located on the other side of the villages. "Tyali wasn't here." A slightly younger man proposed a related but slightly different idea, saying, "Our allegiance is to Chief Zulu, but the chiefs are absent in this area." Echoing the perspective that chiefs were absent were many local youths. "It's as if they don't exist," a woman in her twenties observed to me.

13. Robins (2008, 11).
14. Thipe and Buthelezi (2014).
15. Greene (2004).
16. Green (2004, 222).
17. "They conducted workshops for us," one resident explained. "I can also say they were here to help us get a fair deal (*ngokufanalekileyo*) in all this trade. They wanted us to benefit (*sincedeke*) just like the Germans were doing." Funeka, a Masakhane CPA leader, echoed this opinion. At the conclusion of the meeting led by ACB in a Masakhane village, Funeka said the following to the NGO representatives: "I had thought that this pelargonium issue was a closed chapter already. I'm very thankful that all along, ACB has not rested or backed away. You have been tirelessly pursuing our cause. I would like to commend you by saying, please keep on with the good work and march forward. I can assure you that we, as this community, shall not derail or go astray but will keep on treading on the track we've been shown."
18. Bergh and Visagie (1985).
19. Mostert (1992).
20. According to Nomthunzi, "On the rare occasion, some of us did have to leave for a short time. There was this rule from the White farmers that a family could reside on the farm only if that family's head was employed. In the late 1970s, when my father grew old and could no longer work, we had to briefly move across the road to a village. We returned when the White farmers left."
21. Delius (2008).
22. Bergh and Visagie (1985).
23. Peires (1989a). According to Peires (2012, 349), "The resuscitation of the amaRharhabe as a political identity was mainly due to the decision of the apartheid government to establish Ciskei as a separate homeland distinct from Transkei. It was only then that Archie Velile Sandile was plucked from the obscurity of Centane and resettled at the original Rharhabe's old Great Place of Mnqesha to become King of the amaRharhabe rather than Chief of the amaNgqika."
24. Cocks, Dold, and Grundy (2001).
25. Such nostalgia is not uncommon in South Africa, as Dlamini (2009) and Bank and Mabhena (2011) have shown.

26. Cocks, Dold, and Grundy (2001).

27. I requested numerous times to meet with and interview Chieftainess Tyali. She eventually invited me to visit with her and her council, and I gratefully accepted. I was never permitted to interview her directly, however.

28. Peires (1989b, 321).

29. See Lund and Boone (2013).

30. Hayden (quoted in Greene 2004, 229).

31. Hayden (quoted in Greene 2004, 229).

32. See Peck and Tickell (2002).

33. See Castree (2007).

34. Vandergeest and Peluso (1995).

35. Vandergeest and Peluso (1995, 388; emphasis added).

36. See Agrawal and Redford (2009) and Neumann (2015). In their highly cited review of the social science literature concerning neoliberal conservation, Jim Igoe and Dan Brockington (2007) emphasize the human displacement territorialization can engender. A section of the article about territorialization's effects on local people is titled "Exclusion and Impacts," and this section concludes with a quotation from a rural interlocutor: "'It is like you are no longer a citizen of your own country. Wherever we go we are told: you can't stay here'" (2007, 445).

37. See Dowie (2009).

38. To be clear, I do not contend that expansional processes of territorialization and belonging (what I have also termed "ethnic capture") are new or limited to the context I explore in this book. Anthropologists have long described how precolonial African polities were often expansional in character, incorporating and subjecting new members to grow their "wealth in people" (see, e.g., Miers and Kopytoff 1977). More recently, Emily Yeh (2013) has detailed Chinese state-run programs of territorialization in Tibet from the 1950s to the 2000s.

39. The argument brings to mind a long-running discussion among Africanist anthropologists. The discussion concerns how systems of wealth in Europe and Africa have interreacted and changed over the past centuries and into the present (Guyer 1995). Roughly sketched, Europe is a historical context in which contests over capital and political power hinged on the control of land, which was a limited resource. Such contests in precolonial African settings were different. Land was plentiful. Subjects (as followers and laborers) were more difficult to pin down, however. After all, James Ferguson argues, these "were strikingly dynamic and open social systems, characterized by very high levels of mobility and a profusion of exit options" (2013, 226). Political elites consequently maintained and expanded their powers by controlling their "wealth in people," to use Suzanne Miers and Igor Kopytoff's (1977) terminology. The picture is an overly simplified one, as scholars readily admit. But it is heuristically valuable; it helps us talk about sociopolitical relationality and how variables involved in the accumulation of power articulate(d) with one another (Geschiere 2018). In the view of some scholars,

decades of market liberalization have propelled a shift away from previous patterns; wealth-in-things has come to replace "wealth-in-people" in contemporary Africa. But as anthropologist Peter Geschiere stressed to me in a personal communication, we should remain open to surprises when examining a contingent and historically shifting range of possibilities. In fact, as historian Sara Berry has shown, connections between "wealth-in-people" and wealth-in-things have also intensified in places where free-market conditions dominate (2013).

INTERLUDE: "THE DOOM OF 150,000 PEOPLE" (1915–1953)

1. Newsom (2002).
2. English Physician (1931, 9–10; emphasis in original).
3. Wilson (1990).
4. Daniel (2006).
5. Bryder (1988).
6. Worboys (1992).
7. *Lancet* (1905b).
8. Wilson (1912, 37).
9. Worboys (1992, 62–63).
10. Worboys (1992, 55).
11. Bynum (2012).
12. Bryder (1988).
13. English Physician (1931, 22–23; emphasis added).
14. Stevens (1912, 21).
15. Sechehaye (1930, 19–20).
16. The two case studies come from a report from the Committee of Investigation on Treatments of Tuberculosis, dated February 27, 1936, Wellcome Collection SA/BMA/C363.
17. Newsom (2002, 466).

CHAPTER 4: WAITING

1. See Bayart (2007), Jeffrey (2010), and Janeja and Bandak (2018).
2. See Walker (2011).
3. Hornby et al. (2017).
4. See Peires (1989b).
5. Peires (1989b).
6. Dold and Cocks (2012) and Peires (1989b).
7. Peires (1989b, 321).

8. Peires (1989b).
9. Peires (1989b, 4).
10. Smith (2011).
11. Navaro et al. (2021).
12. See Smith (2011).
13. Bolt and Rajak (2016, 806).
14. Smith (2015, 4).
15. Guyer (2007, 416-17).
16. For example, according to Kingwill's research, over a period of five months in 1997, the residents sold over $8,000 worth of livestock on the local market.
17. In the words of Tara Weinberg (2021, 218), CPAs were "devised to provide land claimants with official legal recognition of their land rights as a group—in the form of title deeds in the name of the CPA."
18. If the CPAs and chiefs were at loggerheads, then Gumbi had reluctantly found himself at the epicenter of the conflict. In his role as registrar, he faced intimidation to the degree that, for a period, he required a security escort (Weinberg 2021). Sociologist Sonwabile Mnwana (2021) details the story and reveals the kinds of tensions and stakes faced by CPAs in former homeland regions. In 2005 a group of rural people established a CPA in what was previously a homeland but is now an area of North West Province. During apartheid, the people had been forcibly moved from their homes. They successfully lodged a restitution claim to seven farms they had lost. However, after a local chieftaincy protested the CPA's formation, the then national land affairs office elected to register the CPA as "provisional" rather than permanent. The move proved consequential. In the years that soon followed, the chieftaincy entered royalty-sharing agreements with mining companies to extract platinum from land that included portions under the management of the CPA. Making matters worse, the chieftaincy allegedly hoarded the royalties. Around 2008, the then minister of agriculture and land affairs directed Sithe Gumbi to deregister the provisional CPA. When Gumbi refused, he received threats. It was at this time that he received a security detail. But the story was not over. On the grounds that the CPA was only temporary, the chieftaincy then sought in 2012 to transfer a portion of the contested land to a commercial developer (who intended to build a shopping mall). The CPA took the matter to the courts, and a series of difficult legal contests ensued. Eventually, in what Mnwana (2021, 74) calls "a landmark judgment" for communal landholding institutions in South Africa, the Constitutional Court rejected the chieftaincy's claims to the land and ordered that the CPA be permanently registered.
19. See Beinart, Delius, and Hay (2017).
20. Hall (2015).
21. Hall (2015, 140).
22. Hall (2015).

23. Cocks, Dold, and Vetter (2012, 1).

24. Minister Nkwinti was correct when he said that chiefs were not alone in taking issue with CPAs. As I have suggested previously, some scholars have noted how CPAs threaten to sever long-standing social ties between groups, excluding those unable to secure land of their own (see Weinberg 2021). Others question the assumption that extending the system of title deeds to the third of the population who live in "communal areas" under chiefs will resolve problems of tenure insecurity. Nevertheless, members of the Masakhane and Iqayiyalethu CPAs insisted that title deeds would be their best means of transforming their circumstances. Their position was sensible; as Hornby et al. (2017, 390) argue, "the benefits of private ownership through a deeds registration system lie partly in its strong linkages to the cadastre, the financial system (bonds, credit, public development financing), spatial planning, and the land use management system)." The CPAs continued to be denied any such benefits. In fact, in 2011 they wrote a letter to the Eastern Cape director of the DRDLR stating that their relationship with the provincial official servicing their case had "irretrievably broken down." The official had ceased communication, leaving the plans for capitalization funds stalled. Farm infrastructure had "broken down," and former lessees continued to graze large numbers of cattle on the land without permission.

INTERLUDE: THE RED LIST (1920–2024)

1. Report to British Medical Association from the Committee of the Investigation on Treatments of Tuberculosis, February 27, 1936, Wellcome Collection SA/BMA/C363.

2. Correspondence between G. Russell Chapman, General Secretary of the British Advertising Agency, and Alfred Cox, Medical Secretary of the British Medical Association, June 4, 1931, Wellcome Collection SA/BMA/C362. Note that the British Pharmacy and Medical Act of 1941 included a clause prohibiting advertisements relating to tuberculosis and other disease.

3. Correspondence between G. Russell Chapman, General Secretary of the Advertising Association, and G. C. Anderson of the British Medical Association, October 18, 1933, Wellcome Collection SA/BMA/C362.

4. Correspondence between G. Russell Chapman, General Secretary of the British Advertising Agency, and Alfred Cox, Medical Secretary of the British Medical Association, June 4, 1931, Wellcome Collection SA/BMA/C362.

5. Correspondence between Alfred Cox, Medical Secretary of the British Medical Association, and G. Russell Chapman, General Secretary of the Advertising Association, June 9, 1931, Wellcome Collection SA/BMA/C362.

6. Wellcome Collection SA/BMA/C366.

7. Bladt (1974).
8. Brendler and van Wyk (2008).

CHAPTER 5: ROYAL PHARMACEUTICALS

1. Phillips and Chipkin (2014).
2. Stoler (2016).
3. Phillips and Chipkin (2014).
4. See De Wet and Leibbrandt (1994, 159).
5. Jensen and Zenker (2015, 944).
6. Peires (1989a, 395).
7. See White (2015).
8. This meeting was conducted in both English and isiXhosa.
9. Gollin (1993, 191).
10. Hayden (2003a, 52).
11. UN Secretariat of the Convention on Biological Diversity (2010), 2.
12. Hayden (2003a) and Hirsh (2010).
13. Hayden (2003a, 65).
14. Comaroff and Comaroff (2009), Greene (2004), and Posey (1996).
15. Hodgson (2002, 1042).
16. Pelican (2009, 52). See also Igoe (2006), Kuper (2003), and Robins (2008).
17. Peters (quoted in Li 2010, 404–5).
18. Chennells (2013, 166).
19. Department of Environmental Affairs (2012, 51). The ABS provisions of South Africa's National Environmental Management: Biodiversity Act of 2004 outline the country's obligations to the CBD. In 2008 the DEA gave effect to these provisions through the Bioprospecting Access and Benefit Sharing (BABS) regulations. South Africa ratified the Nagoya Protocol in January 2013.
20. Greene (2004, 222).
21. Castree (quoted in Greene 2004, 227).
22. Hayden (quoted in Greene 2004, 229).
23. Coombe (2005).
24. Van Niekerk and Wynberg (2012, 541).
25. Taylor and Wynberg (2008).
26. Van Niekerk and Wynberg (2012).
27. Goldstein (2007).
28. Lund and Boone (2013, 4).
29. Claassens (2014).
30. Cooper (2002, 157).
31. Castree (quoted in Greene 2004, 227).
32. Castree (quoted in Greene 2004, 227).

33. Englund (2006, 47).
34. Ntsebeza (2005).
35. Oomen (2005, 115).
36. Koelble and LiPuma (2011).
37. Cook and Hardin (2013).
38. Cook and Hardin (2013, 228).
39. Koelble and LiPuma (2011, 6).
40. As far as directing use of royalties, Mavuso expressed enthusiasm for programs addressing hunger (soup kitchens specifically) and childhood education (he and his wife had already initiated such a program at a local elementary school).
41. Nhlapo Commission on Traditional Leadership Disputes and Claims (2010).
42. Prince (2012).
43. Comaroff and Comaroff (2009).
44. The label for Ukhohlokhohlo indicates that the medicine be used "for the infections of upper respiratory tract, ears, nose and throat." But at least one traditional leader I interviewed in 2011 was selling the product as a therapy for tuberculosis and HIV—diseases for which the medicine has never been clinically assessed.
45. See Brown (2003) and Sylvain (2005).
46. Crais (2011).
47. Claassens (2014). These laws include the Traditional Leadership and Governance Framework of 2003, the Communal Land Rights Act of 2004, and a variety of provincial regulations enacted pursuant to the national Framework Act and the Traditional Courts Bill of 2012.
48. Peires (1989a).
49. Peires (1989a).
50. Peires (1989a).
51. Hayden (quoted in Greene 2004, 229).
52. See for example Nelson and Agrawal (2008); Fabricius et al. (2004); and Benjaminsen, Cousins, and Thompson (2002).
53. Ribot (2003).
54. Cousins and Kepe (2004).
55. Murphree (1999).
56. Moore (1998). See also Maré (1993).
57. Claassens (2014, 762).
58. Claassens (2014, 769).
59. See Bennett, Ainslie, and Davis (2013).
60. Bennett, Ainslie, and Davis (2013, 35).
61. Fay (2008, 179).
62. See Wotshela (2004). In 1980, one year before the Ciskei was declared an independent state, the Thembu Tribal Authority was created. To serve as chief of this authority, President Sebe installed his brother-in-law, Simon Hebe, a

man who "was not from a chiefly family and knew little about the role of a chief" (Mager and Velelo 2018, 161). Hebe used his position to secure state funds and build a significant patronage network—one that saw nonfollowers denied sites for residential or agricultural development (Wotshela 2004). Opposition to Hebe grew, but Sebe mostly curtailed it via threats and actual violence (one opponent was arrested and beaten). After Brigadier Oupa Gqozo ousted Sebe and became president, Simon Hebe's chieftaincy was invalidated but just as quickly reinstated with the assistance of King Mxolisi Sandile. Simon Hebe died in 1999, but a struggle over legitimacy continued for his son and successor, Viwe Hebe (Mager and Velelo 2018). Hebe was eventually investigated by the Mndende Commission, which in 2013 ruled that someone else was the rightful chief.

63. See Mager and Velelo (2018).
64. Mager and Velelo (2018).
65. Law, Race, and Gender Research Unit (2010).
66. Mkentane (2020).
67. Comaroff and Comaroff (2009, 111).
68. Claassens (2014, 769).
69. Westaway (2012, 116).
70. Bank and Mabhena (2011).
71. Mager and Velelo (2018).
72. Van Kessel and Oomen (1997).
73. Marais (2011).
74. Crais (2011). I stress that the ANC is far from monolithic and is characterized by competition and significant internal divisions over a range of issues (Hoeane 2011), including the powers of traditional leaders.
75. Appadurai (1988) and Gupta and Ferguson (1992); Fabian (1983); and Ferguson (1992).
76. Williams (1973).
77. Ferguson (1992).
78. Gupta and Ferguson (1992, 7).
79. Lund (2016, 1209).
80. See Guyer (2004).
81. Claassens (2013) and Robins (2008).
82. Ives (2014, 700).

CONCLUSION

1. Cook (2007).
2. Griffin (2020). At the same time, the Native Americans whose knowledge formed the basis of ideas about the tree's medicinal uses perished from colonial violence and the virgin-soil epidemics it wrought.

3. See Schiebinger and Swan (2005) and Cañizares-Esguerra (2018).
4. Laird et al. (2020).
5. Laird et al. (2020, 1201).
6. IPBES (2019).
7. See Wynberg (2023).
8. See Robinson (2010).
9. Masinjila, Lewis, and Mayet (2022).
10. Department of Forestry, Fisheries, and the Environment (2023).
11. Department of Forestry, Fisheries, and the Environment (2023, 19).
12. Department of Forestry, Fisheries, and the Environment (2023, 36–37).
13. The effort to link them arguably resonates with McKusker, Moseley, and Ramutsindela's (2015, 104) observations on the lingering "spatial hegemonies" of apartheid: "The spatial legacy of apartheid continues to linger in the imagination for a democratic dispensation."
14. Wynberg (2023, 11; emphasis added).
15. Wynberg (2017b, 306).
16. Some observers will undoubtedly suggest that the situation calls for biocultural community protocols, an instrument I have not discussed as it was never implemented in the context of pelargonium. See Bavikatte, Robinson, and Oliva (2015) for a discussion of such protocols. For an analysis of their relative strengths and weaknesses, see Rutert (2020).
17. Berliner, Clarke, and McGregor (2020).
18. Kingwill (2018).
19. See Wynberg (2017a).
20. Hendriks (2022).
21. See Smith (2015).
22. Gómez-Barris (2017).
23. My use of "archive" borrows from Fairhead and Leach and their vivid language describing socionatures shaped by colonial ruination (2019).
24. See Besky and Padwe (2016).
25. See Sassen (2006, 415).
26. See Hendriks (2022).
27. See Tsing (2013).
28. Lund (2016).
29. Lund and Boone (2013).
30. Lund and Boone (2013, 6).
31. Lund (2016).
32. I thank Sara Berry for making me see this point.
33. Geschiere (2009) and Mbembe (2001).
34. Englund and Nyamnjoh (2004), Goodale and Merry (2007), and Robins (2008).
35. Englund (2006).

36. Englund (2006, 32).
37. Tsing (2005).
38. See also Badiou (2001), Brown (2006), and Povinelli (2002).
39. Obarrio (2014).
40. Von Benda-Beckman, Von Benda-Beckmann, and Eckert (2009).
41. Geschiere (2009, 1). See also Li (2007a).

References

African Center for Biosafety (ACB). 2008. "Knowledge Not for Sale: Umckaloabo and the Pelargonium Patent Challenges." Briefing paper, African Center for Biosafety, Johannesburg.
———. 2010a. "Biopiracy under Fire: The *Pelargonium* Patent Hearing." Briefing paper, African Centre for Biosafety, Johannesburg.
———. 2010b. "Joy as Pelargonium Patent Revoked." January 26. https://acbio.org.za/gm-biosafety/joy-pelargonium-patent-revoked/.
———. 2010c. "Major Breakthrough in the Fight against Biopiracy: Pelargonium Patents." March 26. https://biosafetyafrica.org.za/index.php/20100426305/Major-breakthrough-in-the-fight-against-biopiracy-Pelargonium-patents/menu-id-100029.html.
———. 2010d. "Submission On: Intellectual Property Laws Amendment Bill." October 18. https://static.pmg.org.za/docs/101020biosafety_0.pdf.
———. 2011. "Objections and Comments to the Biodiversity Management Plan for *Pelargonium sidoides*." Briefing paper, African Centre for Biosafety, Johannesburg.
Agrawal, Arun, and Kent Redford. 2009. "Place, Conservation, and Displacement." *Conservation and Society* 7 (1): 56–58.
Anders, Gerhard. 2009. *In the Shadow of Good Governance: An Ethnography of Civil Service Reform in Africa*. Leiden: Brill.

André, Georgina, and Victoria Baux, dirs. 2011. *Pelargonium, Trading Traditional Knowledge*. www.youtube.com/watch?v=r_rMsVovjto&list=PL7QRO aqdavIEHECooCJwdy430HeKCon65&index=2.
Anonymous. 1912. *Medical Evidence Given in the Consumption Cure Libel Action: Stevens v. The British Medical Association*. London: n.p.
Anonymous. 1931a. *Tuberculosis—Its Treatment and Cure with the Help of Umckaloabo*. London: B. Fraser.
Anonymous. 1931b. *The Doom of 150000 People*. London: Reason Publishing.
Appadurai, Arjun. 1988. "Putting Hierarchy in Its Place." *Cultural Anthropology* 3 (1): 36–49.
Asad, Talal, ed. 1973. *Anthropology and the Colonial Encounter*. Reading: Ithaca Press.
Badiou, Alain. 2001. *Ethics: An Essay on the Understanding of Evil*. London: Verso.
Bagley, Margo. 2017. "De-Materializing Genetic Resources: Synthetic Biology, Intellectual Property, and the ABS Bypass." In *Routledge Handbook of Biodiversity and the Law*, edited by Charles R. McManis and Burton Ong, 219–36. New York: Routledge.
Bank, Leslie, and Clifford Mabhena. 2011. "Bring Back Kaiser Matanzima? Communal Land, Traditional Leaders, and the Politics of Nostalgia." In *New South Africa Review*, vol. 2, edited by John Daniel, Prishani Naidoo, Devan Pillay, and Roger Southall, 119–41. Johannesburg: Wits University Press.
Barchiesi, Franco. 2011. *Precarious Liberation: Workers, the State, and Contested Social Citizenship in Postapartheid South Africa*. Albany: State University of New York Press.
Baschin, Marion. 2014. "'Globules at Home': The History of Homeopathic Self-medication." *Social History of Medicine* 29 (4): 717–33.
Bavikatte, Kabir, Daniel Robinson, and Maria Julia Oliva. 2015. "Biocultural Community Protocols: Dialogues on the Space Within." *IK: Other Ways of Knowing* 1 (2): 1–31.
Bayart, Jean-Francois. 2007. *Global Subjects: A Political Critique of Globalization*. Cambridge, UK: Polity Press.
Bear, Laura, Karen Ho, Anna Lowenhaupt Tsing, and Sylvia Yanagisako. 2015. "Gens: A Feminist Manifesto for the Study of Capitalism." Theorizing the Contemporary, *Fieldsights*, March 30. https://culanth.org/fieldsights/gens-a-feminist-manifesto-for-the-study-of-capitalism.
Beinart, William. 2012. "Beyond Homelands: Some Ideas about the History of the African Rural Areas in South Africa." *South African Historical Journal* 64 (1): 5–21.
Beinart, William, Peter Delius, and Michelle Hay. 2017. *Rights to Land: A Guide to Tenure Upgrading and Restitution in South Africa*. Auckland Park: Jacana.

Beinart, William, Rosalie Kingwill, and Gavin Capps. 2021. *Land, Law, and Chiefs in Rural South Africa: Contested Histories and Current Struggles*. Johannesburg: Wits University Press.

Beinart, William, and Luvoyo Wotshela. 2011. *Prickly Pear: The Social History of a Plant in the Eastern Cape*. Johannesburg: Wits University Press.

Benjaminsen, Tor Arve, Ben Cousins, and Lisa Thompson, eds. 2002. *Contested Resources: Challenges to the Governance on Natural Resources in Southern Africa*. Cape Town: PLAAS.

Bennett, James, Andrew Ainslie, and John Davis. 2013. "Contested Institutions? Traditional Leaders and Land Access and Control in Communal Areas of Eastern Cape Province, South Africa." *Land Use Policy* 32: 27–38.

Bergh, J. S., and J. C. Visagie. 1985. *The Eastern Cape Frontier Zone 1660–1980: A Cartographical Guide for Historical Research*. Durban: Butterworths.

Berlant, Lauren. 2011. *Cruel Optimism*. Durham, NC: Duke University Press.

Berliner, Derek, Jeanette Clarke, and Gillian McGregor. 2020. "Principles for and Suitable Approach to a Long-Term National Monitoring Programme That Considers Important Indigenous Bio-Traded Species in South Africa and a Regional Resource Assessment." Draft final report prepared on behalf of LIMA, November 20.

Berry, Sarah. 2013. "Questions of Ownership: Proprietorship and Control in a Changing Rural Terrain—A Case Study from Ghana." *Africa* 83 (1): 36–56.

———. 2018. "Chieftaincy, Land, and the State in Ghana and South Africa." In *The Politics of Custom: Chiefship, Capital, and the State in Contemporary Africa*, edited by John L. Comaroff and Jean Comaroff. Chicago: University of Chicago Press.

Besky, Sarah, and Jonathan Padwe. 2016. "Placing Plants in Territory." *Environment and Society: Advances in Research* 7: 9–28

Bethge, Philip, Rafaela von Bredow, and Christian Schwägerl. 2008. "What Would It Cost to Save Nature?" *Spiegel International*, May 23, 2008. www.spiegel.de/international/world/the-price-of-survival-what-would-it-cost-to-save-nature-a-554982.html.

Biko, Steve. 1987. *I Write What I Like: A Selection of His Writings*. London: Heinemann.

Bisseker, Claire. 2002. "Biodiversity Bloom Is Off Natural Cure." *Financial Mail*, July 19, 2002.

Bladt, Sabine. 1974. "Zur Chemie der Inhaltsstoffe der Pelargonium Reniforme Curt. Wurzel (Umckaloabo)." PhD thesis, University of Munich.

Bladt, Sabine, and Hildebert Wagner. 2007. "From the Zulu Medicine to the European Phytomedicine Umckaloabo." *Phytomedicine* 14 (Suppl. 6): 2–4.

Bolt, Maxim, and Dinah Rajak. 2016. "Introduction: Labor, Insecurity and Violence in South Africa." *Journal of Southern African Studies* 42 (5): 797–813.

Boone, Catharine. *Property and Political Order in Africa: Land Rights and the Structure of Politics.* New York: Cambridge University Press.

Bourdieu, Pierre. 1981. "Men and Machines." In *Advances in Social Theory and Methodology: Toward an Integration of Micro-and Macro-Sociologies,* edited by Karin Knorr Cetina and Aaron Cicourel, 304–18. New York: Routledge.

Brendler, Thomas, and Ben-Erik van Wyk. 2008. "A Historical and Commercial Perspective on the Medicinal Use of *Pelargonium Sidoides* (Geraniaceae)." *Journal of Ethnopharmacology* 119 (3): 420–33.

British Medical Association. 1909. *Secret Remedies: What They Cost and What They Contain.* London: British Medical Association.

Brown, Michael. 2003. *Who Owns Native Culture?* Cambridge, MA: Harvard University Press.

Brown, Wendy. 2006. *Regulating Aversion: Tolerance in the Age of Identity and Empire.* Princeton, NJ: Princeton University Press.

Brummitt, Neil. A., Steven P. Bachman, Janine Griffiths-Lee, Maiko Lutz, Justin F. Moat, Aljos Farjon, Eimear M. Nic Lughadha, et al. 2015. "Green Plants in the Red: A Baseline Global Assessment for the IUCN Sampled Red List Index for Plants." *PLoS ONE* 10: e0135152.

Brush, Stephen. 2004. *Farmers' Bounty: Locating Crop Diversity in the Contemporary World.* New Haven, CT: Yale University Press.

Bryder, Linda. 1988. *Below the Magic Mountain: A Social History of Tuberculosis in Twentieth-Century Britain.* Oxford: Oxford University Press.

Bynum, Helen. 2012. *Spitting Blood: The History of Tuberculosis.* Oxford: Oxford University Press.

Cañizares-Esguerra, Jorge. 2018. *Entangled Empires: The Anglo-Iberian Atlantic, 1500–1830.* Philadelphia: University of Pennsylvania Press.

Cantero, Lucia. 2017. "Sociocultural Anthropology in 2016: In Dark Times; Hauntologies and Other Ghosts of Production." *American Anthropologist* 119 (2): 308–18.

Careddu, Domenico, and Andrea Pettenazzo. 2018. "*Pelargonium sidoides* Extract EPs 7630: A Review of Its Clinical Efficacy and Safety for Treating Acute Respiratory Tract Infections in Children." *International Journal of General Medicine* 11: 91–98. https://doi.org/10.2147/IJGM.S154198.

Castree, Noel. 2007. "Neoliberalizing Nature: The Logics of Deregulation and Reregulation." *Environment and Planning A* 40 (1): 131–52.

Chennells, Roger. 2013. "Traditional Knowledge and Benefit Sharing after the Nagoya Protocol: Three Cases from South Africa." *Law, Environment and Development Journal* 9 (2): 165–84.

Claassens, Aninka. 2013. "Recent Changes in Women's Land Rights and Contested Customary Law in South Africa." *Journal of Agrarian Change* 13 (1): 71–92.

———. 2014. "Denying Ownership and Equal Citizenship: Continuities in the State's Use of Law and 'Custom,' 1913–2013." *Journal of Southern African Studies* 40 (4): 761–79.

Claassens, Aninka, and Ben Cousins, eds. 2008. *Land, Power, and Custom: Controversies Generated by South Africa's Communal Land Rights Act*. Cape Town: University of Cape Town Press.

Cocks, Michelle. 1997. "Towards an Understanding of Amayeza Esixhosa Stores (African Chemists): How They Operate, and the Services They Offer in the Eastern Cape." MA thesis, Rhodes University.

Cocks, Michelle, Anthony Dold, and Isla Grundy. 2001. "Challenges Facing a Community Structure to Implement CBNRM in the Eastern Cape, South Africa." *African Studies Quarterly* 5 (3): 57–71.

Cocks, Michelle, Tony Dold, and Susi Vetter. 2012. "'God Is My Forest': Xhosa Cultural Values Provide Untapped Opportunities for Conservation." *South African Journal of Science* 108 (5/6): 1–8.

Comaroff, John L., and Jean Comaroff. 2009. *Ethnicity, Inc*. Scottsville: University of KwaZulu-Natal Press.

———. 2018. *The Politics of Custom: Chiefship, Capital, and the State in Contemporary Africa*. Chicago: University of Chicago Press.

Cook, Harold J. 2007. *Matters of Exchange: Commerce, Medicine, and Science in the Dutch Golden Age*. New Haven, CT: Yale University Press.

Cook, Susan. 2011. "The Business of Being Bafokeng: Corporatization in a Tribal Authority in South Africa." *Current Anthropology* 52 (S3): S151–59.

Cook, Susan, and Rebecca Hardin. 2013. "Performing Royalty in Contemporary South Africa." *Cultural Anthropology* 28 (2): 227–51.

Coombe, Rosemary. 1998. *The Cultural Life of Intellectual Properties: Authorship, Appropriation, and the Law*. Durham, NC: Duke University Press.

———. 2005. "Legal Claims to Culture in and against the Market: Neoliberalism and the Global Proliferation of Meaningful Difference." *Law, Culture and the Humanities* 1 (1): 35–52.

———. 2016. "The Knowledge Economy and Its Cultures: Neoliberal Technologies and Latin American Reterritorializations." *Hau: Journal of Ethnographic Theory* 6 (3): 247–75.

———. 2017. "Frontiers of Cultural Property in the Global South." In *Routledge Companion to Cultural Property*, edited by Haidy Geismar and Jane Anderson, 373–400. New York: Routledge.

Cooper, Frederick. 2002. *Africa since 1940: The Past of the Present*. Cambridge: Cambridge University Press.

Cooper, Melinda. 2008. *Life as Surplus: Biotechnology and Capitalism in the Neoliberal Era*. Seattle: University of Washington Press.

Cousins, Ben. 2008. "Contextualising the Controversies: Dilemmas of Communal Tenure Reform in Post-Apartheid South Africa." In *Land, Power, and Custom:*

Controversies Generated by South Africa's Communal Land Rights Act, 3–31. Cape Town: University of Cape Town Press.

Cousins, Ben, and Thembela Kepe. 2004. "Decentralization When Land and Resource Rights Are Deeply Contested: A Case Study of the Mkambati Eco-Tourism Project on the Wild Coast of South Africa." *European Journal of Development Research* 16 (1): 41–54.

Cousins, Steven R., and Ed T. F. Witkowski. 2017. "African Cycad Ecology, Ethnobotany and Conservation: A Synthesis." *Botanical Review* 83 (2): 152–94.

Cowie, Robert, Phillipe Bouchet, and Benoît Fontaine. 2022. "The Sixth Mass Extinction: Fact, Fiction, or Speculation?" *Biological Reviews* 97: 640–63.

Crais, Clifton. 2011. *Poverty, War, and Violence in South Africa*. New York: Cambridge University Press.

Crouch, Neil, Errol Douwes, Maureen M. Wolfson, Gideon F. Smith, and Trevor J. Edwards. 2008. "South Africa's Bioprospecting, Access and Benefit-Sharing Legislation: Current Realities, Future Complications, and a Proposed Alternative." *South African Journal of Science* 104 (9–10): 355–66.

Crouch, Neil, and Maureen Wolfson. 2009. "Complying with South African Bioprospecting Legislation: The Case of the *Pelargonium* Phytomedicines Industry." In *Plants People and Nature: Benefit Sharing in Practice*, edited by Denzil Phillips. Port Louis: AAMPS Publishing.

Daniel, Thomas. 2006. "The History of Tuberculosis." *Respiratory Medicine* 100 (11): 1862–70.

Davis, Colin. 2005. "Hauntology, Spectres and Phantoms." *French Studies* 59 (3): 373–79.

de Castro, Antonio, Jan Vlok, and W. McLellan. 2010. "Field Survey of the Distribution of *Pelargonium sidoides* and Size of Selected Sub-Populations." Resource Assessment Study Conducted for the South African National Biodiversity Institute (SANBI).

de Wet, Chris, and Murray Leibbrandt. 1994. "Separate Developments: The Different Effect of Homeland Policy on Two Ciskei Villages." *Development Southern Africa*, 11 (2): 159–76.

Delius, Peter. 2008. "Contested Terrain: Land Rights and Chiefly Power in Historical Perspective." In *Land, Power and Custom: Controversies Generated by South Africa's Communal Land Rights Act*, edited by Aninka Claassens and Ben Cousins, 211–37. Cape Town: University of Cape Town Press.

Department of Environmental Affairs. 2012. "South Africa's Bioprospecting, Access and Benefit-Sharing Regulatory Framework: Guidelines for Providers, Users and Regulators." www.dffe.gov.za/sites/default/files/legislations/bioprospecting_regulatory_framework_guideline.pdf.

Department of Forestry, Fisheries and the Environment. 2023. "White Paper on the Conservation and Sustainable Use of South Africa's Biodiversity as

Approved by Cabinet." www.environment.gov.za/sites/default/files/docs/sa biodiversity2023whitepaper.pdf.

Department of Science and Technology (DST). 2007. "Innovation Towards a Knowledge-Based Economy: Ten-Year Plan for South Africa (2008–2018)." https://pmg.org.za/policy-document/169/.

Derrida, Jacques. 2006. *Specters of Marx: The State of the Debt, the Work of Mourning, and the New International*. New York: Routledge.

Descola, Phillipe. 2014. *Beyond Nature and Culture*. Chicago: University of Chicago Press.

Desmond, Cosmas. 1971. *The Discarded People: An Account of African Resettlement in South Africa*. New York: Penguin.

Deutsche Welle. 2010. "EU Patent Ruling on German Drug Highlights Biopiracy Debate." January 27. www.dw.com/en/eu-patent-ruling-on-german-drug-highlights-biopiracy-debate/a-5174318.

Dlamini, Jacob. 2009. *Native Nostalgia*. Auckland Park: Jacana.

Dold, A. P. 2009. "Traditional Use of Pelargonium sidoides in the Eastern Cape." Presented at TRAFFIC/SANBI Workshop: Management Plan for *Pelargonium sidoides*. Grahamstown, South Africa, February 3.

Dold, Tony, and Michelle Cocks. 2012. *Voices from the Forest: Celebrating Nature and Culture in Xhosaland*. Auckland Park: Jacana.

Dolder, Fritz. 2008. "Traditional Knowledge and Patenting: The Experience of the Neemfungicide and the Hoodia Cases." *Biotechnology Law Report* 26 (6): 583–90.

Dowie, Mark. 2009. *Conservation Refugees: The Hundred-Year Conflict between Global Conservation and Native Peoples*. Cambridge, MA: MIT Press.

Drahos, Peter, and John Braithwaite. 2002. *Information Feudalism: Who Owns the Knowledge Economy?* London: Earthscan Publicans.

Dutfield, Graham, Rachel Wynberg, Sarah Laird, and Sarah Ives. 2020. "Benefit Sharing and Traditional Knowledge: Unsolved Dilemmas for Implementation." Voices for Biojustice Policy Brief. www.voices4biojustice.org/wp-content/uploads/2017/12/Traditional-Knowledge-Policy-Brief-1.pdf.

Eastern Cape Department of Economic Development, Environmental Affairs, and Tourism. 2014. *The Eastern Cape Socio-Economic Review and Outlook*.

Eastern Cape Department of Environmental Affairs and Tourism. 2004. *State of the Environment Report*. https://soer.environment.gov.za/soer/Upload LibraryImages/UploadDocuments/170318070512_ECape_full_report_sKnNF.pdf.

English Physician, An. 1931. *Tuberculosis: Its Treatment and Cure with the Help of Umckaloabo (Stevens)*. London: B. Fraser.

Englund, Harri. 2006. *Prisoners of Freedom: Human Rights and the African Poor*. Berkeley: University of California Press.

Englund, Harri, and Francis Nyamnjoh. 2004. *Rights and the Politics of Recognition in Africa*. London: Zed Books.

Escobar, Arturo. 2008. *Territories of Difference: Place, Movements, Life, Redes*. Durham, NC: Duke University Press.

European Medicines Agency. 2011. *Assessment Report on* Pelargonium Sidoides DC *and/or* Pelargonium Reniforme. March 31. www.ema.europa.eu/en /documents/herbal-report/superseded-assessment-report-pelargonium -sidoides-dc-andor-pelargonium-reniforme-curt-radix-first-version_en.pdf.

Evans, Laura. 2014. "Resettlement and the Making of the Ciskei Bantustan, South Africa, c. 1960–1976." *Journal of Southern African Studies* 40 (1): 21–40.

———. 2019. *Survival in the "Dumping Grounds": A Social History of Apartheid Relocation*. Leiden: Brill.

"Exposure of a Quack." 1910. *Journal of the American Medical Association* 55 (10): 872.

Fabian, Johannes. 1983. *Time and the Other: How Anthropology Makes Its Object*. New York: Columbia University Press.

Fabricius, Christo, Eddie Koch, Steven Turner, and Hector Magome, eds. 2004. *Rights, Resources and Rural Development: Community-Based Natural Resource Management in Southern Africa*. London: Earthscan.

Fairchild, Amy, and Gerald Oppenheimer. 1998. "Public Health Nihilism vs Pragmatism: History, Politics, and the Control of Tuberculosis." *American Journal of Public Health* 88 (7): 1105–17.

Fairhead, James, and Melissa Leach. 2019. "Environment and Anthropology: Socio-natures in a Politicized Anthropocene." In *Exotic No More: Anthropology for the Contemporary World*, edited by Jeremy MacClancy, 209–21. Chicago: University of Chicago Press.

Fay, Derick. 2008. "Democracy and Traditional Authorities in South Africa." *Political and Legal Anthropology Review* 31 (1): 174–80.

Feiter, Louisa. 2018. "In Pursuit of Pelargonium in the Eastern Cape." Parceval Pharmaceuticals. https://parceval.co.za/in-pursuit-of-pelargonium/.

Ferguson, James. 1992. "The Country and the City on the Copper-Belt." *Cultural Anthropology* 7 (1): 80–92.

———. 1994. *The Anti-Politics Machine: "Development," Depoliticization, and Bureaucratic Power in Lesotho*. Minneapolis: University of Minnesota Press.

———. 2013. "Declarations of Dependence: Labor, Personhood, and Welfare in Southern Africa." *Journal of the Royal Anthropological Institute* 19 (2): 223–42.

———. 2015. *Give a Man a Fish: Reflections on the New Politics of Distribution*. Durham, NC: Duke University Press.

Fisher, J. 1994. "Is the Iron Law of Oligarchy Rusting Away in the Third World?" *World Development* 22(4): 129–44.

Flint, Karen. 2008. *Healing Traditions: African Medicine, Cultural Exchange, and Competition in South Africa, 1820-1948*. Athens: Ohio University Press.

Foster, Laura. 2017. *Reinventing Hoodia: Peoples, Plants, and Patents in South Africa*. Seattle: University of Washington Press.

Foucault, Michel. 2000. "Truth and Juridical Forms." In *The Essential Works of Foucault, 1954-1984*, vol. 3, *Power*, edited by James D. Faubion, 1–89. New York: New Press.

Frein, Michael, and Hartmut Meyer. 2008. *Die Biopiraten: Milliardengeschäfte der Pharmaindustrie mit dem Bauplan der Natur*. Berlin: Econ.

Friedrich, Christoph, Ulrich Meyer, and Caroline Seyfang. 2016. "Die Firma Willmar Schwabe in der NS-Zeit." *Medizin, Gesellschaft, und Geschichte* 34: 209–40.

Gerardy, Justine. 2002. "Nine Arrests for Digging Out EC Medicinal Plant." *Daily Dispatch*, June 8, 2002.

Geschiere, Peter. 2009. *The Perils of Belonging: Autochthony, Citizenship, and Exclusion in Africa and Europe*. Chicago: University of Chicago Press.

———. 2018. "Belonging." In *Critical Terms for the Study of Africa*, edited by Guarav Desai and Adeline Masquelier, 27–39. Chicago: University of Chicago Press.

Gieryn, Thomas F. 1983. "Boundary-Work and the Demarcation of Science from Non-Science: Strains and Interests in Professional Ideologies of Scientists." *American Sociological Review* 48 (6): 781–95.

Glewwe, Paul, and Gillette Hall. 1998. "Are Some Groups More Vulnerable to Macroeconomic Shocks than Others? Hypothesis Testing Based on Panel Testing in Peru." *Journal of Development Economics* 56 (1): 181–206.

Goldstein, Donna. 2003. *Laughter Out of Place: Race, Class, Violence, and Sexuality in a Rio Shantytown*. Berkeley: University of California Press.

———. 2007. "Life or Profit? Structural Violence, Moral Psychology, and Pharmaceutical Politics." *Anthropology in Action* 14 (3): 44–58.

Gollin, Michael. 1993. "An Intellectual Property Rights Framework for Biodiversity Prospecting." In *Biodiversity Prospecting: Using Genetic Resources for Sustainable Development*, edited by Walter A. Reid, Sarah A. Laird, Carrie A. Meyer, Rodrigo Gomez, Ana Sittenfeld, Daniel H. Janzen, Michael A. Gollin, and Calestous Juma, 159–97. Washington, DC: World Resources Institute.

Gómez-Barris, Macarena. 2017. *The Extractive Zone: Social Ecologies and Decolonial Perspectives*. Durham, NC: Duke University Press.

Goodale, Mark. 2017. *Anthropology and the Law: A Critical Introduction*. New York: NYU Press.

Goodale, Mark, and Sally Engle Merry, eds. 2007. *The Practice of Human Rights: Tracking Law between the Global and the Local*. Cambridge: Cambridge University Press.

Greene, Jeremy, Flurin Condrau, and Elizabeth Siegel Watkins, eds. 2016. *Therapeutic Revolutions: Pharmaceuticals and Social Change in the Twentieth Century*. Chicago: University of Chicago Press.

Greene, Shane. 2004. "Indigenous People Incorporated? Culture as Politics, Culture as Property in Pharmaceutical Bioprospecting." *Current Anthropology* 45 (2): 211–37.

Griffin, Clare. 2020. "Disentangling Commodity Histories: *Paume* and Sassafras in the Early Modern Global World." *Journal of Global History* 15 (1): 1–18.

Groenewald, Yolandi. 2010. "Locals Win Patent Dispute." *Mail and Guardian*, 29 January 29, 2010. https://mg.co.za/article/2010-01-29-locals-win-patent-dispute/.

Gupta, Akhil, and James Ferguson. 1992. "Beyond 'Culture': Space, Identity, and the Politics of Difference." *Cultural Anthropology* 7 (1): 6–23.

Guyer, Jane. 1995. "Wealth in People, Wealth in Things—Introduction." *Journal of African History* 36 (1): 83–90.

———. 2004. *Marginal Gains: Monetary Transactions in Atlantic Africa*. Chicago: University of Chicago Press.

———. 2007. "Prophecy and the Near Future: Thoughts on Macroeconomic, Evangelical, and Punctuated Time." *American Ethnologist* 34 (3): 409–21.

Hall, Marc. 2013. "EU Debates Biopiracy Law to Protect Indigenous People." *Guardian*, May 1, 2013.

Hall, Ruth. 2015. "Who, What, Where, How, Why? The Many Disagreements about Land Redistribution in South Africa." In *Land Divided Land Restored: Land Reform in South Africa for the 21st Century*, edited by Ben Cousins and Cherryl Walker, 127–44. Auckland Park: Jacana.

Harding, Sandra, ed. 2011. *The Postcolonial Science and Technology Studies Reader*. Durham, NC: Duke University Press.

Harvey, David. 2005. *The New Imperialism*. Oxford: Oxford University Press.

Hayden, Cori. 2003a. *When Nature Goes Public: The Making and Unmaking of Bioprospecting in Mexico*. Princeton, NJ: Princeton University Press.

———. 2003b. "From Market to Market: Bioprospecting's Idioms of Inclusion." *American Ethnologist* 30 (3): 359–71.

Hebinck, Paul, and Charlie Shackleton. 2011. *Reforming Land and Resource Use in South Africa: Impact on Livelihoods*. New York: Routledge.

Helmstädter, Axel. 1996. "Umckaloabo—Late Vindication of a Secret Remedy." *Pharmaceutical Historian* 26 (1): 2–4.

Hemmungs Wirtén, Eva 2008. *Terms of Use: Negotiating the Jungle of the Intellectual Commons*. Toronto: University of Toronto Press.

Hendriks, Thomas. 2022. *Rainforest Capitalism. Power and Masculinity in a Congolese Timber Concession*. Durham, NC: Duke University Press.

Hirsch, Eric. 2010. "Property and Persons: New Forms and Contests in the Era of Neoliberalism." *Annual Review of Anthropology* 39: 347–60.

Hodgson, Dorothy. 2002. "Introduction: Comparative Perspectives on the Indigenous Rights Movement in Africa and the Americas." *American Anthropologist* 104 (4): 1037-49.
Hoeane, Thabisi. 2011. "Political Contestation and the ANC in the Eastern Cape." In *The Fate of the Eastern Cape: History, Politics, and Social Policy*, edited by Greg Reuters, 93–101. Pietermaritzburg: University of KwaZulu-Natal Press.
Hofmann, Cornelia, and Ortun Riha. 2015. "Werbung und Zeitgeist: Die Inserate der Firma Dr. Willmar Schwabe." *Medizin, Gesellschaft, und Geschichte* 33: 247–82.
Hornby, Donna, Rosalie Kingwill, Lauren Royston, and Ben Cousins, eds. 2017. *Untitled: Securing Land Tenure in Urban and Rural South Africa*. Pietermaritzburg: University of KwaZulu-Natal Press.
Igoe, Jim. 2006. "Becoming Indigenous Peoples: Difference, Inequality, and the Globalization of East African Identity Politics." *African Affairs* 105 (419): 1–22.
Igoe, Jim, and Dan Brockington. 2007. "Neoliberal Conservation: A Brief Introduction." *Conservation and Society* 5 (4): 432–49.
Ingold, Tim. 1987. *The Appropriation of Nature: Essays on Human Ecology and Social Relations*. Iowa City: University of Iowa Press.
IPBES (Intergovernmental Science-Policy Platform on Biodiversity and Ecosystem Services). 2019. *Summary for Policymakers of the Global Assessment Report on Biodiversity and Ecosystem Services of the Intergovernmental Science-Policy Platform on Biodiversity and Ecosystem Services*. Edited by Sandra Diaz, Josef Settele, Eduardo S. Brondizio, and Hien T. Ngo. Bonn, Germany: IPBES Secretariat.
Ives, Sarah. 2014. "Farming the South African 'Bush': Ecologies of Belonging and Exclusion in Rooibos Tea." *American Ethnologist* 41 (4): 698–713.
Janeja, Manpreet K., and Andreas Bandak, eds. 2018. *Ethnographies of Waiting: Doubt, Hope, and Uncertainty*. New York: Bloomsbury.
Jeffrey, Craig. 2010. *Timepass: Youth, Class, and the Politics of Waiting in India*. Stanford, CA: Stanford University Press.
Jenkins, Martin, Anastaysia Timoshyna, and Marcus Cornthwaite. 2018. "Wild at Home: Exploring the Global Harvest, Trade and Use of Wild Plant Ingredients." www.traffic.org/site/asset s/files/9241/wild-at-home.pdf.
Jensen, Steffen, and Olaf Zenker. 2015. "Homelands as Frontiers: Apartheid's Loose Ends—An Introduction." *Journal of Southern African Studies* 41 (5): 937–52.
Keck, Tilman, Andreas Strobl, Andreas Weinhaeusel, Petra Funk, and Martin Michaelis. 2021. "Pelargonium Extract EPs 7630 in the Treatment of Human Corona Virus-Associated Acute Respiratory Tract Infections: A Secondary Subgroup-Analysis of an Open-Label, Uncontrolled Clinical Trial." *Frontiers in Pharmacology* 12 (666546). https://doi.org/10.3389/fphar.2021.666546.

Kingwill, Rosalie. 2018. "Title Deeds for All—Nice Idea Versus Complex Praxis." *Daily Maverick*, October 17, 2018.

Koch, Robert. 1890. "Über Bakteriologische Forschung." Verhandlungen des X Internationalen Medizinischen Kongresses, Berlin, Germany.

Koelble, Thomas, and Edward LiPuma. 2011. "Traditional Leaders and the Culture of Governance in South Africa." *Governance: An International Journal of Policy, Administration, and Institutions* 24 (1): 5–29.

Koyama, Michelle M. 2008. "Marine Bioprospecting: Key Challenges and the Situation in South Africa." Briefing paper, African Centre for Biosafety, Johannesburg.

Kuper, Adam. 2003. "The Return of the Native." *Current Anthropology* 44 (3): 389–402.

Laird, Sarah, and Rachel Wynberg. 2013. *Bioscience at a Crossroads: Access and Benefit Sharing in a Time of Scientific, Technological and Industry Change: Botanicals*. Montreal: Secretariat of the Convention on Biological Diversity.

———. 2021. "Connecting the Dots: Biodiversity Conservation, Sustainable Use and Access and Benefit Sharing." BioInnovation Africa, University of Cape Town. https://bio-economy.org.za/wp-content/uploads/2021/08/Laird-and-Wynberg-2021-Connecting-the-Dots.pdf.

Laird, Sarah, Rachel Wynberg, Michelle Rourke, Fran Humphries, Manuel Ruiz Muller, and Charles Lawson. 2020. "Rethink the Expansion of Access and Benefit Sharing." *Science* 367 (6483): 1200–1202.

Lancet. 1905a. "The Latest Quackery." July 22, 1905, 264.

Lancet. 1905b. "The Prevention of Tuberculosis in Trinidad." August 26, 1905, 640.

Lancet. 1905c. "Sacco." August 26, 1905, 640.

Laplant, Julie. 2015. *Healing Roots: Anthropology in Life and Medicine*. New York: Berghahn Books.

Law, Race, and Gender Research Unit. 2010. "Thembani: Headman in a Township?" July. https://open.uct.ac.za/bitstream/handle/11427/2456/CLS_newsletters_Law_Custom_and_Rights_2010-07.pdf?sequence=1&isAllowed=y.

Levine, Susan. 2012. "Testing Knowledge: Legitimacy, Healing, and Medicine in South Africa." In *Medicine and the Politics of Knowledge*, edited by Susan Levine, 55–76. Cape Town: HSRC Press.

Li, Tania Murray. 2007a. "Practices of Assemblage and Community Forest Management." *Economy and Society* 36 (2): 264–94.

———. 2007b. *The Will to Improve: Governmentality, Development, and the Practice of Politics*. Durham, NC: Duke University Press.

———. 2010. "Indigeneity, Capitalism, and the Management of Dispossession." *Current Anthropology* 51 (3): 385–414.

Lis-Balchin, Maria. 2002. "History of Nomenclature, Usage and Cultivation of *Geranium* and *Pelargonium* Species." In *Geranium and Pelargonium*:

History of Nomenclature, Usage and Cultivation, edited by Maria Lis-Balchin, 5–10. London: CRC Press.

Lock, Margaret, and Vinh-Kim Nguyen. 2018. *An Anthropology of Biomedicine*. Malden, MA: Wiley-Blackwell.

Lodge, Tom. 2003. *Politics in South Africa: From Mandela to Mbeki*. Bloomington: Indiana University Press.

Lund, Christian. 2016. "Rule and Rupture: State Formation through the Production of Property and Citizenship." *Development and Change* 47 (6): 1199–1228.

Lund, Christian, and Catherine Boone. 2013. "Introduction: Land Politics in Africa—Constituting Authority over Territory, Property, and Persons." *Africa* 83 (1): 1–13.

Luxemburg, Rosa. 2003. *The Accumulation of Capital*. New York: Routledge.

Mager, Anne. 1995. "Patriarchs, Politics, and Ethnicity in the Making of the Ciskei, 1945–1959." *African Studies* 54 (1): 47–72.

Mager, Anne, and Phiko Velelo. 2018. *The House of Tshatshu: Power, Politics, and Chiefs in the North-West of the Great Kei River c 1818–2018*. Cape Town: University of Cape Town Press.

Mains, Daniel. 2007. "Neoliberal Times: Progress, Boredom, and Shame among Young Men in Urban Ethiopia." *American Ethnologist* 34 (4): 659–73.

Manning, Erin. 2016. *The Minor Gesture*. Durham, NC: Duke University Press.

Manona, Cecil. 1980. "Ethnic Relations in the Ciskei." In *Ciskei: A South African Homeland*, edited by Nancy Charton, 97–121. London: Croom Helm.

Manson, Andrew. 2013. "Mining and 'Traditional Communities' in South Africa's 'Platinum Belt': Contestations over Land, Leadership and Assets in North-West Province c. 1996–2012." *Journal of Southern African Studies* 39 (2): 409–23.

Marais, Hein. 2011. *South Africa Pushed to the Limit: The Political Economy of Change*. Claremont: University of Cape Town Press.

Marcus, George. 2003. "The Unbearable Slowness of Being an Anthropologist Now: Notes on a Contemporary Anxiety in the Making of Ethnography." *Xcp: Cross-Cultural Poetics* 12: 7–20.

Maré, Gerhard. 1993. *Ethnicity and Politics in South Africa*. London: Zed Books.

Margulies, Jared, Leigh-Anne Bullough, Amy Hinsley, Daniel Ingram, Carly Cowell, Bárbara Goettsch, et al. 2019. "Illegal Wildlife Trade and the Persistence of 'Plant Blindness.'" *Plants People Planet* 1 (3): 173–82.

Marx, Karl. 1977. *Capital: A Critique of Political Economy*. New York: Vintage.

Masco, Joseph. 2002. "Lie Detectors: On Secrets and Hypersecurity in Los Alamos." *Public Culture* 14 (3): 441–67.

Masinjila, Sabrina, Linzi Lewis, and Mariam Mayet. 2022. "Playing Chess with the World's Biodiversity: The Post-2020 Global Biodiversity Framework and Africa's Future." https://acbio.org.za/corporate-expansion/playing-chess

-with-the-worlds-biodiversity-new-gambit-needed-to-avoid-a-stalemate-for-the-post-2020-global-biodiversity-framework-and-africas-future/.

Mazzarella, William. 2003. *Shoveling Smoke: Advertising and Globalization in Contemporary India*. Durham, NC: Duke University Press.

———. 2004. "Culture, Globalization, Mediation." *Annual Review of Anthropology* 33: 345–67.

Mayor, Susan. 2011. "Tree That Provides Paclitaxel Is Put on List of Endangered Species." *BMJ* 343: d7411.

Mbembe, Achille. 2001. *On the Postcolony*. Berkeley: University of California Press.

McCusker, Brent, William G. Moseley, and Maano Ramutsindela. 2015. *Land Reform in South Africa: An Uneven Transformation*. Lanham, MD: Rowman & Littlefield.

McKune, Craig. 2010. "Ground-Breaking Victory for Community against Drug Giant." *Cape Times*, January 28, 2010.

Meiu, George Paul. 2019. "Who Are the New Natives? Ethnicity and Emerging Idioms of Belonging in Africa." In *A Companion to the Anthropology of Africa*, edited by Roy Richard Grinker, Stephen C. Lubkemann, Christopher B. Steiner, and Euclides Gonçalves, 147–72. Malden, MA: Wiley-Blackwell.

Mertz, Elizabeth. 1994. "A New Social Constructionism for Sociolegal Studies." *Law and Society Review* 28: 1243–65.

Mgbeoji, Ikechi. 2006. *Global Biopiracy: Patents, Plants, and Indigenous Knowledge*. Ithaca, NY: Cornell University Press.

Miers, Suzanne, and Igor Kopytoff, eds. 1977. *Slavery in Africa: Historical and Anthropological Perspectives*. Madison: University of Wisconsin Press.

Miller, Diana M. 2002. "The Taxonomy of *Pelargonium* Species and Cultivars, Their Origins and Growth in the Wild." In *Geranium and Pelargonium: History of Nomenclature, Usage and Cultivation*, edited by Maria Lis-Balchin, 11–19. London: CRC Press.

Mkentane, Luyolo. 2020. "Report to Rule on Communities' Land Rights in Eastern Cape." *Business Day*, November 19, 2020.

Mnwana, Sonwabile. 2014. "Mineral Wealth—'In the Name of Morafe'? Community Control in South Africa's 'Platinum Valley.'" *Development Southern Africa* 31 (6): 826–42.

———. 2021. "When Custom Divides 'Community': Legal Battles Over Platinum in North West Province." In *Land, Law, and Chiefs in Rural South Africa: Contested Histories and Current Struggles*, edited by William Beinart, Rosalie Kingwill, and Gavin Capps, 60–80. Johannesburg: Wits University Press.

Moodie, T. Dunbar, and Vivienne Ndatshe. 1994. *Going for Gold: Men, Mines, and Migration*. Berkeley: University of California Press.

Moore, Donald. 1998. "Clear Waters and Muddied Histories: Environmental History and the Politics of Community in Zimbabwe's Eastern Highlands." *Journal of Southern African Studies* 24 (2): 377–403.

Morris, Christopher. 2017. "Biopolitics and Boundary Work in South Africa's *Sutherlandia* Clinical Trial." *Medical Anthropology* 36 (7): 685–98.
Mostert, Noël. 1992. *Frontiers: The Epic of South Africa's Creation and the Tragedy of the Xhosa People*. New York: Knopf.
Motjotji, Liseabo. 2011. "Towards Sustainability of Harvesting the Medicinal Plant *Pelargonium sidoides* DC (GERANIACEAE)." MA diss., University of the Witwatersrand.
Moyo, Mack, Adeyemi O. Aremu, Jiri Cruz, Michaela Subrtová, Lucie Szüčová, Karel Doležal, and Johannes Van Staden. 2013. "Conservation Strategy for *Pelargonium sidoides* DC: Phenolic Profile and Pharmacological Activity of Acclimatized Plants Derived from Tissue Culture." *Journal of Ethnopharmacology* 149 (2): 557–61.
Mulligan, Shane P. 1999. "For Whose Benefit? Limits to Sharing in the Bioprospecting 'Regime.'" *Environmental Politics* 8 (4): 35–65.
Murphree. Marshall. 1999. "Governance and Community Capacity." Paper prepared for the Centre for Applied Social Studies/Programme for Land and Agrarian Studies inaugural meeting on CBNRM in Southern Africa: A Regional Programme of Analysis and Communication, Harare.
Myburgh, André F. 2010. "Lessons from a Town Like Alice: Intellectual Property." *Without Prejudice* 10 (8): 4–7.
———. 2011. "Legal Developments in the Protection of Plant Related Traditional Knowledge: An Intellectual Property Lawyer's Perspective of the International and South African Legal Framework." *South African Journal of Botany* 77 (4): 844–49.
Navaro, Yael, Zerrin Özlem Biner, Alice von Bieberstein, and Seda Altuğ. 2021. *Reverberations: Violence Across Time and Space*. Philadelphia: University of Pennsylvania Press.
Neimark, Benjamin D. 2012. "Industrializing Nature, Knowledge, and Labor: The Political Economy of Bioprospecting in Madagascar." *Geoforum* 43 (5): 980–90.
Neimark, Benjamin D., and Richard A. Schroeder. 2009. "Hotspot Discourse in Africa: Making Space for Bioprospecting in Madagascar." *African Geographical Review* 28 (1): 43–69.
Nelson, Fred, and Arun Agrawal. 2008. "Patronage or Participation? Community-Based Natural Resource Management Reform in Sub-Saharan Africa." *Development and Change* 39 (4): 557–85.
Neumann, Roderick P. 2015. "Nature Conservation." In *The Routledge Handbook of Political Ecology*, edited by Tom Perreault, Gavin Bridge, and James McCarthy, 391–405. New York: Routledge.
Neumann, Roderick P., and Eric Hirsch. 2000. *Commercialization of Non-Timber Forest Products: Review and Analysis of Research*. Bogor Barat: Center for International Forestry Research.
Newsom, S. W. B. 2002. "Stevens' Cure: A Secret Remedy." *Journal of the Royal Society of Medicine* 95 (9): 463–67.

Ngubane, Harriet. 1977. *Body and Mind in Zulu Medicine: An Ethnography of Health and Disease in Nyuswa-Zulu Thought and Practice*. New York: Academic Press.

Nhlapo Commission on Traditional Leadership Disputes and Claims. 2010. "Determinations on the Position of the Paramount Chiefs." https://static.pmg.org.za/docs/100729determination-chiefs.pdf.

Normand, Valerie, María Julia Oliva, Susanne Müller, Suhel al-Janabi, Yannick Zohren, Nicole Nöske, Luciana Zedda, and Axel Paulsch. 2021. *The Contribution of Access and Benefit-Sharing (ABS) to the Sustainable Development Goals: Lessons Learned and Best Practices*. https://uebt.org/resource-pages/handoutthe-contribution-of-abs-to-the-sdgs.

Ntsebeza, Lungisile. 2005. *Democracy Compromised: Chiefs and the Politics of Land in South Africa*. Cape Town: Human Sciences Research Council.

———. 2011. "Traditional Authority and Democracy: Are We Back to Apartheid?" In *The Fate of the Eastern Cape: History, Politics and Social Policy*, edited by Greg Reuters, 75–92. Scottsville: University of KwaZulu-Natal Press.

Nyamnjoh, Francis. 2012. "Blinded by Sight: Divining the Future of Anthropology in Africa." *Africa Spectrum* 47 (2–3): 63–92.

Obarrio, Juan. 2014. *The Spirit of the Laws in Mozambique*. Chicago: University of Chicago Press.

Oberthür, Sebastian, and G. Kristin Rosendal, eds. 2014. *Global Governance of Genetic Resources: Access and Benefit Sharing after the Nagoya Protocol*. New York: Routledge.

Olivier de Sardan, Jean-Pierre. 2015. *Epistemology, Fieldwork, and Anthropology*. New York: Palgrave.

Oomen, Barbara. 2005. *Chiefs in South Africa: Law, Power and Culture in the Post-apartheid Era*. Pietermaritzburg: University of KwaZulu-Natal.

Osseo-Asare, Abena. 2014. *Bitter Roots: The Search for Healing Plants in Africa*. Chicago: University of Chicago Press.

Packard, Randall M. 1989. *White Plague, Black Labor: Tuberculosis and the Political Economy of Health and Disease in South Africa*. Berkeley: University of California Press.

Parks, Louisa. 2020. *Benefit-Sharing in Environmental Governance: Local Experiences of a Global Concept*. New York: Routledge.

Peires, Jeff. 1982. *The House of Phalo: A History of the Xhosa People in the Days of Their Independence*. Berkeley: University of California Press.

———. 1989a. "Ethnicity and Pseudo-ethnicity in the Ciskei." In *The Creation of Tribalism in Southern Africa*, edited by Leroy Vail, 395–413. Berkeley: University of California Press.

———. 1989b. *The Dead Will Arise: Nongqawuse and the Great Xhosa Cattle-Killing Movement of 1856–7*. Bloomington: Indiana University Press.

———. 2012. "'He Wears Short Clothes!': Rethinking Rharhabe (c. 1715–c. 1782)." *Journal of Southern African Studies* 38 (2): 333–54.
Pelican, Michaela. 2009. "Complexities of Indigeneity and Autochthony: An African Example." *American Ethnologist* 36 (1): 52–65.
Peters, Pauline. 2004. "Inequality and Social Conflict Over Land in Africa." *Journal of Agrarian Change* 4 (3): 269–314.
Phillips, Laura, and Igor Chipkin. 2014. "Bantustans Are Dead—Long Live the Bantustans." *Mail & Guardian*, July 11, 2014. http://mg.co.za/article/2014-07-10-bantustans-are-dead-long-live-the-bantustans.
Pickard, Louis A. 2006. *The State of the State: Institutional Transformation, Capacity and Political Change in South Africa*. Johannesburg: Wits University Press.
Pollock, Anne. 2019. *Synthesizing Hope: Matter, Knowledge, and Place in South African Drug Discovery*. Chicago: University of Chicago Press.
Posey, Darrell. 1996. *Traditional Resource Rights: International Instruments for Protection and Compensation for Indigenous Peoples and Local Communities*. Gland, Switzerland: International Union for the Conservation of Nature.
Povinelli, Elizabeth A. 2002. *The Cunning of Recognition: Indigenous Alterities and the Making of Australian Multiculturalism*. Durham, NC: Duke University Press.
Prince, Chandre. 2012. "Queen Fights for Her Kingdom." *Times Live*, July 11, 2012. www.timeslive.co.za/thetimes/2012/07/11/queen-fights-for-her-kingdom.
Ramphele, Mamphela. 1996. "How Ethical Are the Ethics of This Militant Anthropologist?" *Social Dynamics* 22 (1): 1–4.
Ramutsindela, Maano. 2007. "Resilient Geographies: Land, Boundaries and the Consolidation of the Former Bantustans in Post-1994 South Africa." *Geographical Journal* 173 (1): 43–55.
———. 2016. "Political Dynamics of Human-Environmental Relations." In *The Politics of Nature and Science in Southern Africa*, edited by Maano Ramutsindela, Giorgio Miescher, and Melanie Boehi, 20–36. Basel: Basler Afrika Bibliographien.
Ribot, Jesse. 2003. "Democratic Decentralization of Natural Resources: Institutional Choice and Discretionary Power Transfers in Sub-Saharan Africa." *Public Administration and Development* 23 (1): 53–65.
Ritchie, Mark, Kristin Dawkins, and Mark Vallianatos. 1996. "Intellectual Property Rights and Biodiversity: The Industrialization of Natural Resources and Traditional Knowledge." *St. John's Journal of Legal Commentary* 11 (2): 431–54.
Robins, Steven. 1996. "On the Call for a Militant Anthropology: The Complexity of 'Doing the Right Thing.'" *Current Anthropology* 37 (2): 341–43.

———. 2008. *From Revolution to Rights in South Africa: Social Movements, NGOs and Popular Politics*. Pietermaritzburg: University of KwaZulu Natal Press.

Robinson, Daniel. 2010. *Confronting Biopiracy: Challenges, Cases and International Debates*. New York: Routledge.

———. 2014. *Biodiversity, Access and Benefit-Sharing: Global Case Studies*. New York: Routledge.

Robinson, Jason. 2015. "Fragments of the Past: Homeland Politics and the South African Transition, 1990–2014." *Journal of Southern African Studies* 41 (5): 953–67.

Rosen, Lauren Coyle. 2020. *Fires of Gold: Law, Spirit, and Sacrificial Labor in Ghana*. Oakland: University of California Press.

Ruiters, Greg, ed. 2011. *The Fate of the Eastern Cape: History, Politics, and Social Policy*. Pietermaritzburg: University of Kwa-Zulu Natal Press.

Rutert, Britta. 2020. *Contested Properties: Peoples, Plants, and Politics in Post-Apartheid South Africa*. Bielefeld: Transcript.

Sassen, Saskia. 2006. *Territory, Authority, Rights: From Medieval to Global Assemblages*. Princeton, NJ: Princeton University Press.

Schiebinger, Londa, and Claudia Swan, eds. 2005. *Colonial Botany: Science, Commerce, and Politics in the Early Modern World*. Philadelphia: University of Pennsylvania Press.

Schippmann, Uwe, Danna Leaman, and A. B. Cunningham. 2006. "A Comparison of Cultivation and Wild Collection of Medicinal and Aromatic Plants under Sustainability Aspects." In *Medicinal and Aromatic Plants: Proceedings of the Frontis Workshop on Medicinal and Aromatic Plants, 17–20 April 2005*, edited by Roger Bogers, Lyle Craker, and Dagmar Lange, 75–95. Wageningen, The Netherlands: Springer.

Sechehaye, Adrien. 1930. *The Treatment of Pulmonary and Surgical Tuberculosis with Umckaloabo (Stevens' Cure)*. London: B. Fraser.

Seuss, Dr. 1961. *The Sneetches and Other Stories*. New York: Random House.

Shackleton, Charlie M., Fiona Parkin, Maphambe I. Chauke, Linda Downsborough, Ashleigh Olsen, Gregg Brill, and Craig Weideman. 2009. "Conservation, Commercialization and Confusion: Harvesting of *Ischyrolepis* in a Coastal Forest, South Africa." *Environment, Development, and Sustainability* 11 (2): 229–40.

Shackleton, Charlie M., and Sheona Shackleton. 2004. "The Importance of Non-Timber Forest Products in Rural Livelihood Security and as Safety-Nets: Evidence from South Africa." *South African Journal of Science* 100 (11–12): 658–64.

Sharma, Aradhana, and Akhil Gupta, eds. 2006. *The Anthropology of the State*. Oxford: Blackwell.

Shiva, Vandana. 1997. *Biopiracy: The Plunder of Nature and Knowledge*. London: South End Press.

Simmel, Georg. 1906. "The Sociology of Secrecy and of Secret Societies." *American Journal of Sociology* 11 (4): 441–98.
———. 2009. *Sociology: Inquiries into the Construction of Social Forms*. Boston: Brill.
Smith, James. 2011. "Tantalus in the Digital Age: Coltan Ore, Temporal Dispossession, and 'Movement' in the Eastern Democratic Republic of the Congo." *American Ethnologist* 38 (1): 17–35.
———. 2015. "'May It Never End': Price Wars, Networks, and Temporality in the '3 Ts' Mining Trade of the Eastern DR Congo." *Hau: Journal of Ethnographic Theory* 5 (1): 1–34.
Solomon, Harris. 2022. *Lifelines: The Traffic of Trauma*. Durham, NC: Duke University Press.
South African Department of Environmental Affairs. 2015. *Biodiversity Economy Strategy*. https://cer.org.za/wp-content/uploads/2019/04/Biodiversity-Economy-Strategy.pdf.
South African National Biodiversity Institute. 2010. *Medicinal plant* Umckaloabo Pelargonium sidoides *Not Threatened*. Report submitted to Convention on Biological Diversity.
Starling, Shane. 2012. "South African Immunity Herb Winning New Community." Nutraingredients, March 14. www.nutraingredients.com/Article/2012/03/14/South-African-immunity-herb-winning-new-community.
Stevens, Charles Henry. 1912. *Medical Evidence Given in the Consumption Cure Libel Action: Stevens v. The British Medical Association*. Leeds: Jowett & Sowry LTD.
Stiglitz, Joseph. 2013. *Selected Works of Joseph Stiglitz*. Vol. 2, *Information and Capital Markets*. Oxford: Oxford University Press.
Stoler, Ann. 2016. *Duress: Imperial Durabilities in Our Times*. Durham, NC: Duke University Press.
Street, Renee, and Gerhard Prinsloo. 2013. "Commercially Important Medicinal Plants of South Africa: A Review." *Journal of Chemistry* 2013: 1–16.
Sunder Rajan, Kaushik. 2006. *Biocapital: The Constitution of Postgenomic Life*. Durham, NC: Duke University Press.
Sunderlin, William D., Arild Angelsen, Brian Belcher, Paul Burgers, Robert Nasi, Levania Santoso, and Sven Wunder. 2005. "Livelihoods, Forests, and Conservation in Developing Countries: An Overview." *World Development* 33 (9): 1383–1402.
Sylvain, Renee. 2005. "Disorderly Development: Globalization and the Idea of 'Culture' in the Kalahari." *American Ethnologist* 32 (3): 354–70.
TallBear, Kim. 2013. *Native American DNA: Tribal Belonging and the False Promise of Genetic Science*. Minneapolis: University of Minnesota Press.
Taylor, Mandy, and Rachel Wynberg. 2008. "Regulating Access to South Africa's Biodiversity and Ensuring the Fair Sharing of Benefits from Its

Use." *South African Journal of Environmental Science and Policy* 15 (2): 217–43.
Theil, Stefan. 2009. "Germany's Technophobia is Holding It Back." *Newsweek*, July 17, 2009.
Thipe, Thuto, and Mbongiseni Buthelezi. 2014. "Democracy in Action: The Demise of the Traditional Courts Bill and Its Implications; Discourse and Debate." *South African Journal on Human Rights* 30 (1): 196–205.
Thompson, Carol. 2009. "The Scramble for Genetic Resources." In *A New Scramble for Africa? Imperialism, Investment, and Development*, edited by Roger Southall and Henning Melber, 299–323. Scottsville: University of KwaZulu-Natal Press.
Trade and Industrial Policy Strategies. 2016. *The Real Economy Bulletin Provincial Review: Eastern Cape 2016*. https://www.tips.org.za/images/The_REB_Provincial_Review_2016_Eastern_Cape.pdf.
Traugott, Ulrich. 2010. "Okay to Harvest Pelargonium." Commentary, *Mail & Guardian*, February 5–11, 2010. https://mg.co.za/article/2010-03-08-february-5-to-11-2010/.
Tsing, Anna. 2005. *Friction: An Ethnography of Global Connection*. Princeton, NJ: Princeton University Press.
———. 2013. "Sorting Out Commodities: How Capitalist Value Is Made through Gifts." *HAU: Journal of Ethnographic Theory* 3 (1): 21–43.
———. 2015. *The Mushroom at the End of the World: On the Possibility of Life in Capitalist Ruins*. Princeton, NJ: Princeton University Press.
UN Secretariat of the Convention on Biological Diversity. 2010. "Nagoya Protocol on Access to Genetic Resources and the Fair and Equitable Sharing of Benefits Arising from Their Utilization to the Convention on Biological Diversity." www.cbd.int/abs/text.
UN Trade and Development. n.d. "BioTrade." Accessed June 10, 2016. http://unctad.org/en/Pages/DITC/Trade-and-Environment/BioTrade.aspx.
United Nations. 2018. "UN Comtrade Database—Export Value of Products Reported in Code HS1211 in 1999, 2005 and 2015." http://comtrade.un.org/db.
van Kessel, Ineke, and Barbara Oomen. 1997. "One Chief, One Vote: The Revival of Traditional Authorities in Post-apartheid South Africa." *African Affairs* 96 (385): 551–85.
van Niekerk, Jaci, and Rachel Wynberg. 2012. "The Trade in *Pelargonium sidoides*: Rural Livelihood Relief or Bounty for the 'Bio-buccaneers'?" *Development Southern Africa* 29 (4): 530–47.
Vandergeest, Peter, and Nancy Peluso. 1995. "Territorialization and State Power in Thailand." *Theory and Society* 24: 385–426.
Vermeylen, Saskia. 2007. "Contextualizing 'Fair' and 'Equitable': The San's Reflections on the Hoodia Benefit-Sharing Agreement." *Local Environment* 12 (4): 423–36.

Vice, Samantha. 2011. "Why My Opinions on Whiteness Touched a Nerve." *Mail & Guardian*, September 2, 2011.
von Benda-Beckmann, Franz, Keebet von Benda-Beckmann, and Julie Eckert. 2009. "Rules of Law and Laws of Ruling: Law and Governance between Past and Future." In *Rules of Law and Laws of Ruling: On the Governance of Law*, edited by Franz von Benda-Beckmann, Keebet von Benda-Beckmann, and Julie Eckert, 1–30. Farnham, UK: Ashgate.
Walker, Cherryl. 2011. "The Big Problem Is Not 'White' Farms." *Cape Times*, July 4, 2011.
Wandersee, James, and Elisabeth Schussler. 1999. "Preventing Plant Blindness." *American Biology Teacher* 61 (2): 82, 84, 86.
Webster, Edward. 2006. "Trade Unions and Challenge of the Informalization of Work." In *Trade Unions and Democracy: COSATU Workers' Political Attitudes in South Africa*, edited by Sakhela Buhlungu, 21–44. Cape Town: HSRC Press.
Weinberg, Tara. 2015. *The Contested Status of "Communal Land Tenure" in South Africa*. Cape Town: Institute for Poverty, Land and Agrarian Studies, University of the Western Cape.
———. 2021. "A History of Communal Property Associations in South Africa." In *Land, Law, and Chiefs in Rural South Africa: Contested Histories and Current Struggles*, edited by William Beinart, Rosalie Kingwill, and Gavin Capps, 208–28. Johannesburg: Wits University Press.
Westaway, Ashley. 2012. "Rural Poverty in the Eastern Cape Province: Legacy of Apartheid or Consequence of Contemporary Segregationism?" *Development Southern Africa* 29 (1): 115–25.
White, Andrew G., Michael T. Davies-Coleman, and Brad S. Ripley. 2008. "Measuring and Optimizing Umckalin Concentration in Wild-Harvested and Cultivated *Pelargonium sidoides* (Geraniaceae)." *South African Journal of Botany* 74 (2): 260–67.
White, Hylton. 2015. "Custom, Normativity and Authority in South Africa." *Journal of Southern African Studies* 41 (5): 1005–17.
Wiersum, K. F., Anthony. P. Dold, M. Husselman, and Michelle Cocks. 2006. "Cultivation of Medicinal Plants as a Tool for Biodiversity Conservation and Poverty Alleviation in the Amatola Region, South Africa." In *Medicinal and Aromatic Plants: Agricultural, Commercial, Ecological, Legal, Pharmacological and Social Aspects*, edited by Robert J. Bogers, Lyle E. Craker, and Dagmar Lange, 43–57. Dordrecht: Springer.
Williams, J. Michael. 2010. *Chieftaincy, the State and Democracy: Political Legitimacy in Post-apartheid South Africa*. Bloomington: Indiana University Press.
Williams, Raymond. 1973. *The Country and the City*. New York: Oxford University Press.

Wilson, Horace. 1912. "The Science and Art of Sanatorium Management." *British Medical Journal of Tuberculosis* 6 (1): 37–39.

Wilson, Leonard. 1990. "The Historical Decline of Tuberculosis in America: Its Causes and Significance." *Journal of the History of Medicine and Allied Sciences* 45 (3): 366–96.

Wood, J. M., and M. Franks. 1911. "Kaempferia natalensis." *The Naturalist: The Journal of the Natal Scientific Society* 3: 112–15.

Worboys, Michael. 1992. "The Sanatorium Treatment for Consumption in Britain, 1890–1914." In *Medical Innovations in Historical Perspective*, edited by John Pickstone, 47–71. New York: St. Martin's Press.

Wotshela, Luvoyo. 2004. "Territorial Manipulation in Apartheid South Africa: Resettlement, Tribal Politics, and the Making of the Northern Ciskei, 1975–1990." *Journal of Southern African Studies* 30 (2): 317–37.

Wreford, Jo. 2005. "'*Sincedisa*—We Can Help!' A Literature Review of Current Practice Involving Traditional African Healers in Biomedical HIV/AIDS Interventions in South Africa." *Social Dynamics* 31 (2): 90–117.

Wynberg, Rachel. 2017a. "One Step Forward, Two Steps Back? Implementing Access and Benefit-Sharing Legislation in South Africa." In *Routledge Handbook of Biodiversity and the Law*, edited by Charles R. McManis and Burton Ong, 198–218. New York: Routledge.

———. 2017b. "Bioprospecting: Moving Beyond Benefit Sharing." In *Global Africa: Into the Twenty-First Century*, edited by Dorothy Hodgson and Judith Byfield, 298–307. Durham, NC: Duke University Press.

———. 2023. "Biopiracy: Crying Wolf or a Lever for Equity and Conservation?" *Research Policy* 52: 104674.

Wynberg, Rachel, and Sarah Laird. 2012. "Governance of Biological and Genetic Resources." In *Moving Forward with Forest Governance*, edited by Guido Broekhoven, Herman Savenije, and Stefanie von Scheliha, 46–52. Wageningen, The Netherlands: Tropenbos International.

Wynberg, Rachel, Doris Schroeder, and Roger Chennells, eds. 2009. *Indigenous Peoples, Consent and Benefit Sharing: Lessons from the San-Hoodia Case*. London: Springer.

Wynberg, Rachel, and Jaci van Niekerk. 2014. "Global Ambitions and Local Realities: Achieving Equity and Sustainability in Two High-Value NTFP Trade Chains." *Forests, Trees and Livelihoods* 23 (1–2): 19–35.

Yeh, Emily T. 2013. *Taming Tibet: Landscape Transformation and the Gift of Chinese Development*. Ithaca, NY: Cornell University Press.

Yousefian, Zeynab, Yousef Hamidoghli, Pooran Golkar, and Mohammad Hossein Mirjalili. 2023. "Growth Patterns and Biological Activities of *Pelargonium sidoides* DC. Hairy Root Cultures: A Commercially-Feasible Industrial Scale-Up to Improve Yields." *Industrial Crops and Products* 194 (116272).

Index

access: access agreements, 164–68, 168*fig.*, 170, 178; access zones, 7, 171, 178–79; and benefit sharing, 10, 13, 14–15, 34, 56, 112, 150, 167, 176
African Center for Biosafety (ACB), 1, 27, 39, 72–73, 175; challenge of against Schwabe, 3–4, 32–33, 42–43, 44, 192n37; criticism of NEMBA by, 73; first publication of ("Knowledge Not for Sale"), 53; meeting with the Alice group, 96–101; as a self-described "activist organization," 43–44
African *muthi* (medicine), 90
African National Congress (ANC), 130, 155, 169
Agamben, Giorgio, 20
Agreement on Trade-Related Aspects of Intellectual Property Rights (TRIPS), 9, 10, 42
AIDS, xviii, 38, 70
Alice/Alice community/group, 44, 52–53, 56; as descended from families of farm dwellers, 104–5; meeting with the ACB, 96–101; as a "new collectivity," 102–3
Aloe ferox, 66, 136
amaRharhabe, as a political identity, 200n23
Amathole District, household income in, 78
Anathi, 121–23, 124–25, 124*fig.*, 126–28, 129, 130
ancestors, 138

Anders, Gerhard, 35
anti-patent activism, 1, 192n29
apartheid, 15, 67; creation of homelands as policy of, 16; environmental legislative legacies of, 14, 72–74, 87; forced migrations under, 17, 203n18; ideology of "proper farming" under, 135; land reform programs addressing legacies of, 132; legacy of in contemporary cultural and spatial divisions, 170–71; legacy of in post-apartheid resource rights, 181; legacy of in post-apartheid traditional leadership structures, 158–59; patronage politics during, 165; population crowding resulting from, 86, 106; role in shaping "access" zones, 178; and segregation, 7, 13; and "separate development," 18, 22. *See also* Bantustans ("Bantu homelands"); Ciskei region/homeland; homelands; "retribalization"; Transkei homeland
autochthony, 95

Bafokeng Nation, border concerns of, 95
Bantustans ("Bantu homelands"), 16, 149
Beinart, William, 16
belonging: and contested notions of indigeneity in Africa, 152; expansion of through

233

belonging (continued)
  benefit-sharing agreements 95–97, 180–82; shaping of through legal processes and property claims, 50, 56; and subjection, 112–13, 169; and territorialization, 201n38
benefit sharing, 13, 15, 186–87n39, 187n43; and biotraders, 161–63, 164–65; and community, 112–13; desire for, 101–3; DEA's ambivalence concerning, 154; expansion of, 173–75; and Indigenous collectives, 150–54; international regime of access and benefit sharing, 34–35; as an offspring of neoliberal conservation, 113; and the plant-commodity trade, 102; South African government's version of, 12–14, 94–95
Berlant, Lauren, 11
Berne Declaration, 39, 194n71
Berry, Sara, 20, 202n39
Bhisho, 17, 85
Biko, Steve, 16
bio/cultural diversities, 189–90n83
biodiscovery, 184n14, 189n82
biodiversity, 8–9; biodiversity commercialization, 16; biodiversity custodians, 15; commodity trade in, 184–85n16; conservation of, 152; drug discovery from biodiversity, 11; UN Biodiversity Convention (COP$_{15}$), 174; UN biodiversity summit, 174
Biodiversity Management Plan, 80
biological resources: as a form of traffic, 6, 7–8; international biological resources, 181; movement of, 172–73; visual of traffic, 6–7
biopiracy, 4, 10, 26, 32–34, 43–44, 50, 102, 174, 184n10, 185nn19–20, 194n75
Biopiracy: The Plunder of Nature and Knowledge (Shiva), 41
Biopirates, The: The Pharmaceutical Industry's Billion-Dollar-Business with Nature's Blueprint, 34, 35, 39, 40
[Bioprospecting and Benefit Sharing] regulations, 72–73
biotechnology, 9
biotraders, xix, 13–14, 67–68, 87, 171, 179; and benefit sharing, 161–63, 164–65
biotraffic, 120, 170; control of, 96; governance of, 12–15, 21, 113, 177; patent activism to address, 33; visual of, 6–7. *See also* biological resources, as a form of traffic
Black commercial farmers, 129, 130–31; development grants for, 131

Bloemfontein, 30
Bolt, Maxim, 126
Boone, Catherine, 179–80
boundaries, 6, 13, 15, 17, 20, 28, 78, 169, 177, 185n19; boundary closure, 95, 192n35; of community, 50, 56–57, 95, 161–62; ethnic boundary construction, 21; geographic boundaries, 113; and human displacement, 113–14; sociopolitical boundaries, 96; "tribal" boundaries, 154
British Kaffraria, 104, 105
British Medical Association (BMA), 195n17; hostility toward Stevens and libel suit of, 61–63, 90–93, 117–19
Bryder, Linda, 116

capitalists/capitalism, 41; extractive capitalism, 21, 177, 179; liberal capitalism, 113; neoliberal capitalism, 181; supply-chain capitalism, 179
Castree, Noel, 154–55
C. H. Stevens and Co., 59, 60; criticism of, 115–16; early success of, 60–61; growth of, 114; libel suit of against the BMA, 90–93, 114, 117
Chennells, Roger, 52, 53–54, 101–2
Chief Gungubele, 165–67
Chief Langa Mavuso, 151, 155–57, 160, 161, 206n40
Chief Mgolombane Sandile, 105
chiefs, 19–20; as afromodern capitalist cosmopolitans, 154–57; chiefly jurisdictions, 181–82; leadership of, 21; re/centralization of chiefly authority, 20; as representatives of communities, xvii; 22, 151–53; warrior chiefs and mafiosos, 158–60
chieftaincies, 178; Imingcangathelo chieftaincy, 139, 142, 163; partnership with pharmaceutical companies, xvii–xx; perspectives concerning CPAs, 109–11; relationships with CPAs, 133–34; Thastshu chieftaincy, 165–66, 167
Chieftainess Tyali, 98, 103, 105, 106, 110–11, 112, 200n12, 201n27; and the harvesting of pelargonium, 99
China root (*Smilax china*), 172
Church Development Service, 39
Ciskei region/homeland (South Africa), xv, xviii, 13, 15, 18–19, 20, 65, 71, 78, 158, 169, 170; assembling of by the apartheid regime, 105; attempt to "retribalize" its system of government, 106; colonial

consolidation of, 128–29; compared with Transkei homeland, 18, 150, 162; control over biotraffic in, 96; farms and farm dwellers in, 106–8; as an independent homeland, 17, 105, 106, 206–7n62; opposition to hereditary leaders in, 105–6; reintegration into South Africa, 107; uniqueness of, 170
citizen-rights, of post-colonial citizen-subjects, 100–1
Claassens, Aninka, 154, 162, 169
Cocks, Michelle, 138
Comaroff, Jean, 49, 95, 169
Comaroff, John, 49, 95, 169
communal property associations (CPAs), 108, 131, 162, 203n17, 204n24; criticism of, 141; missing title deeds of, 108–11; number of registered CPAs in South Africa and complaints concerning, 134–35; questions concerning the legal status of, 130–35; relationships with chiefs, 133–34; title deeds and formal CPA qualification, 128
Communal Property Associations (CPA) Act, 108
community, boundaries of, 50, 56–57
conservation, 10–11, 14, 16, 66, 79, 80, 81, 85, 113, 138–39, 173, 175; of biological diversity, 152; homeland conservation, 69, 73, 87; neoliberal conservation, 201n36; and the trope of economic incentivization, 152
Convention on Biological Diversity (CBD), 9–10, 11, 12, 15, 39, 49, 53, 83, 153, 175–76; as a legal focal point for many nationalities, 151–52; limitations of, 14; membership of, 173; uniqueness of in environmental governance, 14
Council for Scientific and Industrial Research (CSIR), 50, 52
COVID-19 pandemic, 144, 157
cultural differentiation, 95
culture: commodification of, 194n60; legality of, 49

Dabula, 17–18, 19, 20
dagga (marijuana), 65
Davis, W. H., 117–18
Department of Environmental Affairs (DEA), 37, 153, 171; ambivalence concerning benefit sharing, 154; amendment of its legislation, 38–39; granting of "amnesty" to continue Schwabe's activities in South Africa, 140, 191n26; hostility of toward drug discovery, 38; and Mandela, 157

Department of Land Affairs, and "beneficial occupiers," 128
Department of Rural Development and Land Reform (DRDLR), 108, 109, 131–32, 133–34, 135; opposition to CPAs, 142; restitution program of, 132
Department of Science and Technology (DST), 12
Der Spiegel, 34
Diamond v. Chakrabarty (1980), 9, 40–41
Didiza, Thoko, 130–31
Dimbaza, 17
Dold, Anthony, 138
Dolder, Fritz, 192n29
Doom of 150,000 People, The, 118–19, 118*fig.*
drug discovery, 11, 12, 15, 72, 184n14; DEA hostility toward, 38; drug discovery/ commodity-trade and export agreements concerning, 164, 185n19; and plant-commodity trading, 12–13
Dutch East India Company, 172

Eastern Cape Department of Economic Development, Environmental Affairs, and Tourism, 68, 198n58
Eastern Cape Province, xxi*map.*, 13, 65, 78–79, 86–87, 102, 162, 165, 169; Eastern Cape frontier zone as "Ceded Territory," 104; former homelands of, 15, 152; land cultivation in, 176
Englund, Harri, 181–82
ethnographic arrival trope, 51
ethnographies, 189n75
European Patent Office (EPO), 4; Munich EPO, 2, 32, 37, 56, 192n29; revocation of patent held by Schwabe Pharmaceuticals, 32–33, 37–43, 54–57
European Patent Convention: Article 53 of, 39, 40–41, 42, 55, 191–92n28; prevention of the EPO from granting patents on animal or plant life forms, 40–41

Ferguson, James, 170, 201n39
First Anglo-Boer War (1880–1881), 31
Foster, Laura, 7, 52, 185n21
Frein, Michael, 39

genetic resources, 10–11
German National Formulary (the Red List [*die Rote Liste*]), 146
Germany, 39; drug laws of, 147; as a medicinal-plant importer, 36–37
germ theory, 29

Geschiere, Peter, 95
Global Biodiversity Framework (GBF), 174–75; criticism of, 175
Greene, Shane, 50, 101
Green Scorpions, 5, 13, 14, 167
Greenwood, Arthur, 118–19
Grün, Edward Ferdinand, 91–92, 117
Gumbi, Sithembiso, 132–33, 133–34, 135, 136, 203n18
Guyer, Jane, 126, 171

Hall, Ruth, 135–36
hauntology, 25, 189n80
Hayden, Cori, 14, 112
herbal healers, 35
Heritage Festival, 158, 159
Heroes' Acre, 158
HIV, 6, 38, 70, 206n44
homelands (South African), 15–21, 149–50; access and benefit sharing in, 15–21; decentralized tiers of government in, 155; dismantling and reintegration of, 155; durability of, 13; homeland reconsolidation, 16, 20; number of in old South Africa, 16; re/centralization of chiefly authority in, 20; as "resilient geographies," 16–17. *See also* Bantustans ("Bantu homelands"); Eastern Cape Province, former homelands of
honeybush (*Cyclopia* spp.), 184n15
Hoodia gordonii, 50, 52, 56, 185–86n21, 187n40
House of Traditional Leaders, 19
Humor, as politics, 188n57
Hurtado, Lorenzo Muelas, 194n75

Ihlathi lesi-Xhosa (Xhosa forest), 137
illiberalism, 15, 177
Imingcangathelo chieftaincy, 105; benefit-sharing agreements with drug companies, 98–99, 101, 102; perspectives concerning CPAs, 109–11
immigration, 170
indigeneity, 50, 95, 152, 154; UN concept of, 171
Indigenous collectives, and benefit sharing, 150–54
Indigenous communities, 152, 153, 154
Indigenous knowledge holders/systems, 14–15, 42, 187n46
Indigenous medicines, 185n17; academic recognition of, 193n52; as a booming business in South Africa, 47
Indigenous movements, 50

Indigenous peoples: ability to direct export to drug companies, 102; ability to establish plant nurseries, 102; ability to establish their own benefit-sharing agreements, 102; aspirations concerning the plant-commodity trade 154–55
Indigenous rights, 182
Integrated Development Plan, 78–79
Intellectual Property Laws Amendment Bill, 56
intellectual property rights, 10, 14, 41, 42, 43, 50, 192–93n38; of indigenous peoples, 101
Interim Protection of Land Rights Act (IPILRA), 130
International Union for Conservation of Nature, 80–81
Iqayiyalethu CPA, 108, 120, 121, 135, 165; national developments concerning, 132–33; productivity of, 136
isiXhosa, 85, 89, 96, 125, 183n2

Johannesburg: mining near, 75
Journal of the American Medical Association, 89
JSO Werks Regensburg, 146, 147
jurisdictions: chiefly jurisdictions, 13, 153–54, 161, 167, 181–82; different types of, 112, 180

Kenneth, 68–70, 72
Khoi people, 14–15, 152
Khwezi, 66–68, 73–79, 197n24
Kijitse, Mike, 31, 58, 190n8
King Maxhoba Zanesizwe Sandile, xvii, 105, 160; death of, xx, 156
King Archie Velile Sandile, 106, 200n23
King Sandile Development Trust, 150, 156–57, 163
Kingwell, Rosalie, 128, 129, 130–31, 132, 141, 176, 203n16
Knysna, 137
Koch, Robert, 29–30
Krameria, 63
KwaZulu-Natal, 134

Laird, Sarah, 173, 187n43
Lancet, article in critical of Stevens, 59–60
"Land Divided" conference/dispute, 140–42
"lawfare," 49, 194n60
legality, culture of, 49
Lesotho, xviii, 32, 34, 151, 168; difficulty of sourcing pelargonium from, 148; as access site for pelargonium, 147

Li, Tania Murray, 26
liberal-democratic rights, 181
Liberia, 61, 93
localities, boundaries of. *See* boundaries, boundary closure
Lock, Margaret, 91
Lund, Christian, 179–80
Luthando, 77–79, 137

Mail & Guardian, 32, 33
Mandela, Nelson, 16, 19, 54, 130, 157; release of from prison, 107
Mbeki, Thabo, 54
Medical Evidence Given in the Consumption Cure Libel Case, 90–91
Medicine of Rharhabe (Amayeza Akwa Rharhabe), 157
Meiu, George Paul, 95
Marx, Karl, 41
Masakhane CPA, 107, 108, 120, 121, 135; national developments concerning, 132–33; productivity of, 136
Matanzima, Kaiser, 17, 165–66
Mava, 96–98, 101, 139
Mazzarella, William, 36
medicinal plants: international trade in, 65–66; valuation of, 65
Mooney, Pat, 184n10
Mr. Makeba, 109–11, 112

Nagoya Protocol, 10, 12, 140, 154, 173, 175–76; and "indigenous and local communities," 153; as a legal focal point for many nationalities, 151–52; limitations of, 14; uniqueness of in environmental governance, 14
National Development of Land Affairs, 130
National Environmental Management: Biodiversity Act (South Africa [NEMBA]), 38, 39, 54, 72–73, 186–87n39, 198n61
nationalism, ethnic, 158
Native Affairs Department of the Cape Colony, 62
Native Americans, 207n2; requirement of DNA testing for membership in, 95
Native Trust and Land Act, 129
Natives Land Act, 129
nature, as a resource that comes with new kinds of potential claimants, 152
Nguyen, Vinh-Kim, 91
Nhlapo Commission, 157, 160
Ninth Conference of the Parties of the UN CBD, 34

Nkayi, Funeka, 96–97, 142, 143, 200n17; interview with, 99–100
Nkwinti, Gugile, 109, 133, 141, 204n24
Nomble, 136–38, 139
Nomthunzi Api, 32–33, 43–46, 49, 51, 52, 97, 101, 103–7, 108, 200n20
nongovernmental organizations (NGOs), xv, xviii, xix, 1, 35, 102, 140, 192n29; global advocacy of, 102; influence of in supporting indigenous intellectual property rights, 101
Ntaba kaNdoda (national temple of the Ciskei), 158, 159*fig*.

Operation Phakisa for the National Biodiversity Economy, 12, 175
Orange Free State, 30

Parceval Pharmaceuticals, 68, 72, 73, 81, 83, 111, 157, 164, 167; agreements of with chieftaincies, 98; money made on wild harvesting of *Pelargonium sidoides*, 85
"pass laws," 74–75
Peires, Jeff, 125–26
Pelargonium sidoides (*uvendle* in isiXhosa [hereafter pelargonium]), xvi, xvii, 7, 13, 42, 124*fig*., 157, 178, 185–86n21, 196–97n23; access of, 72–73; conservation status of, 79–80; cultivation of as an alternative to harvesting, 82–83, 83*fig*; described as *izifozonke*, 46; harvesting of (including wild harvesting), 70–71, 72–73, 77–78, 80–81, 82*fig*., 83–85, 121–23; illegal harvested pelargonium, 71*fig*; as indigenous to South Africa and Lesotho, 2; international trade in, 65–66; juxtaposition of the pelargonium industry's operations in South Africa and Germany, 122–23; knowledge of, 53; as a member of the Geraniaceae family, 2, 183–84n2; national environmental management plan for, 164; popularity of in South Africa, 48–49; tubers of, 3*fig*.; value chain involving, 67–68. *See also* Umckaloabo
Peluso, Nancy, 113
Perils of Belonging, The (Geschiere), 95
peri-urban settlements, uncontrolled grazing in, 138
"Permission to Occupy" certificates, 129
Peters, Pauline, 152
plants: assumption they are coterminous with people and knowledge, 14, 180
"policy intellectuals," 22, 188–89n74

Portfolio Committee of the Department of Trade, 56
poverty, 15, 16, 78, 80, 193n52; structural poverty in rural spaces, 86
primitive accumulation, 41
Proactive Land Acquisition Strategy (PLAS), 133; narrow focus of on "production discipline," 135–36
productivity, broad conception of, 139

Queen Noloyiso Sandile, 156; death of, 157
Qonce: medicinal plant (*amayeza*) area of, 48; taxi-rank area of, 47; Xhosa chemists in, 47–48

Rajak, Dinah, 126
Ramaphosa, Cyril, 12, 157
Ramutsindela, Maano, 16–17
Reconstruction and Development Program, 76
Reinventing Hoodia (Foster), 52, 185–86n21
representation: and claims of authority over people and resources, 151–53, 180; of indigenous peoples by NGOs, 50; and the politics of "community," 103, 112, 142; politics of, in CBD and Nagoya Protocol frameworks, 154; and the production of knowledge and value in academic writing, 25; role in fostering political legitimacy and recognition, 156, 160
Republic of South Africa, 16, 166
reregulation, 113
resources: indigenous claims to, 21; resource movement, 12–13
"Rethink the Expansion of Access and Benefit Sharing" (Laird), 173
"retribalization," 18–19, 106, 166
Rharhabe kingdom, 102, 105, 157, 159–60, 179; Great Place of, 99, 100, 150, 156, 166, 199n11, 200n23
rights-bearing citizenship, and the accommodation of centralized chiefly authority, 171
Riverman, 123, 126
Robben Island, 158
Robins, Howard, 117
Robins, Steven, 100
rooibos tea (*Aspalathus linearis*), 184n15

"Sacco," 59, 60
sanatoria, 30, 115–17, 118, 119
San people, 14–15, 56, 152. *See also* South African San Council
Sassafras trees, 172

scale: interacting dimensions of in biotraffic, 6–7, 122; of plant trade in Eastern Cape 5, 65; political construction of in government approaches to plant trade, 87; in relation to space and time in biotraffic governance, 171, 177–78; in wild harvesting versus cultivation of pelargonium, 84–86
Schwabe Pharmaceuticals, xvi, xvii–xviii, 27, 83, 164, 167, 183n1; advertising of, 35–36; agreements of with chieftaincies, 98, 139–40; annual sales of, 34; domination of the Umckaloabo market, 5–6; granting of "amnesty" by the DEA to continue Schwabe's activities in South Africa, 140; investment of in fruit-tree planting, 110, 111*fig*; involvement in the plant-commodity trade, 36–37; procedure for making Umckaloabo, 42; processing of harvested pelargonium into Umckaloabo, 121–22; proposal by for a benefit-sharing agreement with CPAs, 142–43; rejection of ACB's claims against, 103; role of in the plant-commodity trade, 39–40; use of JSO Werks supply chain by, 147–48. *See also* European Patent Office (EPO), revocation of patent held by Schwabe Pharmaceuticals
Sebe, Lennox, 17, 19, 107, 158, 206–7n62
Sechehaye, Adrien, 31, 145–46; number of patients prescribed Umckaloabo by, 145
Second Anglo-Boer War, 58
Secret Remedies: What They Cost and What They Contain (BMA publication), 61, 62, 90–91, 119, 146–47
segregationism, 169–70; racial segregation, 187n49
Shiva, Vandana, 41
South Africa, xx, 8, 39, 44, 79, 140; access to wild plants in, 13; annual production of Indigenous medicines in, 47; "bioeconomy" of, 12; biotechnology in, 12; genetic and biological resources of, 175; as a leader in market-driven environmental policy, 177
South African Constitution, 158
South African National Biodiversity Institute (SANBI), 38, 80, 81
South African San Council, 50, 52
spatiality: of access zones in former homelands, 13, 178–79; in benefit-sharing agreements and territorialization, 112–13; distance between knowledge holders and

biological/genetic resources, 14; of homeland-associated spaces in plant trade and conservation, 87–88; interacting dimensions of in biotraffic, 6–7; legal disjunctures exploited by biotraders, 14; and mobility as solution to problems of time, 137; role in contemporary segregation and subjection, 169–70; role in legacies of apartheid, 149, 208n13

Spur Steak Ranches, 155–56

"state land," government definition of, 128–29

Stevens, Charles Henry, 27, 29, 58–63, 89–93, 119, 145; allies of in the newspaper business, 146; criticism of, 59; patients of in India and Australia, 146; pursuit of his recovery from tuberculosis with Indigenous medicine, 30–31; supporters of, 117–18. *See also* C. H. Stevens and Co

stewardship, 14

Stoler, Ann, 21

"strategic essentialism," 51–52

streptomycin, 30

subjection, 112, 169, 177

Swartzia madagascariensis, 39

Taplin, Dr., 29, 30, 31

Taxus contorta, 6, 185n18

temporality: of access zones in former homelands, 178–79; in biotraffic value chain, 122; of homeland-associated spaces affecting plant trade, 87; interacting dimensions of in biotraffic, 6–7, 14; problems of accumulating unstructured time, 137; slow growth of plants 13, 85–86; and temporal dispossession, 126; and temporal lags in policing of plant trade, 171. *See also* waiting

territorialization, 113, 201n38

Therapeutic Revolutions (eds. Greene, Condrau, and Watkins), 11

therapeutics, plant-derived, xv

Thompson, Carol, 41

Tom, 68–71, 74, 79–80

TRAFFIC, 80, 85, 198n45

Transkei homeland, 13, 20, 65, 71, 158, 170; compared with Ciskei homeland, 18, 150, 162

Treatment of Tuberculosis with Umckaloabo, The (Sechehaye), 145

"tribal authorities," 19

"tribalism," 105

Trinidad, 115

Trinidad Association for the Prevention and Treatment of Tuberculosis: hygiene leaflets of, 116; objectives of, 116

"trust plots," 129

Tsing, Anna, 181–82

tuberculosis, xviii, 2–3, 6, 29–30, 89–90; BMA's position concerning, 115–16; "contingent contagionism" of, 116; decline of across Europe in the early twentieth century, 115; mortality rates of in Cape Town, 58; powder-form preparation for, 146; "prevention as treatment" model of, 116–17; rise in tuberculosis mortality rates after World War I, 118–19; shift in the treatment of, 116

Tuberculosis: Its Treatment and Cure with the Help of Umckaloabo, 114–15

turmeric, and the Indian government, 186n28

Ukhohlokhohlo, 157, 206n44

Umckaloabo, 3, 5, 35, 36, 90, 91, 145, 196–97n23; advertisement for, 114; newspaper promotion of, 146; noted improvements in the treatment of tuberculosis because of, 117–18; prevalence of, 37; processing of harvested pelargonium into Umckaloabo, 121–22; sales growth of, 114; Umcka version of, 37

Umckaloabo Stevens Corporation, 146

UN Human Rights Declaration, 49

universalism, 181

urbanization, 170

Verwoerd, Hendrik, 18–19

Vetter, Susi, 138

Vice, Samantha, 24–25

Victoria East District, 105

violence: historical, 18, 123–24; in conservation efforts, historical displacements and exclusions, 113; legacy of colonial conflicts on present-day experiences, 125–26; in contemporary rural settings, 127–28; in mining industry, 75–76; role in displacement of Indigenous knowledge holders, 14–15. *See also* Wars of Dispossession (the Cape Frontier Wars)

Von Bojanowski, Irene, 146

waiting: as feature of biotraffic value chain, 121–22; for economic opportunities in former homelands, 74–76; for land transfer and economic funding, 130–31, 143;

waiting (*continued*)
	for plant regeneration and sustainable harvesting, 79–82. *See also* temporality
Wars of Dispossession (the Cape Frontier Wars), 18, 66–67, 105; British triumph in, 124; Eighth War of (War of Mlanjeni), 123–24, 125–26; War of the Axe, 104
wealth in people, 201n38, 201n39
White farms, purchase of from the national trust, 129
White nationalists, 16
"White Paper on Biodiversity Conservation and Sustainable Use," 175
Wilkinson, William Camac, 116

Worboys, Michael, 30
World Trade Organization (WTO), 9
Wynberg, Rachel, 15, 175, 184n15, 187n43

Xhosa forest. See *Ihlathi lesi-Xhosa* (Xhosa forest)
Xhosa people, 54, 67, 104–5, 109; Xhosa cattle-killing movement, 125–26; Xhosa resistance fighters against the British, 123–24
Xhosa nation/territory, 104, 105. *See also* Wars of Dispossession (the Cape Frontier Wars)

Zambia, 170

Founded in 1893,
UNIVERSITY OF CALIFORNIA PRESS
publishes bold, progressive books and journals
on topics in the arts, humanities, social sciences,
and natural sciences—with a focus on social
justice issues—that inspire thought and action
among readers worldwide.

The UC PRESS FOUNDATION
raises funds to uphold the press's vital role
as an independent, nonprofit publisher, and
receives philanthropic support from a wide
range of individuals and institutions—and from
committed readers like you. To learn more, visit
ucpress.edu/supportus.

www.ingramcontent.com/pod-product-compliance
Lightning Source LLC
Jackson TN
JSHW020916020125
76325JS00002B/9